Dublin v. Kerry

Dublin v. Kerry

*The Story of the Epic Rivalry
that Changed Irish Sport*

TOM HUMPHRIES

PENGUIN
IRELAND

PENGUIN IRELAND

Published by the Penguin Group
Penguin Ireland, 25 St Stephen's Green, Dublin 2, Ireland
(a division of Penguin Books Ltd)
Penguin Books Ltd, 80 Strand, London WC2R 0RL, England
Penguin Group (USA) Inc., 375 Hudson Street, New York, New York 10014, USA
Penguin Group (Australia), 250 Camberwell Road,
Camberwell, Victoria 3124, Australia (a division of Pearson Australia Group Pty Ltd)
Penguin Group (Canada), 90 Eglinton Avenue East, Suite 700, Toronto, Ontario, Canada M4P 2Y3
(a division of Pearson Penguin Canada Inc.)
Penguin Books India Pvt Ltd, 11 Community Centre,
Panchsheel Park, New Delhi – 110 017, India
Penguin Group (NZ), cnr Airborne and Rosedale Roads, Albany,
Auckland 1310, New Zealand (a division of Pearson New Zealand Ltd)
Penguin Books (South Africa) (Pty) Ltd, 24 Sturdee Avenue,
Rosebank, Johannesburg 2196, South Africa

Penguin Books Ltd, Registered Offices: 80 Strand, London WC2R 0RL, England

www.penguin.com

First published 2006
I

Copyright © Tom Humphries, 2006

The moral right of the author has been asserted

Set in 12/14.75 pt Monotype Bembo
Typeset by Rowland Phototypesetting Ltd, Bury St Edmunds, Suffolk
Printed in Great Britain by Clays Ltd, St Ives plc

A CIP catalogue record for this book is available from the British Library

ISBN-13 978-1-844-88085-0
ISBN-10 1-844-88085-0

To Mary, Molly and Caitlín, with love as usual

We mortals cross the ocean of the world
Each in his average cabin of a life.
                                    Robert Browning

Contents

Prologue   1

Chapter 1   15
Chapter 2   27
Chapter 3   34
Chapter 4   46
Chapter 5   57
Chapter 6   69
Chapter 7   82
Chapter 8   95
Chapter 9   119
Chapter 10   131
Chapter 11   145
Chapter 12   156
Chapter 13   169
Chapter 14   177
Chapter 15   191
Chapter 16   204
Chapter 17   218
Chapter 18   227
Chapter 19   245
Chapter 20   260

Epilogue   265
Acknowledgements   277
Index   279

Prologue

Up Kerry, Up Catch and Kick

The Kerryman, 1955

For the Dubs it began with Kevin Heffernan and it ended with Kevin Heffernan. He was their throw-in, their final whistle and pretty much everything in between.

For Heffernan himself it began in 1955. That iridescent summer would become part of what he is. Before, there were to be bonfires along Griffith Avenue, there was to be happy revolution. After? There was just the time to learn hard lessons.

He'd grown with his club towards greatness. He shared St Vincent's obsession with excellence and bought fully into the club's unique and high-minded ambitions for Dublin football. He would be an instrument of their philosophy, the spearhead of a movement for Dublin teams to be filled with Dublin natives and for football to be played not just with a frank toughness but with the intelligence and discipline to create spaces on the field and then to exploit them.

By 1955 Kevin Heffernan's name was already etched on to the stones as one of the greatest players the game had known. That summer ended in tears but enhanced his legend.

The summer also provided an indelible Leinster final between Dublin and the All-Ireland champions, Meath. Dublin pushed up against brawny men with the rural neighbour's disdain for the city and its team of fancy dans. The old city brimmed with innocent hope, though. This might, at last, be a team to brag about. Dublin had beaten Meath in a league final, but even as that trophy was being hoisted they could see engraved on its base the traditional caveat: 'Warning! Only The League.'

It was said that Meath possessed the wheel upon which they would break Heffernan. His name was Paddy 'Hands' O'Brien. A fine turret of a man, Paddy's glint came from the two All-Ireland medals already in his back pocket. His nickname referred to the principal tools deployed in his gravity-defying catches.

Heffernan was no scrapper but his path was set to intersect with that of Hands O'Brien. When asked to move in from left corner forward to full forward that summer he surveyed the majesty of O'Brien's fielding and decided that altitude work wasn't for him. So he continued with the habit of a lifetime and set the rules for O'Brien.

Movement would be Heffernan's *métier*. He went about his business with a winner's confidence. Heffernan ran the big man into the ground, smithereened his great heart under a merciless sun. It was pitiless, this exhibition of a new style of football built on motion and speed rather than long kicking and high catching.

Heffernan won the first ball that came in to them. Won it with a yard to spare. He turned and ran at his marker. Hands didn't foul as such, but the surprised groping cost him a free.

Next ball. Same thing. Heffernan wins, runs at Hands again. Hands thinks of the free already given against him. Won't get fooled again, he thinks, but the hesitation has killed him. Heffernan dukes him. Hands turns. Ball in net, iron sky and green grass and no place to hide in between.

Heffernan had two goals for himself in the first twenty minutes. He roved ever further, heedless now of the intentions of Hands.

Dublin trimmed Meath that day 5–12 to 0–7, the worst drubbing ever dished to reigning All-Ireland champions. It was said that Paddy O'Brien sagged into the Meath dressing room and complained softly that Heffernan wouldn't stand shoulder to shoulder and play him fair.

Summer ground on. On a day punctuated by thunder and lightning Dublin needed Nicky Maher to kick a late free from thirty yards with a heavy sodden ball to earn a draw with Mayo in the All-Ireland semi-final. Dublin wiped themselves off and finished the job in the replay. It was a fine preparation for the big dance itself. Dublin and Kerry in September.

For the All-Ireland final the official attendance was announced as 87,102, but the GAA issued a disclaimer, pointing out that this was merely the figure at which they'd had to stop the counting. Two gates had been broken down by the sea of humanity.

A couple of gossoons from Kerry might almost have regretted paying their admission when they saw the swell of freeloaders that hit the terraces, but Eric Murphy and Mick O'Dwyer had made the pilgrimage from Kerry, and left nothing to chance.

Mick and Eric were from Waterville, which meant it was not axiomatic that they were footballers. But footballers they were. They took the train from Cahirciveen. Not a scheduled service but the old ghost train. She pulled out of Cahirciveen at midnight and chugged steadily through the Kingdom, picking up heavy-lidded citizens as it went. On then through the night. From the Kingdom of Kerry to Kingsbridge at the shivering dawn of a September morning in Dublin.

They'd made the journey before, these two. Kerry were playing their third final in succession, after all. They had been there two years earlier, when Kerry gathered back their best players and put down the uprising which was Armagh football. Yet still the city hit them like a bracing wind whenever they stepped into it.

They were worried, but not visibly so. The newspaper chatter about Dublin's 'scientific' football was never-ending. Would Kerry's traditional game suffice? They had heard so much about Kevin Heffernan and Ollie Freeney that they feared they might be giants. Ned Roche and Dan Cronin would be marking them. Good men, but the lads fretted just the same.

Today you can't imagine the fiesta which the All-Ireland of that year sparked. Dublin's team was the first to be composed of Dublin men, as opposed to the usual regiment of country lads playing under a flag of convenience. The phenomenon of Hill 16 was created. Suddenly Gaelic football was being played allegro and the sterility of the high ball contested by two leaping men had been replaced by the sight of Dubs in sky-blue jerseys stabbing balls out into the prairies of space, where colleagues would matierialize quick as sprites.

Heffernan was impossibly glamorous, a luminous presence all summer. He was the blond genius behind a new style of play. His team held the summer in the palm of their hands. If his colleagues were a supporting cast they didn't act that way. They were cerebral and capable and as driven as Heffernan himself.

Collectively they rejected the orthodoxy of catch and kick. They talked football night and day, like scientists figuring out how to put man on the moon. On summer nights, as many of them as possible would be inserted into Jim Lavin's car, shoehorned in, and they'd drive to Sutton. There they'd stretch, get the circulation back and walk the Head of Howth, talking football all the way. If the discussion merited it, they would walk the Head twice.

They were abstemious and obsessive. John Timmons used to moan that for all their talk he knew the opposition better than they did because the opposition were the only ones he could go for a drink with after a match.

By September the yammering of the media, the swaggering boasts of the city and the legend of Heffernan made realism imposs-ible. All-Ireland weekend turned into a carnival. Dublin supporters paraded up and down O'Connell Street, following a drummer. Kerry folk, sniffy about what games will interest them, travelled in large numbers.

This Dublin team was beloved in a way that only native sons can be. They brought to the game the personality of the big city, the swagger of townies. They were a team to make men throw their hats in the air.

Mark Wilson remembers being a beneficiary of the team's sud-den popularity. Injury kept him out of the All-Ireland final that year, but as he lay on his hospital bed in the Bon Secours he heard a gruff enquiry being made in the corridor outside.

'Where's Mark Wilson?'

'Just through there, I think.'

Duly a large man arrived at his bedside carrying an unfeasibly large basket of grapes.

'You're Mark Wilson?'

'Yes.'

'These are for you from all the lads in the docks.'

'Well, thanks very much.'

'Where do the other fellas train?'

'Parnell Park in Donnycarney. Why?'

'We've a couple of barrels of oranges for them.'

The team's heart was in Marino, and the sudden and unprecedented popularity of the team had its root in a decision taken in Marino seven years previously. St Vincent's, the club which Heffernan grew up with, had sensed unease among their own local players who had come through the juvenile ranks. The club was swamped with applications for membership from country-born players who had moved to the city. Players brought through the club's own nursery fretted about their futures.

St Vincent's decided to avoid temptation. The club adopted a ruling for their own purposes which restricted membership to 'persons born in Dublin, persons eligible for juvenile or minor grades though not born in Dublin and persons not born in Dublin, who are ordinarily resident in the parishes of Marino, Fairview or Clontarf'.

In the summer of 1949 St Vincent's won the county championship for the first time. With the county champions having the pick of the inter-county team, the policy of Dublin players for Dublin teams gained a foothold, which was strengthened considerably by each successive championship St Vincent's won.

In 1942 Dublin had won an All-Ireland against Galway and the feat had gone virtually unnoticed in the city. The St Vincent's team, composed entirely of natives, caught the imagination, though. In 1952 a replayed county final between St Vincent's and Garda attracted a crowd of 25,000.

In 1953, when Dublin beat the mighty Cavan in the National League final, all fourteen outfield players were from St Vincent's.

They wore the club's famous white jerseys with the blue band around the chest and back. The city was interested. Very interested.

By 1955 Dublin were applying a new brand of football to the championship. What is mysterious is that it took so long for them to reap reward. Through the early fifties Dublin played with style, but two factors seemed to militate against a journey to the third Sunday of any September.

Firstly, the GAA had abolished the hand pass in 1950, just as St Vincent's – and, by extension, Dublin – had integrated the move into their new style of play. Secondly, having won their first county championship in 1949, St Vincent's embarked on a run of seven years unbeaten. They eventually lost the 1956 Dublin championship to the students from Erin's Hope, before setting out to win a further six in a row. The wear and tear accounted for a few unexpected Leinster championship exits for the county side.

The style which they eventually settled on involved extensive use of a fisted pass and the creation and exploitation of space by means of Heffernan's incessant rovings. It was an approach which drew sufficient suspicion from traditionalists to attract the label 'scientific'. In the GAA, when somebody describes you as being 'scientific' or 'ahead of your time', they are either speaking at your funeral or predicting your downfall.

There was nothing scientific, however, about the way injuries were treated in those days. In trouble with a bad ankle in the approach to the 1955 All-Ireland, Heffernan went to a local doctor, who helpfully produced a syringe the size of a bicycle pump and filled his lower leg with novocaine. The limb swelled till it was the shape of a balloon.

'Now,' said the doctor, 'walk to Howth.'

The doctor's surgery was in Clontarf. Howth is five miles away.

'I can't,' said Heffernan, who doubted at this stage his ability to walk out of the surgery. 'Too much pain.'

'Ah, not now,' said the doctor, triumphantly giving the frozen leg a kick.

So each day he made his pilgrimage to the doctor's surgery and each day the pain got worse. There was a gruesome rhythm to it.

He'd get the leg filled with novocaine and then obey the order to walk to Howth.

Eventually time ran out on the experiment with medical science. Heffernan abandoned the treatments, and on the afternoon of the All-Ireland final took painkilling injections and played, regardless of the risk.

'He should never have played,' says Mark Wilson, who recalls being collected by Nicky Maher and brought to the game on crutches that Sunday and arriving in the dressing room just in time to see the needles go into Heffernan's foot.

Others didn't make it that far. Dublin had lost Norman Allen to appendix trouble and Mark Wilson to leg injury, and the team would line out with midfielder Jim McGuinness injured also.

Still, it was a time before detailed analysis and breaking sports news. The city rode the big wave of good feeling. There was a happy sense that weekend of this being a game that would define the era, a settling between opposing philosophies. While Dublin were struggling with injuries, they had no shortage of panache. And Kerry? Sensing a threat not just to their dominance but to their belief system, they had gone back to fundamentals. Catch it and kick it.

With uncharacteristic sensitivity the GAA chose to mark the occasion of an all-Dublin team wearing the county colours for the first time in an All-Ireland final by introducing the Revd Dr William Fitzpatrick to the team captains before the throw-in. Dr Fitzpatrick was a founder of St Vincent's and a guiding light in the policy of Dublin men for Dublin teams which had its flowering that day.

The match was one of the great games in history. Dublin lost. Kevin Heffernan volunteered to shoulder the blame.

More than half a century later he still isn't flinching. 'I took some wrong options that day. I went for scores where I thought we needed to score a goal. I regret that very much still. If we had popped the points we might have got the goal. That's one thing I learned. In my memory, that afternoon doesn't merge into other games but the hour compacts. I only remember small incidents. I remember putting a ball over the bar instead of giving it on to Johnny Boyle, for instance, early on.

'Then later not taking the points and being closed out. I remember that very well.'

In conversation he never mentions the injury which kept him close to Kerry's full back Ned Roche all day long. No excuses.

Most of what happened afterwards is a dark blur. He thinks there was some kind of collective meal that night for the team, but he escaped out to Skerries for a while to be alone with the grief of the thing. Finally duty summoned him back to the city and the team table.

They should have seen it coming. Perhaps that's what galls the most, even half a century later. The excitement got into their pores. Meanwhile Kerry, knowingly, just let it happen. They watched Dublin's balloon inflate and they smiled through gimlet eyes. Science! Pshaw! They had their own alchemists. Thank you very much.

The practice of collective training, whereby teams entered monastic training camps before big games, had been banned in 1954 as being the thin end of professionalism's wedge. The shifting sands of GAA politics being what they are, the training camps were restored a year later.

The restoration suited Kerry perfectly. Long before the somewhat derogatory phrase, 'the cult of the manager', had been minted, there was Dr Eamonn O'Sullivan. Long before they talked of scientific football Dr Eamonn had perfected the science of catch and kick, wherein players fielded the ball at the highest altitude possible and moved it on quickly until somebody could shoot for a score.

The good doctor's eight All-Irelands as Kerry coach were won between the years 1924 and 1962, making him a winner in five different decades. And he was the author of *the* coaching manual: *The Art and Science of Gaelic Football*, published in 1958. The title was read as a quiet rebuke to Dublin, the fall guys in O'Sullivan's greatest triumph, that 1955 All-Ireland. Only one academy could offer graduation courses in the 'art and science' of Gaelic football, and that was Kerry.

O'Sullivan mixed a traditional view as to how football should be played with a progressive approach to matters of diet (tomatoes were a speciality) and fitness while he had players under his thumb in training camp. Under his guidance Kerry had evolved the training camp system to a point where they were almost unbeatable in All-Ireland finals.

The good doctor offered a full daily programme of work and activity. The squad took a fast walk before Mass, then had a light breakfast, followed by a morning session out on the field, lunch, and then back to the field again for an afternoon session. This went on seven days a week until the Wednesday before the game. Dr Eamonn even incorporated a taper into his regime, easing off the daily regimen in those final days as the game drew nearer.

In 1955, Kerry remained in camp under O'Sullivan's guidance from the time of the replayed semi-final through to the All-Ireland. He instructed his full back Ned Roche not to stray from the square in pursuit of Heffernan. The rest of the plan was catch and kick as usual.

It worked. Mick O'Dwyer watched and never forgot.

By the time Micko and his friend Eric got to stand on the terraces at the 1955 All-Ireland final, Micko was already a minor inter-county player, one with ambitions and a reputation.

He had finished with school at the age of fifteen and gone into his time as a mechanic. In 1954 he had worn the Kerry jersey for the first time. He was a cause célèbre in south Kerry that summer. The first Waterville player ever to wear a county jersey at any grade. The first, they believed, to be victimized.

He had been picked for a replayed Munster semi-final with Waterford in Kenmare. A decent crowd from Waterville came down to enjoy the occasion. They were rewarded by the sight of their boy scoring 1–6.

South Kerry has never had much influence in Kerry GAA, though. O'Dwyer was dropped for the Munster final, and even though Kerry won the game he never received a medal.

He wore number twenty on his back for the Munster final. In the All-Ireland semi-final he had been pushed down to number twenty-one. On All-Ireland final day Kerry didn't even give him a jersey. Dublin beat Kerry that day, winning the first of three minor titles in succession. O'Dwyer watched the game in his street clothes.

O'Dwyer, young and slightly disillusioned, wasn't too interested in the outcome, but that summer brought lessons which he would never forget either.

He had only to wait till the following summer to make his point to those who had overlooked him. 1955 would turn out to be as essential to Mick O'Dwyer's development as it was to Kevin Heffernan's. Still essentially a boy, O'Dwyer played on the South Kerry team which won the Kerry County Championship for the first time in 59 years.

It took two games to decide the final. South Kerry played North Kerry in Tralee in front of 7,100 people. North Kerry took the lead at the death when Dan McAuliffe scored a point. O'Dwyer, the most competitive animal on the park, equalized with just about the last kick of the game.

Three weeks later, South Kerry won the replay by two points. A two-mile convoy of cars drove back to Cahirciveen in triumph. Another seven hundred celebrants arrived on the train soon after. O'Dwyer was nineteen. Mick O'Connell in midfield was eighteen. They would win the next two Kerry titles as well.

And in September Micko would be back in Croke Park with his friend Eric, watching a game which seized the imagination of the country. Dublin versus Kerry. Town versus country. Science versus Catch and Kick. Glory to the green and gold. The wonder of Kerry football was restored to his heart that summer.

Other young men absorbed the lessons of 1955, too. In Tony Hanahoe's mind his teenage summer of 1955 is bookended by two events. On the night of 16 May he sat up all night in the cool of his parents' kitchen, listening to the scratchy transmission of Rocky Marciano's world title defence against Don Cockell, a fight broadcast all the way from Kezar Stadium in San Francisco to the Hanahoe household in Clontarf.

Marciano held the title when the referee stopped the fight with fifty-four seconds of the ninth round left. Young Tony Hanahoe went to bed happy, and a lifelong love of boxing was cemented. To this day, when he reaches for a metaphor or a simile his mind provides him with a line from boxing.

The summer ended less satisfactorily, of course. On 25 September the Hanahoe boys were herded into the back of the family car for one of those interminable trips to the country which generations of Dublin children suffered in some form or other. With the four boys kicking each other in frustration all the way the family took a spin as far as Glendalough.

The lads were let out of the car to release some steam while *mère et père* Hanahoe enjoyed a refreshment. They were just back in the car when Tony spotted a stranger and leaned his head out the window to ask whether Dublin had beaten Kerry in the All-Ireland final.

'He said no, Kerry had won. I remember crying in frustration. It was such a rise to fame for a native-born team from Dublin and they were going to take on Kerry.'

By that summer Hanahoe had become firm friends with a boy in a gabardine coat who, maddeningly, was always in the best spot on Hill 16 before Hanahoe could get there on a Sunday afternoon. No matter how early Hanahoe arrived, the gabardine was there first. They threw in their lot together and developed a system of getting from the Hill out to the sideline seats. You could really appreciate the thunder of players' footfalls out there.

The gabardine was Jimmy Keaveney. He was there in September 1955, lamenting as Dublin lost under a mackerel sky.

'I played almost nothing but soccer till the '55 Dublin team came along. I loved that team. I cried twice in my life over sport. Once when the Dubs lost in 1955. I cried and I cried that day. Then when Dublin lost the 1961 hurling final to Tipperary. I cried then as well. I remember Des Foley coming off the field and the tears coming out of his eyes in 1961. I was crying so much in 1955

I can hardly remember any of them, just Ollie Freaney getting a late goal from a free. It was the worst thing that ever happened, seeing them lose like that.'

Paddy Cullen was there, too. He was eleven years old. Paddy's brother-in-law Johnny Green worked making soap for Lever Brothers, and that weekend Johnny came in from Newtown-mountkennedy and lifted Paddy over the stile. Paddy was already big and gawky and embarrassed by it, but this was a religious observance. He understood.

'I was in thrall to that team of '55. They were this new stylish thing. We all knew what was going on, what it meant. It was the first time you dreamed of being a Dub. That day broke my heart. I remember big Ollie Freaney loping up as usual to take a free and then bang it was in the net. Right at the end there was a lifeline and then it was over. Unbelievable. We didn't talk all the way home.'

In Kerry the joy was fizzed through with relief. 'Up Kerry,' wrote PF, a columnist for *The Kerryman*. 'Up Kerry, Up Catch and Kick, Up Kerry, Up Dr Eamonn, Up Catch and Kick.'

And Kerry weren't yet done with Kevin Heffernan's heart. The ache of losing to the green and gold would become a familiar penance. He lost a minor All-Ireland final to Kerry in 1946. He lost the All-Ireland of 1955 and the semi-finals of 1959 and 1962 as a player. As a selector in the sixties, he was on board for the semi-final defeat of 1965.

His obsession would create the vivid soap opera of the seventies, but when it was done there would be more punishment. Kevin Heffernan oversaw the construction of a new Dublin side in the eighties. They won a remarkable All-Ireland in 1983 but were put back on the seats of their pants in 1984 and 1985. Kerry each time.

And Kevin Heffernan's beloved St Vincent's? They won the Dublin championship of 1984 and went to the All-Ireland final of the following spring and lost a game they should have won when a late high ball was dropped into the net. Their conquerors? Castleisland of Kerry.

St Vincent's had at that point won twenty-three of the previous thirty-six Dublin football championships. The club has failed to win a football title since.

Heffernan absorbed these blows, but the bruises of 1955 remained.

'No defeat as a manager ever hit me like 1955. That was the first time there. It was Kerry. I had great hopes, and so on and so on. That formed a large part of what I became as a person.'

And the person he became shaped a large part of the history of Gaelic football.

I

Being a Dublin player was no help with girls. I'd say it was a
hindrance in fact.

Robbie Kelleher

Jimmy Keaveney thought he was on the pig's back.

Dublin won an All-Ireland in 1963. Nothing hectic about it.
Nobody, least of all Jimmy, knew that the banquet marked the
start of famine.

Kevin Heffernan was a selector that summer and to Jimmy, who
had been raised in Heffernan's shadow on the fields of Marino, it
seemed like the natural order of things when, less than a year later,
he found himself making own his inter-county debut in a challenge
game against Kerry. The match was played in The Oval, the old
St Vincent's club grounds in Raheny. Jimmy did well and earned
his ticket on to the Dublin team. There he stayed. He cleared a
place in the cabinet for the imminent avalanche of All-Ireland
medals.

Two years later, in 1965, Dublin won a Leinster championship.
The adventure ended with an All-Ireland semi-final bout against
Kerry. In the second half Jimmy launched himself for a ball and
came down heavily on his ankle. Lying on the Croke Park sod, he
was tended to by the team selector, Brendan Quinn, who tenderly
poured a bottle of lukewarm water on to the injured area and
asked optimistically if Keaveney could play on. He couldn't.

The game finished and, with it, Dublin's season. Jimmy Keaveney wasn't too distraught. There'd be more chances soon. Anyway,
the wounded ankle had swollen alarmingly and Keaveney couldn't
walk. Liam Ferguson, a sub on the team that day, offered to provide

a lift home to Whitehall, so Keaveney stood alone at the back of Hill 16, waiting for his friend and clubmate as he made the journey back to his own house to fetch the car. Finally Ferguson returned in his red Mini to transport Jimmy Keaveney home to Whitehall.

The next morning brought no good news. Dublin were still out of the championship and Keaveney's ankle was the size of a football. The earnest application of lukewarm water from a bottle hadn't worked. Ignoring the pain hadn't worked either. Resigned to the seriousness of the situation by now, Jimmy hobbled down to the bus stop and caught the number 16 to town. Thus one of the stars of the previous day's All-Ireland semi-final could be seen, hopping in some agony up O'Connell Street and all the way to Jervis Street Hospital. The X-ray showed that the ankle was broken in two places.

The doctors set the ankle, put it in plaster and dispatched Keaveney with a pair of crutches. Without any money for transport, he hobbled home. That was August.

In October he went back to Jervis Street Hospital. All clear this time. The breaks had healed. A nurse went to relieve him of his crutches.

Keaveney demurred. 'Gimme it! I've only the one shoe!'

So, with a crutch and one stockinged foot, he caught the bus home.

In the two months since the semi-final he had not had a word of concern from anybody in the Dublin county board or management team. It was about then that Jimmy Keaveney realized there might be a gap between the dream of being a Dub and the reality of it.

'You play in an All-Ireland semi-final, you break your ankle and nobody gives a shite about you! There wasn't a word about it. Not a call! Nothing! That was Dublin, back then.'

Except it got worse. The '65 semi-final marked the extinguishing of all hope. From 1966 to 1973 Dublin's record in Leinster veered between disastrous and catastrophic. They were beaten by Kildare, Westmeath, Longford, Kildare (again), Longford (again), Laois, Kildare (yet again) and Louth.

The odd thing is that in some of those years Dublin had a

half-decent football team. They had residual ambition. Vital signs were normal. Why the county suffered a near-death experience is still something of a mystery.

In 1967 Keaveney captained a Dublin outfit which went unbeaten through the National League, all the way to the final against the mighty Galway side of that era. Dublin led by five points at half-time but couldn't withstand Galway's second-half response. The team lost by two points and the selectors lost their nerve. By the time Dublin played Westmeath in the Leinster championship five weeks later, half the defence and one midfielder had been dropped. They lost to a last-minute goal.

The selection committees were an unwieldy mess, riven by politics and apathy. Training was poor when it happened and unlamented when it didn't. Men who went on to win All-Ireland medals remember training for Leinster championship games with a couple of laps and a kickaround in Parnell Park. Then they'd repair to the pub for important discussions.

Good footballers came and went. The supporters just stayed at home. Television was more diverting and the couch was more comfortable. Dublin's footballers were in their own private purgatory. Playing for Dublin meant you were a bogballer, a gahman, a culchie. 'Being a Dublin player was no help with girls,' says Robbie Kelleher. 'I'd say it was a hindrance, in fact.'

Paddy Cullen had arrived in 1966. His debut was a challenge game against Derry on the eve of the All-Ireland final of that year. Cullen got a call to say that the great John Timmons had caught the flu. Would Cullen play at full forward?

He was on the pitch for five minutes when he ran for a ball, hit a pothole and broke his ankle. No solicitous words from the county board. No get-well cards. Keaveney told him not to expect bouquets but to use the crutches and a long, sad face to get to the top of the queue when going to the pictures on Saturday nights. Might as well draw some benefit from being an injured Dub.

When Cullen came back to blue, it was as a goalkeeper. He had been playing soccer in goal for his employers, McNaughton's, in an inter-firms league. In the GAA of the time that was a venial sin to those who committed it, and a mortal sin to those who made the rules. It couldn't last. Cullen had attracted some attention from Shelbourne and was pondering an offer to go and play for them when Jimmy Keaveney persuaded Dublin to give him a call.

It wasn't all altruism on Keaveney's part. One of the highlights of the era was an error of judgement by Maxie McCann of St Sylvester's. Maxie was Cullen's immediate predecessor in the Dublin goalkeeping job. At half-time in a league game, just before the teams went back out, Maxie felt an urgent need to evacuate his bowels. He repaired to the bathroom and was thus enthroned when the referee, tired of waiting, threw in the ball for the second half. Dublin conceded a goal into an empty net as somewhere in the depths of Croke Park a cistern flushed.

Paddy Cullen duly received a little blue postcard asking him to report to the dressing room in Croke Park on Sunday. He walked up to the stadium from his house in Seville Place with his kitbag slung over his shoulder, harbouring the illusion that he was entering a world of glamour. He covered the short distance to Croke Park without anybody paying a blind piece of notice. No Cullenmania just yet.

He'd forgotten to bring the postcard and fretted that he might have difficulty gaining entry to the ground. He needn't have worried. His announcement that he was the Dublin goalkeeper was greeted with a shrug of the shoulders. G'wan.

So he walked into the middle of a freefalling Dublin team. There were still some names there, but the photos of their heyday were sepia now. All Cullen remembers is that it was windy and, early on, Greg Hughes hit a ball from forty yards. Paddy moved out too early. The wind suckered him. The ball swung in over his head.

'I said to myself, that's it. You're finished already, Paddy.'

He wasn't. He'd been on the pitch, not in the bathroom. Nobody cared beyond that. He took the number one jersey and kept it.

They couldn't win a game but they looked good. They had the Dublin swagger. The hair was a little longer, the locks a little more flamboyant, the gear always pristine. And, best of all, the transport!

Tom Loftus was the chairman of the board at the time. Tom had connections with the undertaking trade. To save money on coach hire, the Dubs used to travel to matches in the black Austin Princess limousines normally used as mourning cars. A procession of sleek limos would pull up at a godforsaken pitch on a bitter afternoon in November. The Dublin footballers would climb out, endure the local wit, get beaten and clamber back in again. Home, James.

'We looked good arriving,' says Paddy. 'It was hurtful getting beaten by every team in the country but you held on to the dream. You went to the matches knowing you were going to be beaten. We'd lose but we'd look good leaving, too.'

Cullen stayed. Other players suspected that there might have been more to life. They went looking for it. Tony Hanahoe was one who drifted away.

'Everyone had their own priorities and circumstances. Keaveney, Cullen and O'Driscoll and those all continued playing. I was studying in Trinity. I was playing inter-club competition. I got dragged a little into University life and it wasn't hard to leave Dublin behind. As best as I can remember, the Dublin team was poorly organized. It was every man for himself and nobody was going to clap you on the back for taking over his place. Maybe I wasn't dedicated enough at that stage. Maybe they weren't, either!'

Sean Doherty came into the team in the late sixties. He'd played Under-21 football for Wicklow, which was a little unusual for a man who had done most of his growing up on Anglesea Road in Ballsbridge. Either way, he found the Dublin jersey gave him a bit of a shiver any time he put it on.

'I don't know why I liked it! They'd have training sessions, kicking the ball in and out of the square. Paddy Delaney would do a bit of running on his own maybe, and we thought he was mad. We'd laugh behind his back. I sat through from 1968 to 1972. I remember in 1971 we got to a league semi-final. Mayo beat us. J. J. Cribben got a fist to a ball, stuck it in the back of the net. He was full forward, I was full back! Typical.'

Dublin's unkempt team lurched around the highways and

byways, contending with every problem, bar success or popularity. In a league game with Westmeath in 1969, a Dublin official jumped up from the bench, sprinted half the length of the field and decked the Westmeath goalie as he prepared to take a kick-out. Not surprisingly, play was suspended that a brief interval of mayhem might ensue.

The spirit of the times is captured best perhaps in the Babs Keating incident. In the early seventies Dublin played Tipperary in one of the Corn na Casca games which were an annual Easter penance at Croke Park. By then Pat O'Neill had established a reputation for himself as one of the more, ahem, robust defenders at Dublin's disposal. Pat's particular form of play had first gained national attention in the All-Ireland minor semi-final of 1968, when he flattened John Coleman of Cork. He still has regrets about that one: 'I hit him and got away from him and thought I was in the clear, but for maybe the first time in Croke Park the umpire called the referee over and pointed the finger at me. I got sent off.'

Anyway, on this Easter Sunday Pat was more sinned against than sinning. He was playing in the middle on Babs Keating, the Tipperary dual player, and Dublin were experimenting with a forerunner of the wandering corner forward tactic. Kevin Hegarty, a blond corner forward from Raheny, was given what cutting-edge sports writers have for decades termed 'the roving commission'.

At one stage there was a bit of what Pat O'Neill fondly calls 'horsing' in the middle of the field. Keating was a spiky class of opponent and Hegarty, enjoying his freedom, got a few digs in. Unfortunately, Keating got his blond Dubs mixed up and took his retaliation out on Pat O'Neill.

Fortunately for Babs, his victim didn't get up again. Pat O'Neill was carted, out cold, off to Jervis Street.

For Babs the reprieve was temporary. Pat's father, one Bill O'Neill, an irascible Kilkenny man, had serious issues with Tipperary at the best of times. Bill O'Neill could sit in Croke Park with steam issuing from his ears during the national anthem on the days when Kilkenny would hurl against Tipp.

On this occasion, when the final whistle went he strode down the steps of the Cusack Stand and on to the pitch, where he reached out one hand to shake with Babs Keating and hit Babs flush in the face with the other.

He had his escape perfectly orchestrated. He ran down the players' tunnel, into the Dublin dressing room and out through the far door into the exit alley behind. When Babs recovered his senses he tried to give chase, but there were roadblocks. The occupants of the Dublin dressing room had been a little surprised to see Pat O'Neill's father running through, looking flustered. When Babs Keating came knocking, thirty seconds later, it all made sense. 'Sorry, Babs. Your dressing room is down the way.'

By the early seventies the county team were little spoken about, and club football in Dublin was dominated by a blood feud between St Vincent's and University College Dublin.

The sides met in championship games seven years in a row from 1970 onwards, including five consecutive finals (one of which was bitterly conceded as a walkover by the College). There is a separate book to be written by the survivors of those wars, but even the briefest highlights can be upsetting for the faint-hearted.

At a league final in the very early seventies, a game played in the depths of winter in the arctic tundra of O'Toole Park, Crumlin, the sides enthusiastically set about each other, paying little heed to the ball. One haymaker delivered by a College man, partly removed the ear of St Vincent's forward Eugene Mullin.

The larruping stopped briefly to permit the aforementioned Pat O'Neill, then a UCD player and a final-year medical student, to study his opponent's head. To his fascination, O'Neill found that the blood was actually freezing as it poured out from the wound. No danger of infection. Nothing to see here, lads. Seconds out. Resume shemozzling.

The 1972 final between the two teams had far-reaching consequences. Phil Markey of Fingallians, a county board politician who would later be county chairman, claimed that he had been forced to leave Parnell Park after fifteen minutes, so sickened had he been by the bloodshed and violence. There were those who wondered why he had come at all if bloodshed and violence weren't his cup of tea, but Markey ploughed on, stating in an unforgettable moment of rhetoric that 'St Vincent's were running Dublin football and ruining it.' It was a remark for which he would never be forgiven around Marino.

Late in 1972, Markey took over the management and training of the Dublin team. The St Vincent's contingent withdrew their services in protest. Almost a decade and a half later, when Markey became chairman of the county board, Kevin Heffernan withdrew his management team immediately.

'There was bad blood there between Markey and Vincent's,' says Tony Hanahoe with characteristic understatement. 'It could be said that whenever he went and we came back again, neither missed the other.'

By 1973 there was perhaps one bright spot: Frank Murray of Na Fianna. Murray was the only Dublin outfield player getting selected for Leinster in those days. He had come through from a Na Fianna team which defied the odds and won a county championship in 1969. That win in 1969 was remarkable because of the reputation the Na Fianna club had. It was said that whoever trained Na Fianna had to handle more chickens than Colonel Sanders.

John McCarthy remembers playing a championship game as a seventeen-year-old for Na Fianna against St Vincent's and being almost able to smell the fear among his teammates. So much so that, a few minutes after McCarthy's introduction as a sub, a senior teammate came up to him and ordered him to swap positions. 'Not my sort of game in there,' he said, running off merrily to the prairies as McCarthy walked warily down the mean street patrolled by Gay O' Driscoll, the St Vincent's full back.

'If you got into a row with Vincents when you were wearing a Na Fianna jersey, you knew you were on your own,' says McCarthy.

Murray defied convention, though. He was tough, he was brilliant in the air and he could kick. Reared in Clontarf, he had joined Na Fianna when he was seven and the club had just been formed.

He went to school, got signed up and was given a little orange card to show that he was a member. He was hooked. As the years wore on, he found he had a talent for other sports, but he just loved the robust nature of Gaelic football. More than that, he loved catching high balls. He was a natural.

There was an old shed down in the Na Fianna. The shed had a highish ceiling and the younger players were fascinated by how a small group of the senior team who had basketball training could jump and touch the ceiling with the palms of their hands. The youngsters would try for hours and nobody could get within six or seven inches of tippng the ceiling. Then there was Frank Murray. He could leap effortlessly and he just seemed to hang up there as if his hand was holding him to the ceiling.

Murray played for Dublin the following summer. The duty didn't detain him long: Dublin were beaten by Longford in May. He stood out, though, and by 1973 Frank Murray was a legend in the making. Dublin were as hapless as usual that summer, but at least they travelled south and drilled Wexford full of holes in May. Every Dublin player remembers Murray's performance in Wexford Park that afternoon. He scored two goals and resisted the more primal attentions of a series of Wexford defenders.

The Dublin minors played that day as well, and the two teams came home together on the coach, with everyone in good spirits. Murray sat some distance away from the high jinks, though. He was reading a book. Kierkegaard.

He was twenty-five then, with his prime ahead of him. He was married. Sort of. Back in the summer of 1970, some time after Dublin had been removed from the championship by Longford, Frank Murray had come across an American woman, Sharon. They met in Dublin and travelled back to the States together when there was a break in the football. By the time they got to America Sharon was pregnant. She wanted nothing from Frank Murray except a wedding certificate before their child was born. Beyond that she preferred to raise her child on her own. Frank thought that arrangement to be fair enough; he and Sharon had never intended to do anything much more than travel a piece of the road together.

They were married by a preacher in the mountains of western Massachusetts on a sunny Saturday afternoon. Being hippies, Frank, Sharon and the preacher each took off their clothes and went skinny-dipping together as soon as the short ceremony concluded.

They drank a lot of wine and they smoked a lot of dope and they stayed up all night. Next morning, Frank travelled down to New York to play for Cavan in Gaelic Park in a New York championship match. The money he received for lining out would pay for his trip. He remembers that the heat was 103° C. He was a little washed out and dishevelled – so much so, in fact, that it seemed all day as if he was unmarked. He played brilliantly, and through it all there was just one cloud in the perfect sky. Every time he got the ball, Lefty Devine, the famous Gaelic Park announcer, would shout: 'And now to Frank Murray, who was married yesterday.'

Word reached home in Clontarf that Frank Murray was married, long before Frank got home to tell it.

Dublin's time in the doldrums suited Frank. His son grew up on Nantucket Island and during his infant years he saw his father every summer. Frank would play for Dublin until the annual humiliation was visited upon the team, and then he would be free to head to the States to play a little football and do a little Daddying.

Dublin football remained defiantly stagnant and ramshackle. After Frank Murray's greatest game against Wexford in that summer of 1973, the team were due to play Louth in the second round.

John McCarthy was out for a few drinks in The Sunnybank in Glasnevin one night, messing around with a few friends, when he bumped into Phil Markey. The Dublin manager was in high good spirits himself.

'Would you like to come down to Dublin training on Tuesday night?' said Markey.

McCarthy knew that the championship was already in full swing and thought that the offer might be half in jest. He went anyway, delighted with himself at the unexpected elevation. The training transpired to be a joke, which punctured his enthusiasm.

'Off ye go for yer warm-up, lads,' Markey said, clapping his hands.

'How long?'

'Three or four laps. Jogging.'

The players set off at what might have been a moderate walking pace. McCarthy, however, was hoping to make an impression and decided to get a good start in case he got left behind later by the county men.

After a minute or two he realized that he was nearly a lap ahead of everyone else. He was mortified, but now a new problem arose. He didn't know whether to keep ahead of the toiling pack or to stop and let himself be caught. He slowed down a little but remained comfortably ahead of everyone.

He was beginning to realize that no sweat would be broken tonight when Phil Markey ordered twenty press-ups. McCarthy was in good shape and got to it.

He hadn't done ten when he heard an anguished moan.

'Ah Phil, Jaysus Phil, we've had enough.'

They packed it in and, in sympathy for themselves, had a gentle kickaround. McCarthy took a shower afterwards. The Parnell Park showers were legendary, a must-see item for a newcomer. Some players didn't bother with the experience, but others were charmed by the windows, which were broken, and the ivy, which was growing in through the frames. The floor was made of timber and players who came dancing out of the showers when the water turned from warm to ice-cold ran the twin risks of splinters and verrucas.

While McCarthy was washing, he could hear the fellas talking about him.

'Who's that new fucker? Making a bleedin' show of us. Somebody sort him for the next night.'

There wasn't enough time for that. Dublin lost to Louth in a replay and said goodbye to the 1973 championship at roughly the same time as they'd said goodbye to championships for years. Still, some made it to Croke Park on All-Ireland final day.

Brian Mullins, yet to even join the panel, sold final-day

programmes. Sean Doherty and Jimmy Keaveney worked up on Hill 16 as stewards. An extraordinary Cork team beat Galway. The Hill emptied out quickly, but the two old Dubs hung on to watch Billy Morgan take the Cup and make his speech.

Keaveney had stopped playing for Dublin a couple of summers previously, but the romance hadn't left his heart.

'Wouldn't it be great all the same, Doc, to be up there getting that oul cup?'

Sean Doherty rolled his eyes.

'C'mon, Jim. We'll go to Meagher's.'

2

He was ruthless. If there was a fella up in Mountjoy doing life for
stabbing his wife and Heffernan thought he could help win an
All-Ireland for us, then he'd bust him out. And when he'd busted
him out and needed to make room on the team he'd drop
his best friend if he had to. Nothing would stand in his way.
You understood that. And you got on with it and you
were grand! I'm saying that as a friend!

Jimmy Keaveney

Jackie Gilroy has a memory of a small detail from the seventies.
Kevin Heffernan recalls it another way. The difference is revealing.

It was the late spring of 1974 and Heffernan had been back managing the Dublin team for six months. Jackie was chairman of Heffernan's club, St Vincent's. The two men were close friends. Still are.

'And Kevin came to me one evening and he said, "I think we
can do something this year but I'm going to need the lads for the
summer or as long as it takes."'

The lads were the eight or nine St Vincent's players who made
up the nucleus of the Dublin panel. To take so many players
away from the club for county training could have devastating
consequences. Still. It was Kevin Heffernan who was asking. And
this was St Vincent's, a club that took its role in the welfare of the
county very seriously. Jackie Gilroy said yes, and the St Vincent's
players trained with Dublin.

Kevin Heffernan's memory is different in one respect.

'I don't think I would have asked,' Heffernan says with a smile.
'In fact, I'm sure I wouldn't have.'

★

Long ago, back in 1957, Dublin lost a Leinster championship game
to Louth and Kevin Heffernan came off the field, sick with shame.
It was the only time in a long history of playing that he felt he had
been part of a side that had let themselves down.

He was going to be captain of the team the following year. So
he made a decision. He'd quit hurling, concentrate on football.
Something else. He'd go to Wicklow and persuade Joe Timmons
that he was to come back and play for his county. Then he'd get
John Timmons back.

'And we won it the next year,' he says of the 1958 All-Ireland.

He was just a player. Was he really at liberty to be going getting
fellas and putting them back on the team?

He frowns. 'I wasn't at liberty, I suppose. I just did it.'

Five years later, he was a selector when Dublin scraped their
way to the 1963 Leinster final, against Kildare. The day before
the match, Heffernan famously travelled to Kells and intercepted
Snitchy Ferguson in his garden. One of Heffernan's 'just passing'
routines.

The next day, Ferguson appeared in the Dublin dressing room,
unannounced. Played. Made the difference.

Dublin were on their way to another All-Ireland. Nobody
argued. People tended not to argue.

Turlough Parade, Marino, has eight small houses which line up,
four a side, as a stout guard of honour on the path to Griffith
Avenue.

The Parade was a microcosm of Marino's teeming diversity.
Eddie Wall from next door would play for Arsenal. Two doors
down are the Lawlers. Paddy would play second row for Ireland,
famously sitting down once during the playing of 'God Save the
Queen'. His brother John would throw the hammer in the
Olympic Games. And from that house at the bottom of the parade,
the one with the signature cherry tree, would spring Kevin
Heffernan.

He will overshadow them all eventually. Hurling and football
will forge the identity of the entire parish. Also, the games will

shape him and he will shape them. First though they must take
seed in the fertile underworld of childish imaginations. Later they
will change the country.

He learned early the value of movement. John Heffernan, a
guard, would come around on his bike off Shelmartin Avenue and
in the distance see a sliotar or a football flying heedlessly above the
blossoms in his perfectly flowered garden – yet when he'd get to
his own gate there wouldn't be a soul to be seen.

His colleague, the local guard, one Baby Face Malone, would
cycle home twice a day up dusty Griffith Avenue. Each time Baby
Face loomed he interrupted a full-scale hurling game, played from
the top of Turlough Parade down towards the big white church
and the Christian Brothers primary school.

At first sight of Baby Face, in a curious ritual of deference and
respect, the players would vanish like sprites and hide in the
gardens. Baby Face would ride passively by. Play would resume.

Ah, the place teemed. Kids everywhere. They arrived in Marino
together, the children by and large of country folk. They schooled
together. They played together. They made friends easily and they
stayed friends forever.

And in the upper circle, as the orange sun went missing each
evening, at some point, at the distant top of Griffith Avenue, you'd
find him out with his friend and mentor, Budger Keely. Hurling
away.

'Left side.'

'Right side.'

'Pull.'

'Pull.'

'Pull.'

'You're Mick Mackey. I'm John Mackey. Pull.'

Football and hurling was all of life. On Thursday nights they'd
play the boys from the red, austere O'Brien Institute, up near the
Casino. Thursday after Thursday he'd mark his neighbour, Paddy
Lawler, who was five stone heavier and as nimble and tender as
any rugby second-row ever was. Thursday after Thursday Kevin
Heffernan would be flattened. Things like that he never forgot.

It was a tumbledown sort of childhood, but in his head he stored away what needed storing.

On those Thursday nights they called him Heffo. It didn't stick. It was a name he wouldn't hear again till he was in his fifties.

Only twice in the course of his son's epic career did John Heffernan come to see his son play. He was dragged along both times.

'He saw me in the 1958 All-Ireland and in a Railway Cup game. I think in the end he took a pride in not being interested. I'd come home and he'd want to know what happened for when he got asked in the station, but he went his own way. Sometimes he would be on duty outside Croke Park when we would be playing. He'd make a point of not going in.'

An Offaly man, John Heffernan fished, ran gun dogs, went shooting, footed and drew turf from the featherbed and worked his allotment. Those were his interests and passions. His allotment was a little plot of land, uphill in Beaumont, where he grew vegetables.

He built a little cart and put the axle and wheels of a motor car underneath and pneumatic tyres on to the sides.

His eldest son remembers the crushing weight of the thing, the long pull up the hill on Beaumont Road. It seems quirky to have built such a contraption but then, if you sit and listen to Kevin Heffernan discussing the benefits of tacking lumps of wood to the hurleys of young players to improve their strength and swing, you get the same sense of fiercely intelligent difference.

His mother May was more supportive. He remembers coming home from hurling one day as a child with his head bruised and bleeding quite spectacularly. He was tended to unquestioningly.

The next day the Christian Brother quizzed him. 'What did your mother say about the state you were in?'

'Nothing, Brother.'

'Did she say to give it up?'

'No, Brother.'

'Well, maybe it would be as well to.'

'Yes, Brother.'

And loyalty. He learned that early. One Sunday morning in a

St Vincent's jersey he found himself playing Faughs in Croke Park. Half-eleven matches in Croker on a Sunday were the norm then. Suddenly (but not unexpectedly) a row broke out.

Heffernan was about to wade in when his maternal grandfather, a small, stocky horseman from Kilkenny, appeared at his shoulder, sleeves rolled. 'Grandfather? Where did you come from! Would you get off the stage outta that.'

He was a fine student, one of the first GAA men to enter Trinity College. A bishop objected at the time, but Kevin Heffernan was as much his own man at nineteen years of age as he was thereafter. He was a Trinity pink at a time when Gaelic footballers being such a thing was unheard of.

Those he played with, those he managed, categorize themselves two ways. Those who got close and those who voyaged around him. Those who feared him, those who loved him. They all understood. And as the years went past, those who got close came to understand something else: Heffernan's loyalty was absolute.

Jackie Gilroy met Heffernan in 1963 when he was a young fella just busting through on to the St Vincent's panel. Heffernan was the captain and his influence on Gilroy's life began then.

'He used to have this expression. A small thing. We were playing Sean McDermott's. He took me aside. I was feeling under pressure. He said to me: "Remember, Giller, we just want to be one point ahead at the end." I had to think about it but he gave the example. Him and his life. He gave everything he possibly could to whatever he was doing. To be one point ahead at the end.'

Gilroy was about twenty or twenty-one. Heffernan was a god.

'He can be a little bit intimidating. I know what people mean. He can be that way till he decides you are on his team or in his group. Then you are there forever. He was the leader, just naturally the leader. Then he'll do anything for you. Anything.'

Another old friend, Dick O'Sullivan, the Kerryman who now runs Punchestown Racecourse, remembers a night in Tralee in the mid-sixties. Kevin and Mary Heffernan would do a house swap each summer with the man who lived next door to the O'Sullivans.

One night, Dick O'Sullivan and his wife, not too long married, were at a dinner dance in Tralee, and a small crowd came back to the house afterwards. It was a summer's night in the small hours and the merriment spilled out into the back garden and evolved into a game of football.

After a while the Heffernans' curtains were twitching next door. Mary Heffernan heard voices and suspected there might be trouble. Kevin Heffernan got up, peered out and announced happily that the Kerrymen were playing football. He got dressed and disappeared over the garden wall to play.

Through the summer of 1973 he surveyed the state of his beloved Dublin with increasing despair. He spoke to the county chairman, Jimmy Gray, about the future. Gray was convinced that there was only one way forward for the county team, and that was to give a manager his own selectors.

Jimmy had known Heffernan for more than thirty years. He's known him for twice that long today, 'But I still don't know him really.' He knew enough to know that Heffernan was the man.

'Before the appointment of the three lads [Heffernan and his assistants, Donal Colfer and Lorcan Redmond] it was chaotic. Five selectors. Three from county board, two from the county champions. There was no progress being made. I asked the board for permission to go to three selectors and to pick the three. I thought there would be opposition, but the majority agreed. I believed then and I believe now that Heff could manage Manchester United comfortably. Lorcan had been there with Phil Markey. I knew Donal. He was very sound. It was all conditional on Heff coming with the other two.'

Heffernan was the hinge. None of the members of the proposed management team knew each other. Heffernan had played against Redmond often 'and carried the scars from him long before I knew him'; and both remembered Donal Colfer playing with Synge Street with a pair of glasses tied around his head.

Redmond might have been tainted in Heffernan's eyes by his involvement with the Markey regime, but Heffernan kept his ear close enough to the ground to know that Redmond was disillusioned and isolated within the set-up.

'I was there in 1973 with Phil Markey and Paddy Delaney,' Redmond recalls. 'It was a funny old set-up. We trained the Thursday before the matches. Old style. Very few fellas would turn up for training. There was no communication with the manager. It was all whispering behind doors. No sign would be given to me of what was happening. Everything was a secret. I had rows with the other guys because there was no proper training and nobody seemed to know what was happening. Phil and Paddy Delaney were close friends. They knew what was happening but they'd keep it to themselves.'

So Jimmy Gray, having secured the rights to pursue his dream team and having nailed down the commitment of Redmond and Colfer, rang Kevin Heffernan. Jimmy was told regretfully and respectfully that Heffernan had committed himself to managing St Vincent's for the following year. In June of 1973 Nemo Rangers had beaten St Vincent's in a replayed All-Ireland club final in Thurles. St Vincent's were determined to come back and go further.

Gray had a diplomat's instincts and didn't push too hard. He promised Heffernan that he would be coming back to him. He let it lie for a week. Gray had hurled with distinction for Dublin. As had his friend and Heffernan's near neighbour, Sean Óg Ó Ceallacháin, who was working with the *Evening Press*. Ó Ceallacháin was perhaps alone in the journalistic community in having any interest in who became the next Dublin football manager, but nevertheless he harassed Gray with phone calls.

Keen to suggest some progress, Gray told him one day that he was hoping to get Kevin Heffernan and the two lads to do the job. On a Wednesday evening it appeared on the back of the *Evening Press* as a fait accompli. Heffernan for Dublin!

Gray braced himself. Heffernan duly called. He poured battery acid down the phone line into Gray's ear for a few minutes, before commenting that he supposed he'd have to do the job now.

Gray smiled to himself. He was the producer and he had secured his director of choice. Time to begin casting.

3

We're leavin', on a jet plane.

Paddy Cullen

On Easter Sunday in 1974 Dublin won the dowdy old Corn na Casca tournament, beating Sligo in the final in Croke Park. The place happened to be deserted at the time.

UCD, the county champions, had nominated Paddy Cullen to be the inter-county side's captain for the year. Heffernan was having none of what UCD wanted and had installed Sean Doherty as captain instead. Doherty climbed the steps and lifted the modest silverware.

Croke Park being almost silent, his players were able to hear him when he shouted down to them, 'This won't be the last time we're on these steps, lads!'

They all laughed. G'wan Doc, ya good thing!

There were no formalities, no introductory sessions, no getting-to-know-you lunches. Heffernan shook hands with Lorcan Redmond and Donal Colfer one night in September 1973, in Parnell Park, and that was that. There were no instructions as to how their relationship would operate, just the assumption that Heffernan was number one. Colfer and Redmond found their own roles around that.

They held a meeting in the Hollybank Hotel in Clontarf. So many glazed, cynical faces looking back at them. They said that this year was serious. That this year was going to be different. The real thing. They said that they believed there was an All-Ireland in this team. Maybe not this summer, but some summer soon.

They asked the faces, were they in or out. Mostly, the faces just nodded. The faces had heard many speeches like this before: at least one for every season they had been involved in football. Robbie Kelleher, an introverted member of the group, imbued with a flinty realism that would inform his life's work as an economist, said he was in, but frankly he doubted the talk of an All-Ireland.

'If you don't believe it, why don't you fuck off then?' said Frank Murray. The intemperance was uncharacteristic, but Frank was an optimist. He'd liked what he'd been hearing.

The team needed optimists. They'd played one game together by now. In September, just after Heffernan had taken over management of the team, Dublin had travelled to Castlerea to play Roscommon in a long-postponed game from the 1972–3 league.

They needed to win the game by eight clear points to avoid being evicted from Division One of the league for the first time in history. Those who reckon Heffernan got especially lucky with the players he had often point out that Tony Hanahoe, Bobby Doyle, Paddy Cullen, Sean Doherty, Paddy Reilly, Pat O'Neill and David Hickey were in the team that day. They lost by 3–7 to 0–11.

Privately Heffernan wasn't displeased. Getting down and dirty in Division Two for a year was no chore for a man looking to give his team the nutrition of a few handy wins. It made it a little harder to make them believe in the promised land, but nobody had said it would be easy.

The winter that followed was cold and unglamorous. While the ground froze though, Heffernan knew that he had seeds bedded underneath. Plans were taking shape. Players were working. He was blowing the chaff off the wheat.

At the time, winter training was considered to be a cruel and unusual punishment to inflict on any team. In Dublin, where even the perfunctory physical preparations carried out for championship games were resented, the idea of collective training all through the winter was considered to be a flagrant human rights abuse.

The first sessions took place in a school hall in Finglas. They

were resented by a few, avoided by others. There was a large
turnover of players. They came, they saw, they felt stiff the next
day. They never came again.

Again, Heffernan wasn't unhappy. He wanted men who would
last. Word went around that Heffernan was putting together a
panel for circuit training. In the clubs they were dubious. Players
arrived in Finglas carrying the Chinese-whisper version of what
was about to happen. They were ready for circus training. They
wondered, would be they be taught how to go for the opponent's
juggler?

Heffernan's friend Mickey Whelan was in America at the time,
studying sports science. Whelan became Heffernan's sounding
board for most elements of the revolution. Decades later, the gurus
of speed, agility and quickness would introduce ladders to training
sessions. Heffernan got the same results using tyres in 1974.

He believed in balance, and soon he had big-boned footballers
running daintily along three-inch beams in the manner of Olga
Korbut. They climbed ropes and learned how to change pace
in mid-run. They discovered muscles in hitherto unsuspected
locations.

And when spring came and the evenings got brighter, so the
training got harder.

Players remember two ghosts from those gloamy evenings: Brian
Trimble from Scoil Uí Chonnail and John Furlong from Na
Fianna. Furlong is now the chief executive for the Vancouver
Winter Olympic Games in 2010, but back then he was a rabbit.
So was Trimble.

For the first nine or ten heavy sessions in Parnell Park, Heffernan
would send the pack off on 800-metre runs. Trimble and Furlong
would beat the rest of the squad by half a lap. They were finished
running when the lads at the back were still parting company with
their dinners. When it came to pass that the team were able to stay
with the rabbits, the rabbits vanished back into the hat.

Those who remained went to galaxies which no players had
ever travelled to before. None of the galaxies were pleasant. They
lay on their backs on the damp grass with their hands flat beneath

their buttocks and had medicine balls dropped on to their stomachs. They stood in pairs, facing each other. In turn they punched their partner in the gut as hard as they could.

They conspired at first to go easy on each other, but if you were partnered with a Sean Doherty or a Gay O'Driscoll there was no chance of getting a soft punch to the paunch. Soon the air was blue. 'Fuck you, Doc. How'd you like this then? Bam!'

They did press-ups till their arms ached and sit-ups till they were dizzy. Then they did laps. Lot of laps. Sometimes they went to St Anne's Park in Raheny and ran downhills and uphills, which were straightforward enough. Then they would be paired off and a player standing in the middle of the slope would have to get his body in the way of another player coming downhill at speed. Not so straightforward.

And the one they hated most of all was the circle chase. Heffernan thinks he devised it himself in some dark moment.

A circle would be laid out, fifty yards or more in diameter. Flags would be placed around the circumference, about four or five yards apart, depending on how many players were present. One player stood at each flag and when the whistle blew every man chased the man in front in a flat-out, ballbusting sprint. The incentive was that when you caught the player in front you could drop out. Being caught meant that you stayed in and might be sprinting flat-out for ninety seconds to two minutes. And that meant no rest before the next circle chase. Or the one after.

In Dublin in 1974, Saturday was a day of rest, but Heffernan's team trained on Saturdays. Heffernan would drive from his home in Raheny to training in Parnell Park with a head full of plans. Most mornings he would arrive too early. The great Christy Sweets would be there ahead of him. Christy, so named for his habit of carrying a large shopping bag full of sweets and gums for players, would be laying out whatever was needed for the session that day.

Heffernan had his ways of killing time. There was a slightly ramshackle bookie's shop on the far side of Collins Avenue from Parnell Park, and some Saturday mornings Heffernan would ramble in and study the odds before taking a modest stake on a horse or a dog.

One Saturday when the championship was already rolling he was picking a wager for himself when his eye fell upon the handwritten notice with the prices for the Leinster football championship. Dublin 8 to 1. Offaly, Meath, Kildare ahead of that at meaner prices.

Hmmm.

He mentioned the odds to a pal that evening, and the pal gave Heffernan some money to go back to the bookie's with. Just have a little taste of that 8 to 1. With Heffernan in charge, well, who knew what might happen? Heffernan duly laid the bet.

It never occurred to either man to ask what the price would be for an All-Ireland title. Dublin played Wexford in the first round of the championship that year. It was the curtain-raiser to the National League final between Kerry and Roscommon. Dublin won unimpressively. Heffernan stayed in Croke Park to watch the main match.

'I remember they looked like men, while we had looked like wanton boys. I think we went out to 10 to 1 for Leinster after that.'

At that stage Dublin were 33–1 to win the All-Ireland.

On the field of play the improvements were demonstrable in a limited way. They were wrestling with minnows. They lost to Limerick 1–8 to 0–6. They had wins against Carlow (1–9 to 0–4) and, praise the Lord, they beat Kilkenny 6–16 to 0–4 on a miserable day when the entire attendance in Nowlan Park left the ground after the curtain-raiser, a club minor hurling final.

They beat Waterford 2–15 to 0–5 and then lost to Clare 4–9 to 2–9. They beat Antrim. It was just enough.

On 5 May 1974, Dublin lost a league play-off game to Kildare. Dublin scored two goals early. Kildare came back and put Dublin on the canvas. And that was that. Their first championship game was scheduled for two weeks hence.

It wasn't ideal, but Heffernan had learned lessons. He had his team fit. He had an idea, too, of how he wanted them to play.

As a young man in Trinity College, Heffernan had played basketball for a while. It's not hard to picture Heffernan as a young hoopster. The confined space, the quick transfer, the tactical sophistication. Were he raised in Indiana rather than Ireland, it would have been his game.

'Once we played UCG in a blitz above in Cathal Brugha Barracks. It was after the war and a lot of people in Trinity and especially in Galway were there on the GI Bill. We would have fancied ourselves a little as ball-players.

'We were standing about when UCG went past us. Out come all these fat guys with American accents, each of them as big as a ranch. I looked at them and laughed to myself. I said, "We'll run these fellas into the ground." Well, they murdered us. We chased shadows all through. They moved around the place and they showed you the ball if they felt like it; mostly though they kept it moving and us chasing it. I'll never forget the disbelief in my head when the game was over. We were journeymen, they had exposed us. I couldn't believe what I had just seen. That stayed with me.'

Other things. Those Thursdays as a child when he would be flattened by bigger boys each week up in the O'Brien Institute. The memory of 1955 against Kerry and 1957 against Louth. Kerry's triumph of catch and kick. The realization that Dublin had footballers, but the teams that beat them had big footballers.

He had the desire to build a team built on the premise that a good big guy will always beat a good small guy. And a good big smart guy will be nearly impossible to beat. He went after the big smart guys. Then he got them fit. Then he got them transferring the ball in a new way.

The rest was down to him. He believed in the small benefits of out-psyching the opposition. The season was a game of chess, a time for semiotics and smoke signals.

Take Kildare. A few weeks after the league final, with the championship already under way, Dublin were invited to Naas for a challenge game. Kildare were looking for a little meat to devour. Heffernan gave it to them.

Back then, Kildare were waiting patiently for the good times to come. They had won an All-Ireland Under-21 title in 1965 and three more Leinster Under-21 titles since then. They could hear that Lilywhite Express coming from afar.

For the challenge game Heffernan played half of the team which he had mentally picked for the championship. He watched impassively as they lost by sixteen points.

Six weeks later, on 14 July, the teams met in the championship. Kildare, who had an eye on the main prize already, lost by six points. Young Brian Mullins scored a penalty. Kildare deserved to lose by more.

Pat Gogarty remembers coming off the pitch in the company of Olly Crinnigan of Kildare, with Crinnigan muttering all the way about the shrewdness of Heffernan. 'We never saw that coming, Pat. That's some shrewd bastard.'

That was the end of Kildare.

The Leinster championship that summer had plenty of twists and turns to it. Dublin beat Wexford in their opening game on 26 May. Frank Murray, struggling for fitness, was left on the bench despite having dismantled Wexford single-handedly a year previously.

Bobby Doyle scored 2–1 against Wexford this time. One of the goals was a penalty in the second half. Tony Hanahoe picked up the ball and handed it to Doyle.

'Here, Doyler, you take it.'

'But I've never taken a penalty in my life.'

'Just fucking take it.'

So he kicked the penalty almost with his eyes shut, and to his relief it went in. As he came off the field later, Heffernan approached him. 'You're not taking any more penalties.'

Some Kerry players sitting in the stand for the first half as they waited to play their league final with Roscommon remember the game as being comically inept. The *Irish Press* the next morning sniffed that, on the evidence of this match, Dublin 'can be written off as serious challengers for Offaly's provincial crown'.

The next week is memorable for all sorts of reasons. The team were training in Parnell Park when Robbie Kelleher spotted a small blue car pulling in. Two big men got out.

Kelleher rolled his eyes. Thought to himself, 'Here we go, one win and they're bringing back the fatties from St Vincent's.'

Anton O'Toole nudged David Hickey. 'Look! They're rolling out all the old shites and I'll be back on the bench.'

Hickey, a regular on the team since 1967, had grown disenchanted and played Gaelic football just during the 1973 season. Heffernan had enticed him back to the fold just in time for the Wexford game. He recognized the gentle dig from his old friend.

Anyway, Jimmy Keaveney and Leslie Deegan were back.

The details of Jimmy Keaveney's resurrection are legend by now. Heffernan driving home in a despair after the first round of the championship in 1974. His wife's friend Lilly Jennings and her seven-year-old son Terry in the car, too. Heffernan wondering aloud if he wouldn't give his kingdom for a free-taker. Young Terry pointing out that he had never seen Jimmy Keaveney miss one. A image of the, by then, portly Keaveney flashing into Heffernan's mind. Heffernan tried to banish the thought but couldn't. So Keaveney returned.

The last pair of Heffernan's fifteen Dublin senior football championship medals had come on St Vincent's teams which had Keaveney as part of them. The younger man knew Heffernan well enough by then to understand that his own comeback wasn't a matter of choice.

On Friday and Saturday nights Heffernan would mount surveillance operations to keep Keaveney out of the bar in St Vincent's – or any other bar for that matter.

'You're not taking this seriously, are you?'

'I am, Kevin.'

'Why are you drinking this, then?' Heffernan would say, gently sliding the pint glass away from Keaveney.

Keaveney opted out of the weekend nights in St Vincent's, but the underlying habit died hard. One night Heffernan arrived in St Vincent's for a routine sweep of the bar and found no Keaveney.

His friend, the late Joe Drumgoole, whispered the word. 'He's down in Meagher's.'

Heffernan was in the car and down to Meagher's of Fairview in a flash.

One Saturday morning Keaveney arrived for training, quite pleased with himself. He'd been out the night before and had ended up in, of all places, a nightclub. Uneasy in the surroundings at first, it dawned on him that nightclubs might be the solution to all his problems. While the rest of the world danced the night away a man could have a pint or two in a darkened corner. The chances of Heffernan's network stretching to the nightclub scene were slender. He trained, felt grand and went home happy.

The following Tuesday night, hitting the pitch in Parnell Park, he felt the familiar rap of the Heffernan knuckle against his forearm.

'Come here you,' said Heffernan. 'Where were ya, last Friday night?'

Keaveney whose default facial expression is exasperation, weighed the odds calmly. Perhaps Heffernan was bluffing. Stay cool, he told himself.

'Out and about, Kevin. Might have gone for a ramble. Why? Were you looking for me?'

'Listen, do you want me to embarrass you in front of the team later?'

'Ah, bollix!'

Heffernan was in charge of labour relations at the ESB then. ESB staff were everywhere. Heffernan's *stasi*.

Deegan would prove no less important, but he was injury prone to an extent that was almost comical. Joe O'Reilly of Synge Street had dropped off the panel late in spring for family reasons and Heffernan had settled on Deegan as a replacement. He had been out of the Dublin panel since 1971. In the interim he had played some soccer for Bohemians. He got injured playing against Shamrock Rovers in the old Milltown grounds and was advised to pack up the soccer. He had lingering ankle ligament trouble, but he went back to football and hurling with St Vincent's.

Neither he nor Keaveney was ready for what awaited them in

Parnell Park. Deegan lasted just short of twenty minutes. Then he evacuated his stomach and lay on the grass, trying to see the sky but seeing only stars. As he lay there he was vaguely aware of Stephen Rooney, the blond Dublin midfielder, helping Jimmy Keaveney over to the sideline. He could hear the immortal words, 'Jaysus, Stevo, I'm fucked,' but he was too shredded himself to even smile.

Keaveney and Deegan were there for reprise performances on the Thursday. There were some misgivings in the ranks. Having missed the tortures of winter training, were the two Vincent's men going to be fast-tracked straight into starters' jerseys?

On the Saturday morning the team trained again. Frank Murray was bursting out of his skin for a place on the team at this stage. That was exactly what Heffernan wanted from him. Murray was one of the few thoroughbreds available. The session finished with a practice game, and somewhere in the course of the scrimmaging Murray banged into one of his own players and cracked a rib. He was out for the next day. He was desolate. A stupid injury sustained through friendly fire.

Frank Murray was different. In 1969 a UCD student had offered him a joint and he'd laughed for about six hours. Soon afterwards somebody else introduced him to LSD. He liked football and basketball and soccer, and he liked to go out to the Phoenix Park on his own and drop a tab of acid. The park became his Strawberry Fields. Frank says now that he was lucky, lots of his old mates are dead or mad or in jail. In 1974 he felt bulletproof, until his rib got cracked.

His difference insulated and isolated him. Those summers he spent playing in America, Frank would arrive off the plane in Boston or New York carrying no bag, just a pair of football boots hanging by the laces around his neck. He had long, fair hair down to his waistband. The New York Irish above in the dust bowl of Gaelic Park were very tender towards such a creature. He could play, though.

He was different because he had class. He played with Leinster in 1972 and 1973, when only Paddy Cullen and Georgie Wilson were making the team from Dublin. Leinster teams at the time were filled with Offaly men. He remembers playing with Willy Bryan and Tony McTeague, two gods of the midlands. McTeague got a sideline ball one day on the right side of the field. He banged it over with his right foot. About five minutes later he got another one, same spot but on the other side of the field. This time he banged it over with his left foot. Frank Murray had never seen anything like it.

He loved the freedom of expression that Gaelic football gave him. When he'd come on to the panel first, back in 1971, Jimmy Keaveney had yet to take his sabbatical. Sessions were brief and unsatisfactory, and afterwards he and Keaveney, two stylists of the game, would stay out on the field feeding each other passes on the 21-yard line and driving the ball at Paddy Cullen. Happy days.

On the day of the Louth match the Dubs travelled to Louth on the bus. Frank Murray, being injured, wasn't required to travel. The team were in the dressing room listening to Kevin Heffernan when there was a knock on the door. Frank! He was a little the worse for wear – 'I just know that I arrived drunk or stoned or both.' So Frank Murray walks in. John McCarthy, who is nearest the door, gets a big hug. Frank throws a big beaming hello to Heffernan before he is ushered out. He is forgotten about temporarily.

The match starts. Frank Murray appears behind Paddy Cullen's goal, bantering away with the big keeper. Again he is ushered away.

There are fewer than 7,000 people at the match. Jimmy Keaveney who, despite his lack of fitness, has been picked in place of Bernard Brogan at full forward, does what he came to do. He scores seven points.

Afterwards, having pulled off a surprise win, the Dubs repaired to a restaurant in Dunshaughlin. In the middle of a meal marked by high spirits they heard a knocking on the skylight window in the ceiling. Frank Murray was beaming down at them. Unaccountably he was holding in his hand a pair of shoes. That was the last they saw of him.

The following morning he got up early, caught a bus to Dun Laoghaire and emigrated to England. Vanished.

'That's my eternal regret. I walked down, bought a ticket and stepped on to a boat.

'I don't know what possessed me. I just felt I had to go. I think about the rib. That weekend. Often. I suppose life would have been different. Maybe I wouldn't have been good at being famous anyway. Maybe it would have gone to my head. I regret that I had a talent, though, and that I threw it away.'

Frank went to his wild years. Life in Parnell Park rolled on.

4

If you're not ruthless you shouldn't be there.

Gay O' Driscoll

Kevin Heffernan had come up with an exquisite new torture.
Meetings! He loved meetings. After a training session the team
would be shoehorned into a minuscule hut at the top of Parnell
Park and the meeting would begin. It wouldn't end until everyone
had spoken at least once.

Keaveney, as always, had it sussed. Keaveney would speak first.
Thoughtful, sincere words thrown in before the conversation had
assumed a theme. Then he could relax. Let the mind wander while
the others sweated.

It worked for a short while. One night he had his words said
and was daydreaming happily when he heard Heffernan contacting
him from somewhere back on earth.

'What do you think Jimmy?'

'Eh, of what, Kevin?'

'What we've been talking about.'

'Well, in fairness, Kevin, I've already had my say, let somebody
else speak.'

'I want to know what you think.'

'You're some bollix!'

The meetings varied in nature and duration. After games, the
meetings took the form of a post-mortem. Heffernan had enlisted
the film maker Tiernan MacBride to shoot each game from the
top of the Hogan Stand. The view from up there was panoramic
and at any given time the screen showed at least one half of
the Croke Park field. Heffernan could see where every Dublin

defender was when a goal was conceded. The difficulty was that he couldn't always identify who was who. He would pore over the footage like a conspiracy theorist examining the Zapruder film.

There was a serious post-mortem the week after the Wexford match, and a general verdict was passed down of too much bunching at midfield. Anton O'Toole had been given the role of roving corner forward, but Anton hadn't roved enough for Heffernan's liking. He was clogging midfield. The film showed it. By the time of the Leinster final, Bobby Doyle would have become the roving corner forward.

The meeting everyone remembers best from that season came the day before the Offaly match. By that time Gay O'Driscoll had figured that something was happening. His main focus was getting back into the team. Every lunchtime he would hit Seapoint and run for four miles on his own.

If he was known at all at that time, Gay O'Driscoll was known as a hurler. He had captained a Dublin Under-21 team to an All-Ireland final in 1967, and the single-point loss in a game which Dublin should have won haunted him.

By the early seventies he was married and the pressure of playing two games was beginning to hurt. Neither Dublin football nor hurling seemed likely to be popular or profitable in the near future, but for some reason he took a punt on football and Heffernan. He hadn't done so to be a substitute.

From Heffernan's point of view, O'Driscoll brought, in football terms, a touch of political incorrectness. He was a player who would see what had to be done and then do what had to be done. In the county finals of 1970 and 1972, O'Driscoll had been sent off, playing for St Vincent's. He took an opposing player to the line with him both times.

He'd played in the Second Division league final against Kildare and lost his place for the Wexford game. He came in as a sub against Louth and was to be on the subs' bench against Offaly. The commitment he was making in terms of fitness and discipline was beginning to pay off, however. He knew he was close.

Offaly were the dominant Leinster team of the early seventies.

This would be the day when Dublin would discover whether Heffernan was a football genius or a confidence man.

O'Driscoll liked the meetings, the hard and brutal honesty of them. The day before the Offaly match, O'Driscoll stood up and broke the silence. He reminded his colleagues that he was there, sitting on the bench. He felt he was worth his place on the team because he could do a job. He knew he could. And if any of them had any doubts, maybe they should step down now and if they didn't want to step down now they should remember right through the match that Gay O'Driscoll was on the bench, watching and waiting.

A few players glanced up to catch Heffernan's eye. Heffernan smiled. The ethos of the team was in place. The following day in Croke Park, Seamus Darby was giving David Billings a hard time. When Billings was withdrawn. O'Driscoll came on. He kept the place for six years.

'In all the years I was in the team and all the games I played, I never felt secure. I always watched Davy Billings and Jim Brogan. I had to beat them. I was always aware of how they were doing. Overconfidence wasn't something I would suffer from.

'If Jim was in playing, for instance, I'd be willing him to make mistakes. Literally. I'd be sitting on the sideline, willing him to make mistakes. Sure I would. I think people who would say otherwise are being dishonest. You're talking about wanting to be part of a fiercely competitive situation. If you're not ruthless you shouldn't be there.'

For O'Driscoll the proof of the honesty in the room is that the members of the team are still close friends. Everything was accepted in the spirit of the collective good. He doesn't know how he would have felt, being a sub for those six years, but O'Driscoll retains huge admiration for the men who manned the bench. Their hunger pushed him all the way.

After the Louth game Micheál Ó Muircheartaigh had said on the radio that he wouldn't be surprised if the winners of that game went a good way further. There were guffaws. It was a big statement, given that Dublin were playing Offaly next. Even the men of Parnell Park didn't share Ó Muircheartaigh's confidence.

Offaly had contested the five previous Leinster finals and won the last three. When Offaly took the field against Dublin, they had nine All-Star award winners in the squad. Seven of them started. Dublin had Paddy Cullen, who had been a replacement on an All-Star tour and had been dining out on the tales of it ever since.

If there was any feeling within the panel that things were slowly beginning to move, it certainly wasn't shared among the blowhard element of the Dublin county board, many of whose more myopic members were still in a state of grand disgruntlement over Heffernan's decision to have Saturday-morning training sessions. Clubs traditionally felt they had the rights to their players on Saturdays, and if the clubs didn't want the players, well then, the players had the right to stay in bed.

The whingier element of the board had been driven to greater heights of fulmination in May when Dublin had appeared for a game wearing navy shorts. Was it for this that good men died in 1916? Blue shorts?

Mick Dunne of RTE had advised Jimmy Gray that the traditional light-blue jerseys with white trim and white shorts didn't show up well on black-and-white television. Gray had two options. He could have the team colours debated and argued over at board level till infinity or beyond. Or he could just do something.

He asked Paula Lee, the administrative assistant in the county board offices, to come up with a change. Paula designed the classic light-blue and navy strip which would become the colours not just of the county team but of the county itself as civic bodies began to adopt the colours on the back of the team's subsequent popularity.

At first though, Paula was as popular as a prophet in her own land. The next day out, Dublin wore navy shorts, and by the time of the All-Ireland semi-final they would be wearing navy trim on their jerseys, too. The hidebound conservative delegates to the county board would have had Paula Lee burned as a witch, had they got their way.

The last straw for the flat-earthers was the size of the panel.

Heffernan believed in keeping as many players as possible on board. Given that the county board's expenditure on training nights ran to several pints of milk and two packets of plain biscuits, it's hard in retrospect to see why there was such angst over the issue, but nevertheless blood pressure ran dangerously high. Jimmy Gray instinctively saw it as his job to insulate Heffernan from these extraneous pressures and he acted as a lightning rod for all complaints at county board level.

On the day of the game against Offaly, Heffernan brought so many players to Croke Park that there was a small argument about letting them all out on to the field for the kickaround. In the end several of the panel just sat in the Cusack Stand to watch the game. Jim Brogan, who had come into the squad during the previous winter, remembers there being perhaps seven or eight hundred supporters in the entire stand.

At one stage there was a slight altercation between a few fans. A large and stately guard came slowly from the field through the open gate into the stand enclosure and walked up the steps. He pulled on the strap beneath his chin, sorted out the altercation in a manner which didn't involve counselling or arbitration, and walked slowly back down to the pitch.

'That encapsulated it for me. That was a quarter-final against the Leinster champions. You could hear echoes in the ground. By the All-Ireland final there were thousands spilling on to the pitch. The ground was too small to hold everyone.'

The miserable crowd at least got a decent game to watch. Dublin started with coltish enthusiasm, galloping all over the place at top speed. The return for the expenditure of sweat and energy wasn't great. David Hickey rasped a shot off the crossbar. They hit the woodwork twice more. They waited for Offaly to swat them away. Waited.

Leslie Deegan's case for restoration to the Dublin panel had been helped by the fact that he was enjoying a rare period during which he played without suffering some calamitous injury. He was introduced to the game just before half-time.

Paddy Reilly, Dublin's right-wing back that day, was a master at what has become a lost art for defenders: Paddy Reilly could kick the ball. He could field it and drive it downfield to the hands of men who would do damage with it. Just before half-time he did just that. The ball was floating towards a no man's land in front of the Offaly goal. Martin Furlong, the keeper, came confidently towards the interception. Leslie Deegan nipped in and pushed the ball over his head and into the left-hand corner of the goal.

At half-time they led by a point and began to believe that perhaps Offaly weren't about to crush them after all. When they came out for the second half, the Artane Boys Band were tootling the final strains of 'The Offaly Rover' or 'Mary from Tullamore', and Eugene Mulligan, who was marking Anton O'Toole, felt the stirring in his breast.

'D'ya hear that, sonny?' he said.

O'Toole took a second to focus.

'All history now,' he replied cryptically. Had to say something, anything.

The game went to the wire. Dublin, knowing they would never get another bite at this cherry, threw everything at Offaly. With seconds to go the sides were level.

Sean Lowry, the Offaly centre back, emerged with the ball and was about to distribute downfield when Stephen Rooney made a block.

'The only time in his life I saw him do it,' says Heffernan.

'My trademark block,' laughs Rooney.

Rooney passed to young Mullins, who passed again to Leslie Deegan who, with what looked like the entire Offaly defence coming at him, hoofed a high spiralling ball into the heavens. Time stood still. Men grew beards while the ball hung up there. Finally it came down. A white flag was raised.

Thirty seconds later, the final whistle went.

'I remember people running from everywhere,' says Leslie Deegan, becoming the first to identify the miracle of the exponential Dublin support. 'It looked like there were more people running on the pitch than had been in the stands during the match. I threw myself on to the ground and did a somersault.'

For a man as injury-prone as Leslie Deegan the acrobatics were a brave decision. A week later he was playing for St Vincent's against Clanna Gael when he busted the cartilage in his knee. He was out till the Leinster final, when Heffernan told him to warm up with a few minutes left.

'What about the knee, Kevin?' he said.

'Sure, it's only a few minutes,' said Heffernan.

He was crossing the line on to the field when he felt the knee go again. He stayed on the field anyway. There might never be another Leinster final, he thought. And for Leslie, who opened the door to the great era, there wasn't.

Beating Offaly was a watershed.

David Hickey: 'I remember O'Toole and myself hugging each other. I felt then that life couldn't get any better.'

Robbie Kelleher: 'Beating Offaly was the first time we ever beat anyone of any consequence. That was my fifth championship campaign. The previous four were a waste of time. We were hopeless. We could beat nobody. I longed for something beyond playing Westmeath in Mullingar. The only reason I didn't pack it in before then was because I had nothing else to do, really. It was all I knew, really.'

Tony Hanahoe: 'I couldn't repeat the expression I used when the game was over against Offaly. To all intents and purposes it was like being afraid of Becher's Brook, and you got down on the far side and you were alive and the race was on.'

Paddy Reilly: 'One fucking unbelievable day.'

Until the Offaly game the team had been in the habit of having a few good drinks on the evening of a match, just in case they wouldn't be seeing each other for a while after the next game. Now they began to look upwards. There was the stirring of a dream.

Tony Hanahoe, solicitor, outed himself as a Dublin footballer one day down in the Bridewell when the talk turned to GAA. At one point the Garda he was talking with cracked up laughing.

'Tony, you don't really think Dublin will be in the All-Ireland, do you?'

'Maybe.'

The Garda thought it was the funniest thing he had ever heard.

It was a long Leinster campaign during which, through some vagary of the draw, Dublin managed to meet five of the other teams in the province. The matches came thick and fast. Heffernan was learning quickly about what he liked and what he didn't like.

He liked continuity. Before the Kildare game, Gay O'Driscoll went away on a week's holiday – nobody had thought that the postponement of holidays in July would ever be an issue. He came back on the Sunday morning. Match day. Heffernan needed to be sure, so he popped O'Driscoll into one half of a club game for St Vincent's at 11 a.m. He saw enough and stuck O'Driscoll into the team for the afternoon.

They won, and the hurt in Kildare was so palpable that six of the selected team failed to show up for the county's next game.

A Leinster final was the next stop. Meath stood waiting, as they had in 1955.

Heffernan was in his element now. As a player he was used to operating at this altitude. Robbie Kelleher lived not far away from Heffernan at the time and would wait around in Parnell Park some evenings for a lift home. In the week before the Leinster final, the two were driving towards Raheny and Kelleher was expressing his doubts about the big day.

'Don't forget what tradition means,' said Heffernan.

'See, I don't know what you mean by that. Tradition? What does it mean in a game of football?' asked Kelleher.

'It means that, even though as individuals we have never won anything and have performed badly through our careers until now, the tradition of Dublin and the jersey will give you that bit of confidence from now on.'

He was right. In the provincial final they played like the team they would become. They beat Meath by five points.

That night Heffernan again gave Kelleher a lift home. Kelleher was getting out of the car and Heffernan called after him.

'Now do you understand what tradition means?'

★

Gerald McKenna, the chairman of the Kerry county board, watched the Leinster final of 1974 in the company of his late friend, Paddy Driscoll, the great former Cork defender.

Paddy wasn't impressed. He said so to his friend. McKenna has one of the keener intellects in the GAA world. He shared it with Paddy Driscoll. 'I said, that will be the downfall of Cork because Cork won't be impressed. When you beat Meath at any time, it's a good result, but Cork won't see that.'

For Heffernan, tradition meant that no Dublin team should ever lose to a Cork team. Now Cork were up in the All-Ireland semi-final. The day before the game the Dubs gathered in their beloved shed in Parnell Park. Heffernan put it on the table. No Dublin team should ever lose to Cork. He was particularly of the opinion that this Dublin team couldn't lose to Cork.

This was his precise brand of magic. In the shed he analysed the two teams on a player-by-player basis. In truth this analysis should have produced a comprehensive win for Cork, but Heffernan could sell the snake oil when he needed to.

Nothing to fear, he said, nothing to fear. He alluded repeatedly to Cork's arrogance, the Achilles heel, he believed, of all Cork teams. By the time they left the shed, Dublin had forgotten that they were playing the All-Ireland champions the following day. They just wanted a piece of Cork.

Heffernan was relentless.

Billy Morgan's son Brian (the current Nemo Rangers keeper) had been born that summer. Morgan was (and is) close friends with Jimmy Keaveney, and Keaveney and his wife Angela went down to visit for a weekend not long after the birth. Frank Cogan, the Cork defender, lived nearby and he invited everyone up to the house one night for a bit of a party. This was two weeks before the semi-final. As the Keaveneys were leaving, Frank Cogan called Jimmy back. They had the Sam Maguire Cup in the house. Keaveney and Sean Doherty had watched Billy Morgan hoist it the previous September.

'Take a look at that,' said Frank, grinning and waving the cup at two in the morning. 'It'll be the last ye'll see of it!'

All good, clean fun. Keaveney told Heffernan the yarn.

Heffernan recycled it into something less harmless. He used it relentlessly. Cork arrogance, lads, Cork arrogance.

Perhaps he was right. Cork stayed in the Grand Hotel in Malahide that weekend. Mary Morgan and Ann Cogan – twin sisters who had married Billy and Frank – were staying with the Keaveneys in nearby Portmarnock. That weekend Cork had decided to drop Frank Cogan from their team. The corner back had been carrying an injury.

After Mass on the Sunday morning Ann Cogan asked the Keaveneys if she could use the house phone to ring Cork to see if Frank had travelled up for the game. No answer at home. Ann was pleased. Mary Morgan gave her sister's arm a squeeze and said, sure he might even be picked for the final.

And Jimmy Keaveney, standing in his own hallway, said, 'Hold on a minute, girls, ye aren't even in the final and maybe ye won't be.'

That afternoon Dublin blew Cork away. It was one of the great games of the entire era. Cork were flabby, Dublin were lean. Anton O'Toole scored an incredible goal in the second half. Cork then got lucky. Martin Doherty was just coming on as a substitute for Ned Kirby when the ball came straight to him. Cork had sixteen players on the field, but Doherty advanced to the large square, where he was fouled. Despite the fact that Doherty technically hadn't joined the game, the referee Patsy Devlin gave a penalty. Jimmy Barry Murphy cashed it in.

Dublin were unperturbed. They wanted this one badly. Thirteen minutes from the end, Billy Morgan was forced to bring down his old friend, Jimmy Keaveney. Another penalty. Young Mullins scuttered it into the corner. It was plain sailing all the way home.

When Keaveney came out of the back door of the dressing room under the old Cusack Stand, Mary Morgan and Ann Cogan were waiting for him, first with their congratulations.

'We thought that Dublin had reached their peak in the Leinster final,' said Billy Morgan ruefully when asked later. 'We thought they were satisfied with the provincial title.'

On All-Ireland final weekend, Billy Morgan was in Dublin anyway. Nemo Rangers played St Vincent's in a challenge match in Raheny. Afterwards they all went to watch the Dubs play.

Tradition. Do you understand it now?

5

Not even 'Heffo's Army' can get through an
ELEPHANT MAINS FENCER

Evening Press advertisement

Kevin Heffernan wasn't quite sure whether he was lucky with midfielders or just cursed with the species.

The previous autumn he'd had a handsome sheaf of options to choose from. Frank Murray was a fine midfielder. Pat O'Neill often played there, too. Stephen Rooney was thriving. Then he had discovered Brian Mullins quite by accident.

At the time Mullins was playing with a good team in Thomond College. Word had reached Heffernan that there was a very useful player from Ballymun on the Thomond side, Fran Ryder. Thomond were playing St Mary's of Belfast one day and Heffernan went down to have a look at Ryder. He came away with his head full of Mullins.

Naturally, Mullins was no stranger to him. It was just that he had his reservations. The previous autumn Mullins had broken into the St Vincent's senior side, and Heffernan retained an image of him in a Leinster club championship game in Newbridge.

'He was so awkward and so young he did a thing I've only seen once otherwise. He got a ball down there between his knees, with one hand behind his legs and the other in front.

'I remember a fella called Hubie Reynolds doing it when I played with him for Leinster one day. A Louthman. He did that, went to lift the ball and nearly made a gelding of himself. That was my memory of Brian.'

A week or so after the Thomond game, Heffernan brought

Colfer and Redmond to Finglas to see Mullins play in an Under-21 championship game. Mullins did nothing all afternoon. Finally, with St Vincent's losing by two points in the last minute, he caught a ball, drove through a gap, went on going with men bouncing off him, and buried the ball in the net.

Redmond and Colfer nodded. Mullins was in.

Michael Hickey remembers playing Under-19 rugby with Leinster in the spring of 1974. Mullins played in the pack, Hickey behind it. The game was in Ravenhill, and on the train back home the young lads were yarning and yakking and somebody asked Mullins if he was doing anything the following day.

'He said, yeah, he was playing his first game for the Dublin footballers. That was spring and we thought he was mad. The day after an interprovincial game, going playing Gaelic football with those. By September he had an All-Ireland medal.'

A little while earlier the referee Sam Connell had called Heffernan to advise him that he should go and take a look at a player with the junior club Oliver Plunkett's. He took down the name of a rangy young fella called Bernard Brogan. Kept him in mind. A few weeks later, at a loose end, Heffernan went to see Plunkett's playing up in Kinvara Avenue, and he liked what he saw. He approached Brogan after the game.

Brogan was a final-year engineering student at the time. Heffernan asked him to join the squad. Unaware of the force he was up against, Brogan said thanks for the offer, but no thanks. A few weeks later he was playing midfield for Dublin against the Combined Universities in a challenge game. That was the way of things.

This time Heffernan was astounded. At this level Brogan was even better than he'd first thought. He was astonishingly athletic. He was marking John O'Keeffe of Kerry and running the great man ragged. Heffernan clenched his fist with pleasure every time Brogan took the ball and went loping away with it. Nothing beats a lucky general.

At the end of the game Brogan hit the deck. A badly twisted left leg. He was gone for a while. Unlucky, thought Heffernan.

Brogan came back and played at full forward against Wexford in the first round of the 1974 championship. He lost the full forward spot to Jimmy Keaveney against Louth, but against Offaly he came in for the second half as the roving corner forward. Brogan cleaned up. His fitness was back, and in the running role he was a revelation. Heffernan was beaming again.

Then, right towards the end, Brogan twisted his right knee on the heavy turf. He had an operation a fortnight later and was in plaster for six weeks and in rehab for seven months.

So that was Bernard Brogan. Pat O'Neill was an option, but O'Neill had come close to death with a kidney problem the previous Christmas and was only crawling back towards fitness, having returned to the panel in August. He wasn't a real option. And Frank Murray had vanished to London. Through the summer Heffernan would call occasionally to the Murrays' house in Clontarf to see if there was any sign of the prodigal. Finally he gave up.

So Mullins had been trusted, at nineteen years of age, with a midfield position on a team that was trying to punch above its weight. He'd repaid Heffernan handsomely. Heffernan was pleased, not just with the young man's football but with what he brought to the room.

'He had a huge impact on everyone and his grumpiness set him up for everyone to get involved. He had huge intelligence too. He was grumpy as a young fella but you'd never know when he was having you on, when the grumpiness was real or when it was feigned. Lads got a kick out of it. He has a heart of gold though. He was invaluable.'

Then, on 25 August, more bad luck. In the All-Ireland Under-21 semi-final Mullins came off the field, hurt. He went to the Mater Hospital the next day and was told that he had a chipped bone in his foot. They entombed it in plaster and told him to forget about the All-Ireland final on 22 September.

In practice games Stephen Rooney and Pat O'Neill became the starting midfield. It was an awkward situation for O'Neill. Essentially, he was still convalescing after a life-threatening illness, early in the year. In his heart he knew he wasn't fit enough for an

All-Ireland final. He knew too that there might never be another chance. He battled on.

Pat O'Neill was working in the Mater at the time, as intern to Paddy McCauley, who was the chief orthopaedic surgeon in the hospital. One afternoon Heffernan arrived in Casualty with Mullins, who had an appointment. The doctors surveyed the injury again. Heffernan surveyed the doctors.

Pat O'Neill sat with Mullins, whose leg would be in plaster for another week or so, listening as Heffernan and McCauley argued the toss over the subsequent recovery period.

'Heffernan just said he'll play,' O'Neill recalls. 'Paddy McCauley was a tough man. Himself and Heffernan could talk the same language. A decade in medical school didn't impress Kevin.'

He will play, Heffernan says.

He won't, McCauley says.

He will and that's it, Heffernan says.

I'm telling you and I'm telling the patient he will not play, McCauley says.

And I'm just telling you he will play.

Last word.

O'Neill looked at Mullins, and the two young men smiled. Both knew who would be playing midfield on 22 September.

Mullins played. History has shown the impact. Sometimes a very young player shines for a year and then he's gone, like a shooting star faded to black. Heffernan knew that he had something different out there. Lots of others wouldn't have had the courage to play a man in those circumstances. Heffernan had decided that Mullins would be the heart of Dublin football for another decade.

The year was filled with stories like that. Cards falling, until eventually Heffernan had a strong hand. Keaveney rescued from being a Saturday night barfly. Deegan taken out of mothballs. O'Driscoll demanding and claiming a place. Joe O'Neill had been playing for a couple of seasons but had dropped off early in the year when his brother Pat got seriously ill. He was passing through a turnstile into Hill 16 one day in the spring when Heffernan shouted from the other queue. When was he coming back? O'Neill began an explanation that began with words to the effect that at the minute he wasn't that bothered. Before Joe had finished the sentence, Heffernan had vanished through his turnstile. One of the zillion small decisions and actions that make up a season.

David Hickey laughs. He was one of the lucky ones. 1974 was his season. He'd been playing rugby for UCD, and Bective beat them in the Cup. That night the phone rang. Heffernan! Hickey had known Heffernan since he was fifteen and first on the Dublin minors. Heffernan ran through the reasons why Hickey should come back to Gaelic football. No need. He'd had his man at 'Hello'.

By the autumn he would be an All-Star. An emphatic choice. On the field, his athleticism and talent were obvious. Off the field, Hickey was the hidden essence of the charm of the Dubs, the casual aesthete of the team. On the back pages Keaveney and Cullen were the voice and face of the collective. They were witty and confident and garrulous. In the dressing room, large parts of the team's intelligence and confidence came from Hickey. For that Heffernan loved him.

Hickey stories: Playing Laois one day, later in his career, and the Laois defender, a well-known practitioner of his art, having lost the first couple of balls. He has a word with Hickey.

'Next fifty-fifty ball that comes in here I'm going to break you up.'

A chuckle from Hickey. 'I'm afraid I don't do fifty-fifty balls.'

Or the casual dismissal of the art of point-scoring. Anybody can score points, he'd say, as he laid off ball after ball in the hope of being in on a goal-scoring move. He'd tell John McCarthy that he'd rather hit the crossbar with a drive from twenty-five yards than score. Hitting the crossbar was much more spectacular! Macker never knew whether to believe him.

Or a memory drawn from the final of that breakthrough summer of 1974. Anton O'Toole's worst nightmare was that he wouldn't see the ball for the first ten minutes or so of the game, and

Heffernan would get edgy and take him off. Corner forwards are always the first to get lassoed in times of trouble. Thankfully, a ball came in early and, pumped with adrenalin and fright, Anton leapt about ten feet off the ground for it. He came down and laid it off to Hickey. Great feeling. He'd done something. They weren't going to take him off yet.

Then it all went wrong. Michael Rooney punched a goal for Galway, and suddenly Dublin were behind. Anton got a ball not long after that and scored a point. He felt comfortable enough again, but Joe Waldron was marking him. Joe wasn't comfortable. He was starting to make Anton feel very uncomfortable, too. Hickey kept breezing past. Kept saying, 'Don't mind him, Tooler, ignore him.'

So Joe Waldron went over and gave Hickey a quick clout to help him mind his own business.

Hickey turned to Tooler. Huge smile. See. He's got nothing!

The longer the summer lasted the more confident Hickey became. The more confident he became, the more devastating his performances. Against Cork he destroyed Kevin Jer O'Sullivan to the extent that in Dublin it is still believed that Kevin Jer went into the dressing room and announced his retirement immediately after being substituted in the game.

The final was a reprise of this performance. On a dank day with greasy turf, Croke Park hosted two sides who were afraid of losing. Hickey's effervescence was the difference.

You put a Hickey and a Mullins into the same team, and you have a lot of heart and brains already. There's a creationist view of the Dubs of the seventies and there is an evolutionist view. Did Heffernan envisage how they would be, or did they merely blossom as he watched?

The stories tend more towards the idea of a creator with a bit of luck on his side. Heffernan knew what was required. Mostly, he found the men who could meet his needs.

The All-Ireland final was a bad game, but it scarcely mattered. Dublin got out on to the pitch twenty minutes before Galway did and absorbed the carnival atmosphere. When they arrived, it turned out that Galway had neglected to pick up any more scoring forwards than they'd had in losing the previous year's final. When Gay O'Driscoll locked John Tobin out of the game, the jig was up.

Anyway, quality didn't matter. The city was in love.

Records appeared in shops. The streets bloomed an autumn blue. The evening papers couldn't get enough of this new local phenomenon. Kevin Heffernan became Heffo. The vast, garrulous Dublin support became Heffo's Army.

There was madness in the air. Sean Doherty went to Mass on the morning of the final and found that his football gear was on the altar for blessing. Alan Larkin's dad couldn't bear to watch the final. He drove to Baltray to do some fishing. On Hill 16 a man dressed as a woman cajoled the crowd. They needed no cajoling.

A newspaper advertisement in the Sunday papers caught the Zeitgeist.

> STILL THE COUNTRY'S
> GREATEST DEFENDER
> Not even 'Heffo's Army' can get through an
> **ELEPHANT MAINS FENCER**

'I have a distinct memory,' says Heffernan, 'of walking down O'Connell Street some time in the summer of 1974. It was a lovely, sunny Saturday morning and I remember feeling there was a bit of a buzz. I said to myself, it's great to be coming now. The economy was slumped. There was no soccer team going well. The rugby team were struggling. We were arriving. There was a space for us to make a difference.'

They made a huge difference. By Christmas, the Sam Maguire Cup had been to every school in the city. These excursions into academia had a pattern to them.

One day Sean Doherty and a handful of the players brought

the cup to the Technical School on the North Strand. The usual deal: players brought into the staff room, offered a drink. Doherty recalls that principals in those days always had a bottle of whiskey handy for visitors.

The principal took Doherty aside for a word before the cup was displayed to the acned masses.

'I'm sorry, it's great to have ye here but I'm not in a position to offer the kids a half day to celebrate. Could you tell them that when you speak?'

'OK.'

So Doherty stood up and waved the cup and spoke a few words and then he said, 'Listen, I have some bad news. Your principal has told me that unfortunately he's not in a position to give ye a half day . . .'

A great groan went up

'But I am! Go on! GO!!'

The kids vanished like water down a drain. The principal, his staff and the Dubs went across the road to Grainger's for the afternoon.

Frank Murray watched the final in a cinema in London, with tears streaming down his face all afternoon.

Frank was in trouble. He was living in a squat in Finchley and he'd hit a trough of depression.

On the day after he arrived he'd made a mistake. A guy from Clontarf who was living in the squat had sought to make his fortune by buying £250 worth of grass which he hoped to sell on at a profit. He'd ended up buying the world's most expensive bag of birdseed.

Frank wasn't interested in the dealing or the aggro, but as he was tall and strong he was drafted into the posse which would go and put things right.

'Let's go now,' said the Birdseed Man.

'Well, OK,' said Frank.

So immediately the Birdseed Man grabbed a hammer and a breadknife and left. Frank, feeling increasingly uneasy, left too.

On the way out, the third member of the posse grabbed a walking stick from the hall. So into a van with them and through London.

Some knocks on a stranger's door. Frank had no idea where he was and no idea what to say, but he formed the impression it was all being left to him. So now he's eyeballing this little cockney with the face of a hardened grifter. Lenny.

'Yeah?' says Lenny.

They pushed in. One of the Dubs, the one with the walking stick, starts trying to take swings at little Lenny over Frank's shoulder. Frank discerned that this wasn't going to be a philosophical discussion on justice.

He lost his temper. He took the walking stick. He took the hammer and the breadknife and threw them over into a corner of the front room. He pointed Lenny to another corner. You sit there. The Birdseed Man he directed to a third corner, diagonally across from Lenny. You sit there. Frank stood in the middle. A reader of Kierkegaard sorting out a small-time dope deal gone wrong.

'Now we'll talk this out, guys.'

The third party, Mr Walking Stick, adjourned to the garden, his passion spent.

'Did you rip him off?' said Frank to Lenny.

'I did,' said Lenny.

'Well, will you sort it out?'

Lenny shouted to the wife. After some rustling, she produced fifty quid.

'And what about the rest?' said Frank.

'Come back tomorrow?'

'Are you a man of your word?' asked Frank of Lenny, who had sold a bag of birdseed to a fool who thought he was buying primo grass.

'Of course I am.'

'OK then.'

So they are leaving. Frank has won a victory for pacifism. Mr Walking Stick comes through from the back garden. On his way out, Mr Walking Stick turns to Lenny and says, 'If you don't have that money tomorrow, you're in fucking trouble. We're from the IRA. You'll lose your fucking kneecaps.'

And they laughed half the way home at the idea of the hippie provos who came from Clontarf and dealt in birdseed.

Next day, you can guess it. Knock, knock on Lenny's door. And suddenly twelve Panda cars come screeching from every available corner.

Oh, man. Frank felt green as the grass in Croke Park.

Three terrorist suspects arrested.

There was a pre-trial and a free legal-aid lawyer who could scarcely speak English. It all seemed comical in a Kafkaesque way until Exhibit A got pulled out. A breadknife. Then exhibit B, a hammer. Then a walking stick. This wasn't going to be any trial about birdseed.

Silence in court, bar the sound of a penny dropping in Frank Murray's brain.

Oh fuck.

Between pre-trial and trial he watched that All-Ireland final in a cinema somewhere in a city he hated. He cried and cried. His girlfriend, Marianne Muldoon, sat beside him, wondering what it was all about. Then Frank skipped out of London.

He came home for a while and would sit upstairs, depressed, as Heffernan would knock on the front door and speak to his father about coming back to play for the Dubs. He couldn't face it.

He drove trucks. He spent a lot of time in America. He played Gaelic football in Boston a few years, after 1974. He was rusty but he went out to Franklin Field and was more than good enough to star for Connemara Gaels.

The memories aren't entirely happy.

'They were savages,' he laughs. 'Dangerous fuckers. I was play-ing away. They paid me to play. I was avoiding the Irish in America but this guy came to the house, we were talking away. He asked me down to training. They couldn't play to save their lives. I got a grand for four games, which would include the final. In the final there was a brawl, and twenty-nine of them laid into each other. And the stand emptied. I sat on the ball in the middle of the field and watched it. The match was abandoned and re-fixed for the next weekend.'

He missed the replay.

'I'd gone down to Cape Cod because I'd made arrangements to go down there with this coke dealer. I ended up, long story, staying in Faye Dunaway's house on the Cape. As far as I was concerned, I'd done the business. I stayed for the four games. When I got back, the Connemara Gaels didn't see it that way. They told me they didn't want me in Boston.'

He took the hint. He drifted off to New Orleans. Ended up in a Salvation Army hostel, sweeping the steps. There was a swamp across the road, he remembers. His job was to keep the steps swept; most afternoons he sat and smoked his grass and listened to the birds singing. Happy enough, but restless.

On to Houston for a while. Driving a crane on an old missile site, working in a strip joint at night. He ended up listening to a mad Italian who suggested that he try heroin. He took the bait and tried the drug for the first and only time in his life. Bingo! Frank Murray got hepatitis. He came back to Ireland, this time half dead, after a ten-month stint away.

It was six months before he felt well again. He went along to Croke Park occasionally now to see his old comrades play.

'It was never the be-all and end-all for me, I suppose. I just liked playing the game. But it always hurt to see them.'

It was a bad final but it gripped the city of Dublin like nothing good had gripped it in a long time. Fiesta!

On the Monday evening after the game, the team went to Jury's Hotel for a reception. When they left Jury's, they came into the Mansion House for a civic reception. Finally there was an open-top bus ride through the city to the GPO.

The bus moved slowly through the river of citizens. It was a night the like of which the city had never known before, the immense cup glinting in the streetlights and the streets below just rippling rivers of blue.

The bus was crossing O'Connell Bridge on the last two hundred yards of its journey when Robbie Kelleher looked down into the crowd and recognized a face, 'This fella with a hat on him, waving up at us and smiling.'

Heffernan.

6

Where a flag failed to unite them, a football jersey did.

J. J. Barrett

Sometimes late in the morning, when Charlie Nelligan is busy in his coffee shop in Tralee, Darragh Ó Sé will stop by for a chat and a brew. Charlie notices what Darragh doesn't notice: every schoolboy in the place watches Darragh. Every schoolboy watches every move.

It reminds Charlie of a day, long ago, a day when he was just a chiseller growing up in Castleisland. Charlie was in the bakery yard at home and he had a goalpost painted on the back door. Football's grip on the Kerry imagination is such that the painting of goalposts on back doors is considered in no way eccentric.

Charlie had just got a brand new football. It was a time when footballs were a rare commodity and owning one ensured that your door was constantly knocked upon. He was kicking the football in the yard, doing his Micheál Ó Hehir commentary inside his head, when a car pulled in. Out stepped Mick O'Connell. The blessings were raining on Charlie Nelligan.

For perhaps the last time in his life, Charlie stood with his mouth open, unable to think of something to say. O'Connell was on the road for Texaco at the time and the Nelligans used Texaco oil. O'Connell was calling on business to the family bakery. Young Charlie had never known that legends like O'Connell walked the same streets and breathed the same air. He stood with the ball in his hands, just gawping.

'Well,' said O'Connell. 'Give us a kick.'

Charlie threw the ball to O'Connell. O'Connell kicked the ball back. The life was never in Mick O'Connell so much as when he had a football nearby. 'Go on,' he said, 'take a shot.'

He stood at the back-door goals. Charlie kicked it over the bar. O'Connell caught the rebound off the house wall and performed a few elegant solos and shimmies in the Nelligans' backyard, his black hair jetted back, his suit immaculate and his black, shiny shoes dancing on the concrete.

He told Charlie to go in goals. 'Stand in there, son.'

He took a shot at young Nelligan, going handy with it.

Jesus. Charlie just held that ball. O'Connell, finished with footballing, went into the office to do his business. Charlie was too shy to ask him for an autograph.

Suddenly he had a brainwave. He hollered for his father to come down and ask Mick O'Connell, would he sign the football. Done with a smile. The new football went into the Nelligans' attic, never to be touched again.

And for years that was an inspiration. When he was an Under-16 full back with Castleisland, three soft goals went in past his goalie, and next thing Nelligan found himself swapping shirts with his keeper. Most young fellas would regard goalkeeping duty as penal servitude, but Charlie enjoyed it. Hadn't he minded the goal against the great O'Connell?

For Kerry people, football is the glue that binds generations and seals community. It is part of life's expectation, part of the race memory. It seeps into poetry, plays and songs; overlaps with politics, religion and commerce. It is an instrument for living life and surviving bad times. It is a faith that allows the gods to dawdle on bakery yards.

In Tralee the John Mitchel's club squats down beside Austin Stack Park, where Kerry GAA has its headquarters. The address for both is John Joe Sheehy Road. GAA and politics are often intertwined, but in Kerry things are a little different.

Kerry football is blood and bone. It is the soil and much that is buried underneath it. The game is as inescapable as the heartbreaking beauty of the county which loves it, and the business of football is conducted with the same quiet obsessiveness as the business of politics.

In fact the lingering divisions of history and politics are concealed beneath the common passion for the game. It was ever and always will be. In the 1972 All-Ireland final, John Egan, who would spend his life as a guard, came on as a sub for Martin Ferris, who would be imprisoned for gun-running. On the day of Ferris's release from prison, he drove straight to Dingle to play in a charity football match. Egan was playing that day, too.

During the years of the War of Independence, Kerrymen interned at Frongoch played an inter-county game against a team of internees from Louth. Dick Fitzgerald captained the Kerry side. He had captained Kerry to All-Irelands in 1913 and 1914 and was one of the early thinkers of the game. When Gaelic football went from being a 17-a-side scrum to being the 15-a-side game we know today, it was Dick Fitzgerald who figured it all out for Kerry. He wrote the first GAA coaching manual, *How To Play Gaelic Football*, in 1914.

Nowhere did the Civil War years cut deeper than they did in Kerry. At Ballyseedy, nine anti-Treaty men were roped together around a mine and blown up by Free State forces. Miraculously, one, Stephen Fuller, was blown clear into a ditch and escaped, eventually being led to an IRA hideout, run by the great Kerry footballer John Joe Sheehy.

Ballyseedy was a reprisal for a similar atrocity at Knocknagoshel. In the weeks that followed, the killings continued, and another giant of the Kerry game, Tim 'Aeroplane' Lyons, died after a three-day siege in Clashmealcon Caves. Lyons is buried in the graveyard at his home village of Kilflynn, just yards away from Fuller. The graveyard is one of a thousand reminders of that time which exist in Kerry.

Early in 1924 a Kerry team composed entirely of former internees challenged the Kerry inter-county side, who at that time were Munster champions. Both teams trained hard. They played two games, several weeks apart. Each side won one. The Kerry side contained, among others, Con Brosnan. Several of the former internees would soon be his county teammates in the green and gold.

Weeks after those games, Kerry came to Croke Park to play in the 1923 All-Ireland semi-final which had been postponed as a consequence of the Civil War. The team, which now contained many of those men who had been on bitterly opposed sides in that war, came out of the tunnel to delirious applause and then knelt together in prayer at the spot where Michael Hogan had died on Bloody Sunday.

Kerry won, to go through to the All-Ireland final against Dublin. The match had to be delayed until the president of the Kerry county board, Austin Stack, was released from prison.

In one person Stack embodies many of the raw qualities and idealistic strands which defined life in Kerry at that time. Born in Tralee, he was a gifted player and had captained Kerry to the All-Ireland of 1904.

Four years later he became politically active and joined the Irish Republican Brotherhood. By 1916 he was Commandant of the Kerry Brigade of the Irish Volunteers, and in April of that year he suffered his first arrest for his part in the preparations for the landing of arms by Roger Casement. He was sentenced to death but had the punishment commuted to penal servitude for life.

Stack was released under a general amnesty for Republican prisoners in June 1917, but he was arrested again in early 1918. In Crumlin Road jail he participated in hunger and thirst strikes, a sacrifice which would eventually shorten his life. While still a prisoner, he was elected Sinn Féin MP for Kerry in the 1918 general election.

He escaped from prison the following year and continued in political life in the new Dáil. He took an active part in the Civil War and, when captured in 1923, went on hunger strike for forty-one days. During that time the GAA calendar ceased to be of relevance.

In a gesture which typified how things would be between the two counties, Dublin were offered the All-Ireland title by the GAA in June of 1924 but declined. The game went ahead in September, weeks after Austin Stack's eventual release. Kerry lost.

Seven months later, in April 1925, they beat Dublin in what was actually the 1924 All-Ireland final.

Those games redefined the GAA in that time after the national strife. They refocused the nation. One of the more charming stories related in J. J. Barrett's wonderful book on the period, *In The Name of the Game*, was that of the participation of Mundy Prendeville, who played for Kerry in the 1924 final. Prendeville was a seminarian at Maynooth College and he had to climb the walls of the college in order to get to Croke Park. Maynooth refused him ordination as a result of this breach of its rules; later, he was ordained at Clonliffe College, and then moved to Australia, where he eventually became Archbishop of Perth.

Football became the unifying passion of Kerrymen. Everywhere within the county, memories are honoured. The functional plainness of Fitzgerald Stadium is set dramatically between the austerity of St Finian's Hospital and the purple majesty of the Reeks. The stadium is named for Dick Fitzgerald, who died one Friday afternoon in 1930 when he fell from the roof of the courthouse in Killarney.

The Fitzgerald family delayed Dick's funeral so that Kerry might play in the All-Ireland final that weekend. Kerry won the second of what would be four in a row on the Sunday.

The old IRA man, John Joe Sheehy, captained the team that day. Afterwards he was due to hand the captaincy over to Joe Barrett of Austin Stack's, but in a brave and conciliatory gesture, which was not widely welcomed in Tralee, Barrett passed the captaincy over to his former Free State foe, Con Brosnan.

(On the occasion of the Munster final in 1924, John Joe Sheehy had still been on the run as an IRA man. Brosnan had negotiated a guarantee of safe passage for Sheehy so that he could play in the Munster final. Sheehy played, and then vanished again.)

The following year Brosnan handed the captaincy back to Joe Barrett, whom he had played against in the famous Internees v. Kerry match. (Incidentally, Brosnan's son Jim was on the Kerry team which defeated Dublin in the famous 1955 final. Barrett and Sheehy also had sons who won All-Ireland senior medals with Kerry.)

The post-Civil War years saw Kerry football heal itself to the extent that the county won ten of the following eighteen All-Ireland titles. Then things slowed down – or the rest of the world caught up. Three titles in the forties, three in the fifties and two in the sixties: just enough to sustain Kerry's position of pre-eminence in the game.

The sixties were depressing, though. Previously, Kerry had made a point of squashing any challengers for their position as laureates of the game. Kildare, Antrim, Armagh, Roscommon and Dublin were among those who'd had their pretensions shredded. In the sixties, however, things got radical: Kerry had to watch Down win three titles, beating Kerry in two finals, and Galway win three in a row, also beating Kerry in two finals.

Kerry won the 1970 All-Ireland, but nothing about that victory presaged the golden era to come. Cork won three Under-21 Munster titles around the turn of the decade, going on to win two All-Irelands. They also won ten out of twelve minor Munster titles from 1966 onwards, going on to win five minor All-Irelands. In 1971 Cork scored 25 points to beat Kerry, the reigning All-Ireland champions, in the senior Munster final.

Things just got worse. An industrial quantity of salt was applied to Kerry's wounds. Cork won the All-Ireland of 1973 with a side which looked capable of dominating for a decade. In 1974, Cork won Munster again, but had their swagger stolen by a Dublin team who instantly became the media darlings.

Kerry seethed.

The lean times were short, but in the Kingdom of plenty they were keenly resented just the same. In 1973 Kerry travelled as favourites to defend their provincial title in a Munster final at the old Athletic Grounds in Cork. The team got changed in the Imperial Hotel, and their ad hoc dressing room at the Athletic Grounds was a stable in the adjacent Showgrounds. They sat around on the straw bales, a *mixum gatherum* of greybeards and golden boys. They talked confidently about the game ahead.

Finally they stood and stretched and hopped the ditch to get into the ground. Cork were waiting at the table with a strong hand. Cork had Jimmy Barry Murphy, Ray Cummins and Jimmy Barrett in their full-forward line. They duly stuck five goals into the Kerry net. Kerry came in for the half-time break with trembling knees.

Paudie O'Donoghue, at full back, had been dragged here, there and everywhere so quickly that the lads feared he might be dizzy. More stressed perhaps than anyone else at the amount of artillery flying past his ear, he lit up his customary half-time cigarette. If Paudie could have taken a smoke on the pitch, he would have. They sat around with the Munster final already lost and spent the time cautioning Paudie not to set the straw on fire. Jesus, things are bad enough without burning ourselves, Paudie.

Eventually four or five lads lit up cigarettes. It was that sort of a day.

The legendary Johnny Culloty was in charge of the team back then, and Johnny had a hard road to travel. He'd played with many of the lads and he was a little easy-going with them. Culloty had an understanding of football which was and is virtually unrivalled. The trouble was that the old lags knew him too well.

Johnny Culloty's half-century of service to Kerry football has been distinguished by his quiet wisdom and his willingness to learn and adapt quickly. Back then, though, he had inherited an old-school team. Younger players who came into the panel at that time remember one or two senior players not being keen on running laps with the youngsters.

'Call me, I'll be out for the kickaround,' they'd say, bunkering down into the dressing room.

Mickey Ned O'Sullivan had had an underage career which gave him a fame, not just throughout Kerry but in Cork as well. What he lacked in height he made up in courage and ball-carrying ability and, despite the fact that St Brendan's of Killarney were the dominant force in schools football at the time, it was Mickey Ned O'Sullivan from Ballyvourney who played centre back on the Kerry minor team of 1970.

He was promoted quickly to the ranks of the senior squad. As he was making his way in the green and gold of Kerry, he was also dealing with less pressing matters such as life and a career. He was one of the first intake of Irish students to Strawberry Hill College in London, where he was studying physical education.

He remembers coming back in the summer of 1971 when he was a moon-blond teenager with his head brimful of ideas. Kerry were training in Killarney and at the time the great Jackie Lyne was the manager. (Kerry is so densely populated with legendary players that the honorific title The Great . . . can be applied to just about anybody with a connection to the senior inter-county team. Jackie Lyne was more than that.)

Mickey Ned hailed from Kenmare and so had the privilege of sharing the car journey into Killarney with Mick O'Dwyer and Mick O'Connell. They'd hit Killarney early and Johnny Culloty, who lived near Fitzgerald Stadium, would join them in the car for a few minutes' chat and gossip.

Mickey Ned had set off like an explorer to find the brave new world of physical education. The older men were very interested but not prepared to let on they were interested. They had that quintessentially Kerry way of trying to find out something without asking directly. All the time they wondered to themselves if the kid was learning anything that they could use to make them even better footballers.

So they'd hop the ball for Mickey Ned. Set him up.

After a training session one evening they were talking and Johnny Culloty asked innocently, 'Well, Mickey Ned, what did you think of that?'

'Yerra, Johnny, 'twas all right. We'd no warm-up, though.'

Of course this stirred it. Nudges. Swapped looks.

He ploughed on. 'We'd no stretches. We'd no warm-down.'

Warming up and warming down! Fantastic.

O'Dwyer drew him out further. Warming up. 'Why would we warm up on a night like that with the evening sun still on our backs? And why would we warm down then?'

So Mickey Ned gave a short extempore talk on lactic acid. It seemed to go over well. His audience of legends nodded gravely.

He'd expected them to be cynical about this whippersnapper just back from the big smoke with his hatful of half-baked ideas.

He was pleased and grateful for their attention. For a while afterwards, when he'd be passing, he might hear them talking quietly among themselves about lactic acid. He wondered if a supplementary talk on hamstrings might be useful.

And then one day he overheard too much. He realized that he had been re-christened.

'Here comes Lactic Acid!' they'd said.

In Kerry, a football famine is what counts as a time of plenty anywhere else. The county won the National League finals of 1973 and 1974, and in 1973 they also won the All-Ireland Under-21 title, fielding a team which had an unfeasible amount of potential in it. Much of what was to come was on show in that Under-21 final.

Johnny Walsh ran the Under-21 side of 1973 and by then Johnny was in his seventies, with nothing to prove. He was secure enough about his knowledge of football to agree when Mickey Ned, the team captain, asked if he might take a session.

Mickey Ned was a dangerous, long-haired radical. Strawberry Hill College in London had accepted an intake of young Irishmen who nourished themselves on new ideas and experimented wildly while away from an Ireland still bogged down in the tittle-tattle politics of The Ban.

In Strawberry Hill, Mickey Ned played soccer and rugby and anything else which took his fancy. On the rugby field he was joined by Jimmy Deenihan. Deenihan was built and bred for it, though he'd grown up with north Kerry football. Mickey Ned was small and from south Kerry, purist country. He was green, too. When he went down to present himself to the rugby club, there was a big, gnarly, London Welsh guy who looked him over and said, 'You've no neck, you'll be a good prop.'

Mickey Ned established for himself that a prop played among the forwards and decided that he would therefore have ample opportunity to demonstrate his scoring prowess. Happily he signed up.

A little while into his first match he felt that whatever he had where a neck was supposed to be was perhaps in danger of breaking. His conscientious-objector petition was successful and he was given a job away from the front lines. He became a full back and played happily for four years.

He went out for soccer, too. Went with Kevin Kehilly of Cork. They announced that they would be full backs. Mobile and fit, scorching down the wings. Of course they'd be full backs.

'We'd no idea about offside, though. We were playing against Chelsea Reserves. We'd have been comfortable on the ball but we didn't know what we were at. We were beaten 9–0. Dave Sexton was in charge of Chelsea, back then. He'd come to watch. I reckoned he was impressed with his boys. That was my last game.'

The interest grew, however. He went down to Arsenal to do an FA coaching course. Bertie Mee was in charge. Don Revie was there. It was a time when a fella from Kenmare could actually get to talk to these guys in coaching courses. He got ideas and stored them up. One day he had a modest epiphany: the principles of soccer were the same as those of Gaelic football. They were applicable! Penetration, depth, balance. It was just that the GAA had no words for these concepts.

When he took the Under-21 session from Johnny Walsh in that summer of 1973, Kerry had already beaten Cork in a most memorable Munster final, played in a rainstorm in Skibbereen. Cork had acceded to the idea of a game in Skibbereen, which was closer to the Kerry border than to Cork city, because they had a remarkable team that summer and expected that they would win if the game was played up and down Rock Street in Tralee.

Paudie O'Mahoney, the goalkeeper that night, remembers three things clearly. The intimidating size of the crowd. The soft rain. The fact that Jimmy Barry Murphy put the best goal he's ever seen past him that night, a two-fisted swipe which went in off the far post before Paudie's eyes had even registered the impudence.

And finally, when the game was won, they went to the West Cork Hotel and he noticed that Mick O'Dwyer was in there among them, in the best of spirits. Paudie thought nothing of it, but it stuck in his memory, O'Dwyer being there and how happy he was.

And a few nights later, with everyone still riding the wave of happiness, Mickey Ned began spouting his radical ideas and found that the field was full of guys who had thought the same thoughts. Mikey Sheehy, John Egan, Ger Power. This was their game.

'So show me,' said Johnny Walsh.

And they played a game which made catch-and-kick redundant. They transferred and flicked and moved into space. They ran at defenders, scorching the earth with their pace, and then they laid it off. At times they could just walk a ball into the net past bewildered defenders.

One evening that summer, Mickey Ned and the lads did a little evangelizing and got the seniors playing the same way, down in Killarney. When the new style was demonstrated to him, Paudie O'Donoghue, the old full back, shook his head and said, 'You'll get crucified, Mickey Ned.'

Paudie O'Donoghue was no soothsayer, but he was a full back. Perhaps he knew.

That Under-21 All-Ireland win in 1973 gave Kerry a sliver of hope. They needed it. In 1974 Kerry lost the the Munster final to Cork for the second year running. Humphrey Kelleher from Millstreet had an exceptional game for Cork, but in Kerry the game is remembered for Dinny Long pulling a double solo on Mick O'Connell.

It was O'Connell's last game. Dinny Long, who played many years with Austin Stack's in Tralee, was showboating a little. Of course he was. Cork, as All-Ireland champions, were handily winning a Munster final in Killarney. Dinny got a hard time in Kerry afterwards.

Paudie O'Mahoney tended goal for Kerry that day and he heard the crowd's reaction cascading down from the terraces.

'I felt sorry for Mick O'Connell but I also felt sorry for Dinny Long. He was playing well at the time. He was entitled to do what he did because O'Connell would do it to him. I've said it to

O'Connell since. They were that kind of guy, both of them. That sticks out. We all eventually get old. I saw that day that it doesn't pay to stay on.'

Kerry lurched onwards into a league campaign in the autumn of 1974. They started against Offaly, and there was a team meeting in the Bridge Hotel in Tullamore the night before. Lots of stern words and solemn amendments. Mick O'Dwyer was there. He was thirty-nine and had retired in the summer. O'Dwyer was also coaching the Under-21s, who had a large overlap now with the senior team. The players had the impression he was on the verge of playing the next day.

The next day they made a good start in terms of style and intent. They played well but lost by a point. The team was young and built for adventure. Next day out, they drew with Dublin, the new All-Ireland champions, in Killarney. And then they got better. They won the remainder of their league games and qualified for a league quarter-final in Croke Park.

In Kerry a league quarter-final excites about as much comment as a rainy day, but the county was watching this young team with an interested eye. This was a game which might prove something about them, one way or another.

There was a team meeting called in the hotel for the night before. Too hastily, perhaps. It happened at about one in the morning in an open room. Lots of drunk people wandering in and out. There was plenty of abuse handed out to the players. The elders of Kerry football and some hangers-on waded in to offer an opinion. A few players remember one speaker in particular as being 'drunk as a skunk and saying a lot of bad things to a lot of good players that night'.

The players decided that there were to be no more of these humiliations. No more outsiders being let in to talk down to them. That was it. End of story.

And then, as if the whole thing had been a preparation for this *coup de théâtre*, Mick O'Dwyer walked in. Ger McKenna, the county chairman, walked in with him and sat down and asked the players if this was what they wanted. Excoriation by drunks and blowhards for the rest of their days?

No.

Well, this is the way it's going to be from now on, said Ger McKenna, I have control. I have control of everything.

And O'Dwyer spoke a few brief words of encouragement before everyone went to bed.

The story demands a happy ending. Following all that went down that night, they should have gone and mauled Meath the next day. They didn't.

They were useless! John O'Keeffe and Paudie O'Mahoney, despite playing well, had a brief row during the second half. Paudie remembers complaining about something to O'Keeffe and getting a short, sharp answer. 'I said, "Johnno, if that's the way we're going to carry on we might as well not bother." We fell apart that day.'

It was sobering and frightening. The summer was coming over the brow of the hill. Cork were looking to win a three-in-a-row in Munster for the first time ever. Come championship time, the young Kerrymen would be fodder.

If Ger McKenna had a solution and he was called Mick O'Dwyer, well, there was nothing to lose.

7

Gadocha, ya hoor, slow down. Come back, Gadocha!

Timmy Kennelly

There are a couple of versions of the story concerning the precise nature of Mick O'Dwyer's appointment to the job that would change his life.

What's known is this. When Jackie Lyne retired from managing Kerry in 1971, Johnny Culloty was appointed to the job. Johnny said he couldn't take the team for the league. So Mick O'Dwyer of Waterville took them for the winter and won a league.

In 1974 O'Dwyer took the Kerry Under-21 side. They lost a Munster final in Cahirciveen that they should have won. The manner of defeat didn't affect the security of his two-year agreement.

When Johnny Culloty finished up managing after the 1974 Munster final, there was a vacuum. Kerry were in transition but the county board was aware that the renovations to the team would not suffice as an excuse if Cork resurfaced in Croke Park in the summer of 1975.

Kenmare were the 1974 county champions, and Mickey Ned O'Sullivan was top of the queue for the Kerry captaincy, a job it seemed he was born to do. If there was one fly in the ointment of Mickey Ned's contentedness that autumn as Kerry set into the league without a manager, it was that he was increasingly being entrusted with the training of the team. He enjoyed taking the sessions, but he had no intentions of making the arrangement permanent. Given the choice, he wanted the captaincy, not the boot room. He wanted to be thanking the county trainer on the steps of the Hogan Stand, not listening to somebody else make a speech which mentioned him.

Early that spring the county board had a suggestion. There was a coaching course being held in Gormanston, Co. Meath. The course would be run by Kevin Heffernan and Joe Lennon.

Those two names had resonance in Kerry. Lennon was a key part of the Down side which had accumulated three All-Ireland titles in the 1960s, beating Kerry in two finals and one semi-final along the way. O'Dwyer had played in each match and lost each time. Kerry had never been impressed by Down's refusal to doff the cap to the game's brand leaders. Lennon had ventured into print with a book called *Coaching Gaelic Football for Champions*. It was not a best-seller in Kerry.

'Joe Lennon had said Kerry football was twenty years out of date,' Mickey Joe says. 'There was still offence taken at that.'

Heffernan's Dublin, meanwhile, had won the All-Ireland from nowhere the year before, playing a new type of football, and O'Sullivan reckoned that the challenge was one which the young Kerry team should be able for. So he rang Mick O'Dwyer to see, would he come along on the course.

'Dwyer says, "No, I wouldn't go there at all."'

Mickey Ned knew, though, that when he thought about it O'Dwyer would be ready for the trip.

So Mickey Ned was persistent. Eventually O'Dwyer came round and asked what was involved.

'We do a course and there's an exam at the end.'

'Well, I'm not going then,' said O'Dwyer.

'Why?'

'I've no intention of doing any exam.'

'Well,' said Mickey Ned, 'we'll do no exam. We'll see what's happening. The minute it's over, we'll do no exam, we'll just slip away.'

And so O'Dwyer was on the hook.

'I remember Kevin Heffernan gave a coaching session, a physical training session, and it was amazing. Real hard physical stuff. We were coming away and Dwyer says to me, the first team that'll beat Dublin, they'll have to be fitter than them.'

On the way back down to Kerry in the car, Mickey Ned starting chipping at O'Dwyer in the way that O'Dwyer would do with so many charges over the next twelve years.

'Any chance you'd train the team, Mick?'

'No. Too busy.'

Mickey Ned's agenda wasn't restricted to freeing himself up for the captaincy. O'Dwyer was considered by many as a genuine managerial talent. While still playing at inter-county level, he had served as a selector and had trained the team for many sessions. Mickey Ned was keenly aware, too, of O'Dwyer's achievement in coaxing Waterville to unprecedented success. It would be worth nagging him.

So Mickey Ned asked again. 'Will you train the team?'

'Not a hope,' said O'Dwyer.

But Gormanston to Kenmare is a five-hour journey and when Mickey Ned got out of the car he knew he had his man. He went inside and rang Ger McKenna, who hopped into his own car and drove the seventy miles to O'Dywer's house in Waterville. The deal was done before O'Dwyer had time for second thoughts.

The second version is more prosaic but differs only in detail: O'Dwyer recalls that he 'had sort of agreed to it by then anyway'. He was putting together a philosophy of inter-county management for himself.

'That was why I went up with Mickey Ned. I'd played for eighteen years for Kerry, trained under Dr O'Sullivan, Jackie Lyne, Johnny Culloty. I went into All-Ireland finals when I was stiff and tired. I remembered that and had ideas of my own. There was a man in Dublin called Billy Behan, a coach and a scout for Manchester United. I had a good chat with him out in Portmarnock one day, and then I took a trip to Old Trafford and had a look at their heavy training system. I'd got a few ideas which I put into practice after.'

In Gormanston there was the bait of Joe Lennon and Kevin Heffernan. For Kerry football people, the thought of Lennon and Heffernan lecturing on football was both an affront and an attraction.

'Joe Lennon had made a wonderful statement after 1968 that we were out of date and wouldn't be heard of for another twenty years. That didn't go down too well in Kerry,' says O'Dywer. 'We won in 1969 and 1970. We won a lot of All-Irelands in that twenty years of catching up! I went anyway, and Kevin Heffernan showed us a full physical training session. I often wonder since, does he regret it. I knew then what had to be done.'

Ger McKenna remembers this: Kerry had no trainer from the end of the 1974 championship to the following March. The issue didn't arise until the annual county convention at the end of January, after which McKenna went away with a mandate to consult widely with figures around the county.

McKenna himself was keen on O'Dwyer for several reasons. He had seen what he did with Waterville. He had seen O'Dwyer drive sixty miles to play in meaningless challenge games when men who lived a mile from the ground cried off. He remembered that in 1973, when Kerry were short of players for the Wembley Tournament at Whit weekend, exam time, O'Dwyer flew to London on Friday night, played and flew straight home again.

'When I spoke to him, he didn't require much persuading. He says I was very persuasive and that was why he took it. I don't know. If others had asked him to do it, well, perhaps he would have refused – but he knew he'd get on well with me. All other problems were mine. He just had the team to worry about.

'I drove down to Waterville? That's the story and I won't change it. It's a good story, and today it looks well that I thought so much of him that I went down! I met him various places and there was such thing as a telephone in those days!'

Whatever the details, O'Dwyer had arrived. Not so much as a messiah but as an emergency repair man. For the first training session, Mickey Ned made out a rough set of drills for O'Dwyer. Afterwards O'Dwyer asked Mickey Ned what he'd thought of it. Mickey Ned commented that in retrospect it hadn't been tough enough. It was the last time O'Dwyer ever consulted on training and the last time anyone would ever have that complaint about one of his sessions.

The next night he crucified them.

The panel underwent a winnowing process, a natural selection. Older players dropped out or got burned away. O'Dwyer altered the passing style a little, making them kick the ball more. They used the same spaces but released the ball quicker and earlier.

Discarding players who had won All-Ireland titles for Kerry was risky and brave. Around Kerry, people looked on in astonishment, and if O'Dwyer ever paused for thought he would have heard the sound of knives being sharpened on whetting stones.

Instead, he proceeded with utter conviction. He was convinced that he needed flyers. He believed firmly, almost exclusively, in youth. He had seen Heffernan's sessions and wanted the same levels of fitness for his team. As time went on, O'Dwyer never wavered. He became more and more ardent in his beliefs, and his confidence would grow with success.

There would be plenty of that.

Ask one hundred people in Kerry, and ninety will tell you that Mick O'Dwyer is a rogue. Those who deviate from the statistical norm do so only to clarify that O'Dwyer is not a rogue, he is a pure melted rogue, the highest form of roguery there is.

Each of them will love him for the roguery. When it comes to men about whom much is said but nothing is proven, O'Dwyer is the original of the species.

They collect Micko rumours like voracious seagulls at the dock-side. They say that, when he and Mick O'Connell used to drive to Killarney from south Kerry, O'Dwyer would be paid hackney rates by the county board for doing the driving. They say that, when he managed Kildare, he was flown hither and yon in helicopters. They say that his pockets were lined with the money from Arab sheikhs who wanted to see Kildare do well.

And there's scarcely a business in any rural town in the country that somebody won't claim, on good authority, that Mick O'Dwyer has a stake in.

O'Dwyer loves the fun of it. He is as affected by rumour as a duck is by water.

His genius lies in his charm and in his energy. If Kevin Heffernan was analytical, then O'Dwyer was intuitive. If Heffernan was austere, O'Dwyer was loved. Heffernan put a team together from nothing and won All-Irelands with them. O'Dwyer was handed the greatest collection of players the game has ever seen, and won All-Irelands with them. Then he kept them going to win more and more and more.

The two men were never close, but the comparative study of them is one of the joys of running a finger over the contour map of the seventies.

A Kerry training session: O'Dwyer has ordered the boys to be on the field at 7.30 p.m. He himself is there at 6.30. He has brought the boys from south Kerry with him. They like to travel with O'Dwyer because he drives fast and always has a big car, and they like to wind him up.

He drives very fast. On the road and hitting the footpath. The lads find that up around Kells Bay the road gets windy and narrow. They travel Kells Bay with their eyes shut.

And then the wind-ups begin.

Valentia is the favourite topic. In the lean economic years Valentia seemed impervious to the call of emigration. The footballers of Valentia never left for London or Boston or Sydney. Waterville meanwhile lost good players in their droves.

'How they doing out in Valentia this season, Micko?' Somebody asks.

'Christ Jesus,' he says, slapping his forehead in exasperation, 'they live on bread and milk out there. There's none of them that would leave. Oh Jesus, they'd be going for five or six in a row if they don't start leaving!'

In Fitzgerald Stadium, Pat Spillane is always first out on to the field. He likes to kick footballs for three-quarters of an hour before any session. He has Mike Buckley, an outpatient from St Finian's, kicking the balls back out to him.

That's all Spillane does for three-quarters of an hour. Catch, solo, kick. Catch, solo, kick. Catch, solo, kick.

The other Kerry forwards arrive. They look balefully towards the pitch and wonder aloud, will they ever arrive to see Spillane practise his passing. If he wasn't so good, they say, we'd kill him.

It is a regular complaint to O'Dwyer. Spillane is mouthy and he never passes. Nine times out of ten he will shoot rather than pass the ball.

O'Dwyer laughs. Sure eight times out of nine he'll score, boys, let him alone.

In the car park at the top end of the field the cars keep arriving. Ogie and Paudie down from Limerick. John Egan up from Cork. The Tralee boys shoehorned into Ger O'Keeffe's car. Timmy K. and Deenihan in from Listowel.

By seven o'clock they are all out on the field and there's a good smattering of locals perched in the stand. They've come to study the form. There is no harder audience to play to.

Now, those that believe in stretches are doing some exercises to warm up. Others are kicking and catching. There's an air of anticipation, although it's hard to figure out why. It'll be the same as every other session. The only variety for twelve years might be whether they'll be asked to do ten laps or twelve to start off.

Those who are carrying injuries are keeping it to themselves. O'Dwyer hates injuries and firmly believes that the hamstring was invented by Jimmy Deenihan in the early seventies with a view to annoying trainers. Nevertheless, Kerry have good back-up services; the trick is to get yourself seen to and never bother O'Dwyer with your ailments.

He draws them all in and the session begins. No guesswork, no surprises, unless there's a newspaper man in or somebody whom O'Dwyer wants to bamboozle. For the former he will put on a display of ingenious and overly complicated drills which will break down half the time but which will look scientific in the extreme. For the latter he will order a game of 'ground football', aka soccer.

(Here again is a difference with Heffernan. One night, before Dublin played Galway in the All-Ireland final of 1983, the Galway corner back Johnny Hughes appeared on the hill in Parnell Park to watch Dublin train. Heffernan spotted Hughes as quickly as an eagle spotting a lamb in pasture. He landed beside Hughes. Stood

for a minute. 'How's Johnny?' 'Grand. How are you, Kevin?'
'Fine.' Pause. 'Now, Johnny, a quick word, you know that you're
more than welcome here any night of the year, but tonight is the
wrong night for you to be here, so in the nicest way I'm going to
tell you now to fuck off out of here, Johnny.' 'OK, Kevin. Good
luck now.')

Eoin Liston could wake up in the middle of the night, weak
with a fever, and still recite the typical O'Dwyer session. A clatter
of laps to start. Then two 'proper' laps, sprinting the last length
each time. Then walk three-quarters of a lap and then sprint-jog-
sprint-jog for another two laps, making sure to sprint the last fifty
yards. Then the dreaded wire-to-wire. Width of the pitch, one
wire to the other, flat-out sprints in groups of three.

Nothing is random. O'Dwyer has placed a hare into each group
of three. The other two chase the hare. Now Ger O'Keeffe (who
is nicknamed after the great Polish World Cup player) is skimming
the grass and Timmy Kennelly is toiling after him roaring, 'Gadocha, ya hoor, slow down. Come back, Gadocha!'

Over. And back. Want to throw up now? Next thing, an extra
wire-to-wire. And then, for the bigger fellas, the heavies or the
fatties as he called them, the lads who've been out on the soft grass
too long, yet another wire-to-wire.

And all the time for the fatties the voice in their ears, ye're in
terrible shape, ye're in terrible shape, the beer is coming out through
yer pores. And Páidí, the favourite of them all, might turn and
roar, 'Christ, Micko, you'd win fuck-all without the heavy fellas.'

And for his trouble they'll do one last sprint. Goalpost to goalpost
and back. That'll take the winter conditioning off ye!

Meanwhile he'll be stoking the egos of the fit and lithe. Jesus,
boy, you're in great shape. I've never seen anything like you.
You're a greyhound.

Then shorter sprints. Out from the sideline and bending to
touch a football twenty-five yards away, before turning and sprinting back. Man competing against man.

Then, depending on the time of year, some heavy work. Press-
ups, giving each other jockey-backs, and so on. Finally some

backs-and-forwards, and then an all-out game, and the grand finale, an all-out 400-metre sprint around the full perimeter of the Killarney pitch and straight into the dressing rooms.

The five PE teachers on the team would close their eyes and ask the god of warm-downs to forgive them.

Afterwards they'd go to the Park Hotel for steak dinners, paid for by the county board. Most of the players pushed the food around their plates. Their appetites were left behind on the pitch. When they parted, they drove off into the Kerry night, down the narrow, twisting roads of their county. The boys of summer.

They did it without wondering or asking why. And in the winter, when they weren't doing it they were running the roads and the beaches and the hills, getting ready to go training in the spring.

They did it for all manner of high-minded reasons – for the club, for themselves, for the county. Mostly they did it for O'Dwyer, or, as every player he's ever known calls him, for Dwyer. They never feared him personally, but they feared being cut out. Being in the circle of his enthusiasm was addictive.

Those few Kerry players who experienced Kevin Heffernan's management in Australia in 1986, when he managed the Irish International Rules team, came away with immense respect for Heffernan, but they point out the essential difference in player relations. There was always a barrier between Heffernan and his players, a wall over which they could never look. With Dwyer there was just a line. The players never crossed that line, but there was never a big amount made of the line either.

For an ostensibly gregarious man, O'Dwyer is a loner, very much a loner. He is a whirling dervish, running on pure adrenalin all day long, yet he doesn't drink at all or socialize regularly. Pat Spillane reckons that in forty years maybe, Dwyer has bought him two pints. If the lads ever dropped in to Waterville, they always hoped it was Mary Carmel, Micko's wife, who was behind the bar at the hotel the two of them owned and ran.

He was a mystery to them, his life an endless frantic unspooling of nervous energy and enthusiasm. On trips he was first at the airport, first in the check-out queue, first on the plane, first off, straight through because he only brought carry-on luggage because he couldn't bear to stand at a carousel. He was first out of every airport, he was first into each hotel. First always. Rushing everywhere.

And then they wouldn't see him. O'Dwyer would be gone out the door of the hotel early in the morning and he'd be back late at night, and between times they had no idea where he went. A group of them could be loitering in the lobby, drunk, at three in the morning and they'd see O'Dwyer returning, still in a hurry, always pleased to see them but giving off no hint of what filled his days.

'He was part of us and he wasn't,' says Pat Spillane. 'How did he juggle it? You are his friend. You're not his friend. You've known him for forty years and you don't know him at all.'

In 1973 a league semi-final between Derry and Kerry caused such acrimony that the northerners withdrew from the replay. In the pictures of the aftermath of the first match was a shot of O'Dwyer coming off the pitch, holding the match ball and apparently protecting the referee, Paul Kelly, from abuse. The lads came to understand quickly that the match ball was the thing. O'Dwyer would bring one football to a match and invariably come home with two. Next night at training they'd have a new ball with 'Dun na nGall' or 'Uíbh Fhailí' written across it in faded blue marker.

They drove in their cars to National League games through every winter, and O'Dwyer would always leave as if he were making a getaway. Hurry, hurry. Top speed to Waterville, where he would have a band playing in his ballroom every Sunday night. The players swear it was a band called Royal Flush every Sunday for twelve years.

Sometimes on the way home he would stop in a small town and point out a car and ask one of the players to get out and drive the car to Waterville. Once, during a butter crisis which led to rationing and a voucher system, they stopped somewhere in Meath and O'Dwyer disappeared into a house. Five minutes later he reappeared, looking for help, carrying some large boxes of butter to the boot of the car.

Once they were in London for a Wembley Tournament and

somehow O'Dwyer was being driven around by a London Irish millionaire with a Mercedes as big as a house. Graciously O'Dwyer offered several players a lift and hopped into the front passenger seat himself. His eyes fell on a rather unwieldly apparatus between the seats.

'What is that?' he asked his host, picking up what was clearly an early car phone.

'It's a car phone,' said the millionaire, pleased to be asked.

'By Christ is that what that is,' said O'Dwyer, looking at it in apparent fascination. 'How would that work now?'

'Well –' began the millionaire, but he was cut off.

'HELLO?' roared O'Dwyer. 'Hello, Mary Carmel.'

The lads in the back smiled to each other as a ten-minute phone conversation about the following night's dance in Waterville was played out. How would that work now! The Master!

Many of them knew his form, of course. O'Dwyer had played till he was thirty-nine and they had all faced him on a football pitch at some time or other. Charlie Nelligan was a sixteen-year-old goalkeeper playing in the championship for Castleisland, the first time he encountered O'Dwyer.

There was a penalty given against Castleisland. O'Dwyer had a way of co-opting referees onto his side, and on this occasion began making it a joint operation between himself and the referee to make sure that Nelligan stood on his goal line. The debate went on. Nelligan was jumping on his line, nervy as hell. O'Dwyer stood over the ball and engaged the referee again.

'He's moving again, referee.'

Nelligan advanced in exasperation to make his case to the referee. As he came, O'Dwyer sidefooted the ball into the net and trotted off in triumph.

His playing days advertised the man he was. The reputation for cutery thinly conceals the manic competitiveness which he brings to everything he does.

Mikey Sheehy has vivid memories of an early appearance for Kerry, in a league game in Killarney, back when Cork were All-Ireland champions. Kerry were struggling, and O'Dwyer in particular was having trouble with his frees.

Sheehy was a sub with a number on his back somewhere in the high double-digits. At half-time he was kicking the ball around out on the field with the rest of the subs, and his conditioning was such that the effort left him out of breath by the time he hit the dugout again. Just then the county secretary, Andy Molyneaux, stuck his head into the dugout.

'Mikey Sheehy, hurry up, you're going on.'

Sheehy got the slip to give to the referee and strict instructions that he was to take the frees for the rest of the game. So out he went, young, curly-headed and not too limber – 'carrying a big old arse', as Páidí Ó Sé puts it. Sheehy was being marked by Brian Murphy, and that was fine. Murphy wasn't killing himself and Sheehy got a couple of points from play.

Next there was a free given. O'Dwyer was holding on to the ball as if it contained the elixir of life. The free was a handy one, about twenty-five metres out and central. O'Dwyer took a look, put the ball down and placed it over the bar. Sheehy looked to the bench and shrugged his sholders. The bench shrugged back.

'There was no way on earth that day that Dwyer was letting this townie from Tralee come on and kick it. That's not Dwyer!'

He hated to lose. He hated it more than any other human being they'd ever met. Once, a few of them were waiting for him in Waterville, playing cards to kill the time. Knowing he'd be along soon, they fell upon a wheeze. They rigged the deck of cards and tossed some money on the table, and when O'Dwyer came along he couldn't resist joining them for a little poker. In ten minutes he was cleaned out of the modest amount which he had been prepared to wager. The trouble was, he was in such a rage about losing that nobody had the courage to tell him it was a joke. They kept the money for six weeks before finding the right moment to come clean.

He worked every angle with the diligence of a ward boss. When they'd get a job, get selected for Leinster, get something good, O'Dwyer would always have had a word here, a whisper there, a wink to the right person. Whenever they got dropped, he hadn't been able to make that particular selectors' meeting.

'You could get the greatest psychologist in the world,' says Pat Spillane. 'They wouldn't know what to make of that man's brain. He doesn't really have buddies, but he knows everyone. He could play with your head as easy as a child playing with a toy.'

'I don't think we ever got tired of him,' says Jack O'Shea. 'The speech was always the same. Hammering the glass bottle on the table, we'd be on the edge of the seat, expecting it to break every time. On All-Ireland weekends we did the same walkout in Malahide the Saturday night before a match and he said the same things. He never changed. Same old stuff all the time. At the end we were hardly hearing him. No tactics. No pattern. Just make space and play it in. We were just feeding off his enthusiasm.'

8

I knew they had a good team. I knew they were coming. They
didn't take us unawares. They were good, innate footballers.
They could think for themselves on the field. I always think that
in '75 we were unfortunate to concede the first free. A bad free.
A greasy day. Gay O'Driscoll didn't hold it, it spilled on to a
fella's boot and the ball was in the net. That gave them the confidence and the impetus they needed. That's not to detract from
them. They were a great team. We just needed to keep them under.

Kevin Heffernan

Life was less ordinary for the Kerry footballers in the summer of
1975. They were swept along on the torrent of Mick O'Dwyer's
enthusiasm. Their manager was taking the gamble of his life, going
with this callow squad while men with All-Ireland medals in their
pockets and strength in their legs went back to their clubs, there
to live out their playing lives as former inter-county players.

O'Dwyer's enthusiasm was contagious. When he asked his boys
to train for twenty-seven nights in a row in the run-up to the
Munster final, they did so without demur, and when it was over
they asked, what's next? They loved it. Their masochistic sufferings
became a talking point. That was a good thing. The other talking
points around Kerry were their limitations and their heretical style
of play.

In Kerry, they weren't rated. The knowledge of that was as
unavoidable as it was crushing. O'Dwyer was their only shot at
the big time, and vice versa. They'd all go down together if they
were going down.

Kerry started stiffly that summer with no advertisement of the promise which O'Dwyer saw in them. They played Tipperary in Clonmel and settled with a goal in the third minute. They expected to be allowed to express themselves after that, but Tipperary insisted that they get down and dirty and wrestle.

Two second-half goals from John Egan ensured that their dignity was restored to them like a gentleman's hat. Egan! When all around were losing their heads, John Egan was usually whistling a happy tune.

For some, that afternoon was a quiet beginning. For others, it was a high point. Ray Prendiville grew up in Scartaglin, five miles from Castleisland on the Cork side. The football leagues of Kerry are a complicated business, but all you need to know about Scartaglin was that they played in a basement competition known as the Novice League.

The Prendivilles moved to Meath in 1969 and Ray became a Garda two years later. He added a few inches of height around that time, and a couple of pounds of beef on his shoulders, and made the Garda club team at full forward. They had a decent side and it is remembered in the city that they should have beaten St Vincent's in the championship semi-final of 1972. Instead, they lost a replay.

Ray kept playing. He was stationed in Harcourt Terrace at the time, and some days, standing on duty outside the Department of Justice, he'd meet Davey Billings, the St Vincent's and Dublin player. They'd share a line or two of banter, neither of them thinking that they'd ever get near All-Ireland medals.

In February of 1974 Ray played a game for the Gardaí out in Tallaght, which at that time was separated from Dublin by miles of country roads. It was dark when he was driving home and an oncoming car with its headlights ablaze blinded him. He woke up in hospital.

He stayed there for five months. He had damaged a nerve in the spinal cord. He was advised never to play physical-contact sport again. The use of his right hand was gone for a year. People said he never got the best stuff out of himself again on a football pitch. He was happy just to be walking in the world.

He hadn't kicked a ball since the accident, and then out of the blue he had a call-up for Kerry. He thought about what the surgeon had advised him. He thought about the green and gold. He went training with Kerry's Dublin contingent the next week, working in Belfield under Micheál Ó Muircheartaigh. This was late April of 1975. Ray had been almost fifteen months without physical exercise.

At weekends he'd go to Kerry and stay with his sister in Scartaglin. Whatever Ó Muircheartaigh hadn't squeezed out of him, O'Dwyer took.

O'Dwyer stuck him into a few tournament games through May. Kerry played Mayo in Emly the week before the championship got going, and things went well. Come the big day in Clonmel, one Ray Prendiville got picked at full forward. The Resurrection Man wearing fourteen.

He was marked by a big fella called Eddie Webster. A high ball came in between them after three minutes. Ray caught it, turned and hit a sweet left foot. The net bulged. He'd scored the first goal of Kerry's golden era.

He hit the post afterwards and then rattled a crossbar in the second half.

The next week, he played full forward in the challenge with Dublin in Tralee, and the week after, when they played Galway in Limerick in yet another challenge, he was in again. Kerry won both of the games, and yet when it came time for picking the Munster final team Ray wasn't surprised not to be included.

'Looking back, I was more than delighted to just be part of it. I spent the year with one of the greatest teams to ever play football.' He enjoyed the weekend of the All-Ireland final, and that was it. Over. The next spring he played a little O'Byrne Cup football with Meath.

Kerry went back to Kerry on the Monday night after the 1975 final. Going up and down to Kerry for training that summer, Ray Prendiville had used up all his holiday leave from the Gardaí. He had no choice but to go back to work instead. And that was it. Perhaps he'd used up his nine lives, and all his days of grace, too.

His Kerry championship career was over. One game. One goal.

Like being the monk who painted the first letter into the Book of Kells, Ray Prendiville went back to the world, knowing that he'd left his mark.

For the Munster final, the weight of statistics and the weight of betting was with Cork. They had won eight of the previous nine Munster minor championships, four of the previous six Under-21s, and three of the previous four Munster senior finals.

Kerry understood, and it was fine. The last thing any team needs when going to Killarney is to be billed as big shots. Better to back into the limelight, bowing most humbly.

Cork were confident. They had harvested and honed many under-age stars along the way to that afternoon in Killarney. One in particular, Martin O'Doherty, was accustomed to success. An All-Ireland minor football medal-winner in 1968 and 1969, he'd graduated on to teams that won All-Ireland Under-21 titles in 1970 and 1971. He was an under-age hurling star as well, winning All-Ireland minor medals in 1969 and 1970, and Under-21 titles in 1971 and 1973.

In Kerry they remember Martin O'Doherty for a moment just before 3.45 p.m. on 13 July 1975. When Pat Spillane found all avenues of possibility for his pampered right foot blocked, he settled for a weak point attempt from his left hoof. Martin O'Doherty, in one of those moments that men play slowly in their minds for an eternity, managed to turn the ball past Billy Morgan and into his own net. There were thirteen minutes of the match gone. Martin had just become the donor of a life-saving transplant of confidence. If Kerry had been doubting themselves, here was the gift of freedom. Cork responded badly, repeatedly shuffling their players until they were baffling themselves more than anybody else.

Kerry won. 'My name is mud,' commented Martin O'Doherty afterwards. It was to be his last game for the Cork footballers. (As a hurler his name went unsullied, however, and for a time in the late seventies, after he had emigrated to Los Angeles, his county's need was so acute that he was regularly flown home from California for games.)

The 1975 Munster final marked the moment when the most promising generation of footballers which Cork had ever produced were consigned to house arrest. They won just a single Munster title in the following twelve years. Every other year they suffered the twin indignities of defeat and having to grin and bear it when Mick O'Dwyer would come in and tell them that they were the second-best team in the country.

For Kerry, the Munster final of 1975 was the small battle which secured liberation. If O'Dwyer achieved nothing more for the summer, he was off the hook. Cork had been stopped. Many in Kerry still found their team's new style of football offensive, but the eclipse of Cork was sufficient justification for continuing.

No Kerry player used the phrase in the next day's newspapers, but they all use it now when they think back. That day was shit or bust. If they had lost, O'Dwyer was gone and so was the whole experiment.

They celebrated well, with no heed for what the rest of the summer might hold.

Dublin found that being All-Ireland champions was new, un-charted territory. In fact, for the GAA it was new territory, too. Suddenly there were two types of people in this new world. Dubs and culchies.

Jimmy Deenihan witnessed the transformation at first hand and marvelled at the zeal of the converted. For several years in the early seventies Deenihan would work summers in the Dublin factory which canned Batchelor's beans. He worked with Fran Ryder for those summers. The Kerryman and the Dub would talk football softly. It would have been easier to come out as rampant cross-dressing homosexuals than to announce to the factory that they were GAA men.

For Deenihan it was a culture shock. 'The Dubs weren't that interested that much. Most of them were just against the GAA. The All-Ireland final was always a rural event, a country man's occasion. I worked for three summers in Batchelor's and the lads would be making a joke out of football. It was a culchie game. Until they won. I remember I met a bunch of them before the game in 1975; they started shouting at me going up the street and they were all head-to-toe dressed in blue! They told me they were Heffo's Army!

'The Dubs created a wave, a whole mood swing in the country. There were different social movements at the time, but they created this thing. Suddenly there were people proud to be associated with that whole movement. Grown men would dress up for the big match. They brought colour back into the game. The Hill became a focal point of the culture. They, more than us, changed it socially. We were the vanguard of the response. The city had this phenomenon. We represented the country.'

The social revolution was proceeding; but after September 1974, when the Dublin team's private revolution of fitness and style had won them an All-Ireland, nobody in the camp was sure whether or not to stop training for a while.

They took a week off and then ploughed on. The league began in October and they just fell into the same routine. Training Tuesdays and Thursdays and Saturdays. Some say it wasn't a problem, they say that Dublin only lost two games the following year. Others say that they burned out and note that the two games which they lost were the National League final and the All-Ireland final.

In the late spring they didn't care much anyway. All through 1974 Paddy Cullen had goaded them every time he saw an airplane fly over Croke Park. 'We'll be on one of those, going to America next year, boys,' Cullen would say over and over again. So much so that the eyes of the whole squad would roll skywards when he started.

Cullen loved it. He had been to America as an All-Star replacement the previous year and liked to tease the boys about his good fortune. Sometimes he would break into a little burst of John Denver's 'Leaving on a Jet Plane', just to rub the point in.

In 1975 they all flew over Parnell Park together as All-Ireland champions, off to the US to play the All-Stars on the annual tour. They flew to New York, had a three-hour stopover, where they refuelled themselves grandly, and then they flew on to San Francisco. On each flight they had drunk the bar dry within a couple of hours of leaving the ground. They hit San Francisco in a memorably tired and emotional state, taking an inordinate amount of time first to recognize their bags and then to co-ordinate placing them on trolleys. Those who could still stand walked towards the exit gates. Those who couldn't stand sat atop the bags which had been loaded on to trolleys. The men who could walk pushed their more helpless colleagues towards the Arrivals gate.

When they got through the gate into the Arrivals area, things turned surreal. A local Irish-American pipe band had been booked to march Ireland's finest athletes through the airport. The owners of the homes where the players would be staying were on hand to grab their brothy Irish boys and bring them home for a few days. The Dubs paraded through the airport behind the pipe band, looking like dishevelled casualties from a strange and hideous war. They were in holiday mood.

Kevin Heffernan, a teetotaler, wasn't so jolly. The next day, the team attended a function in San Francisco's Irish cultural centre. A new brand of whiskey, Dubliner Whiskey, was being launched. The team launched the drink with such wild enthusiasm that stocks almost ran out before the tipple could hit the shops.

The next morning Heffernan had planned team training at nearby Balboa Park. In the Californian heat the players struggled. Some of them did less than struggle. They surrendered. They just lay down and prayed for death. Heffernan put on his grim reaper face and called a team meeting.

The manager laid it on the line. 'You're here on holidays. Grand. But the way some of you are behaving, you won't be with this group when you go back.'

Cullen, who often acted as a spokesman for the players, interjected brightly with what he felt was a reasonable point. 'Kevin, I think perhaps the problem here is with the shorts.'

'What?' said Heffernan, mystified but none too interested.

'The lads are very used to drinking pints, and the shorts on top of the pints are having a very bad effect, Kevin. If we all stick to drinking pints we'll be grand.'

Heffernan's feelings on this proposed health kick are unrecorded. Players remember, though, that they trained hard several times after that. The Kilkenny hurlers, All-Ireland champions in 1974, were there on tour, too. The hurlers felt that the jury was still out on the benefits of physical training and that the benefits of physical training while on holidays could never be proven. They laughed at the Dubs.

Dublin came back home, sobered up and, a week later, lost the National League final to Meath. On 22 June in Tralee they played a young Kerry team in a challenge game, the proceeds of which went to benefit Sister Consilio's mission for alcoholics. They lost, but thought nothing of it.

It was summer. They were rolling towards September and in the rear mirror they could scarcely see the bad times any more.

There's a graveyard. Keep whistling, boys.

Mickey Ned's year was long and winding. It brought him to Croke Park in September but to a few other spots along the way. Since Gormanston, his relationship with O'Dwyer was such that he felt confident when he approached the manager for a quick word after the All-Ireland semi-final win over a hapless Sligo team.

Mickey Ned announced that he was going on holidays for a month. The All-Ireland final was six weeks away. He'd be back for the start of the school year. He'd send a card and, hey, don't worry.

O'Dwyer may have gaped but he didn't object. The moments after an All-Ireland semi-final win in a historic breakthrough year are precisely the right time to pull one over on O'Dwyer.

So the morning after the semi-final, Kerry's captain began a happy driving holiday across Europe in the company of his friend Donnacha Lucey.

With his back to Fitzgerald Stadium, guilt started to nibble at Mickey Ned's conscience. Fear, too. What was he missing out on? How much fitness would he lose? Mickey Ned trained twice a day, every day. He went up and down more mountains than the Grand Old Duke of York and his men.

His holiday partner had no interest in football, but everywhere they went Donnacha was drafted into the desperate search for a suitable field to train in. Mickey Ned trained in the Alps, in the Black Forest, up the Dolomites and down the Moselle valley. No football. Just running.

He came back as promised to Kenmare for the start of the school year. The town was riven with controversy.

P. J. McIntyre, the Kenmare club secretary who'd started so many local kids playing football in the town, had been sent off in a club match. The Kenmare club felt that McIntyre had been unfairly penalized.

The club were sulking. It was a posture which put Mickey Ned in an awkward position with the county board.

As was traditional in Kerry, there was a church gate collection the week before the All-Ireland for the Kerry training fund. Every parish in the county conducted such a collection, and in places that had a man on the team the take was expected to be especially large.

The Kenmare club decided there was to be no collection if there was to be no justice for P. J. McIntyre.

Mickey Ned was captain of Kerry, however. Loyalty to club had to be weighed against duty for county. He mulled it over, and finally he went across to the church and stood outside all the Sunday Masses himself. The Kerry captain as mendicant holding out a plastic bucket. Alms for the team! Alms for the team!

In the club he was *persona non grata* for a while.

'I felt that it wasn't relevant. I wasn't the flavour of the month, though.'

The buckets filled anyway. The people neither understood nor cared about the crabbed politics of rural GAA. There was a local guy who was captain of Kerry. Of course people were willing to contribute. In a small town there's always a little bit of drama, a little bit of play, but a chance to celebrate comes rarely.

Nobody asked Mickey Ned about the previous month's holiday.

★

Dublin played well through the championship, leaking a lot of goals but scoring promiscuously at the other end.

In September, pitted against a Kerry team who were widely depicted as heading to Croke Park carrying schoolbags on their backs and marbles in their pockets, they were roaring favourites.

Dublin were grown-ups, after all. And they had blossomed into celebrities. They colonized the back pages of newspapers and, as David Hickey says, had got a good smell of themselves and quite liked it.

In Parnell Park the celebrities weren't feeling quite as sanguine as they might have been. The preparation for the game against Kerry is remembered for a few reasons, none of them happy. Most especially it is recalled for the dropping of Bobby Doyle.

On the Sunday before the All-Ireland final, the Dublin team went across the city to Sachs Hotel in Donnybrook for a meeting and a video session. Some of the players remember the Sunday session as coming near the start of a run of six training sessions in a row, the first evidence that Heffernan was a little spooked by Kerry. Others, including Heffernan, remember nothing odd about the amount of preparation done.

Everyone remembers the Bobby Doyle business.

After the Sachs Hotel meeting, the team had something light to eat and headed back across town to Parnell Park for a training session. When they got there Heffernan pulled Bobby Doyle aside and told him that he wasn't playing the next week.

On most sides, corner forwards are disposable parts. If you get a fine one, a rare one, you fix him into things. Otherwise, the lads in the corner are detachable. You haul them off at the first sign of trouble and stick in another fella. G'wan, make a name for yourself.

Dublin were different. For a start, they were a closer-knit side than most. Secondly, the way the corner forwards played – especially Doyle, who ran from the first whistle to the last – was key to the style the team had adopted. Doyle cropped up everywhere, making himself available for loose balls and leaving behind a nice inviting space in the corner of the field.

Now Dublin had three fit first-team corner forwards: Doyle, Paddy Gogarty and John McCarthy. Doyle was dropped, whopped and lollipopped.

Most surprised of all, perhaps, was John McCarthy.

Macker had got himself suspended for three months that summer. He was kicking some ball in training in the run-up to the All-Ireland, but he hadn't played a match in those three months.

Long story abridged. Macker had his jaw broken in Wexford Park at the start of the championship. Three weeks later, Heffernan was keen that McCarthy play against Louth.

Macker wasn't sure. 'I knew he wanted me to play. I had it in my mind that the next guy who would put his elbow in my face, I was going to take the head off him. In the end I wasn't picked to play that day. This lad from Thomas Davis, a fella called Martin Noctor, was selected. Martin called me over before the game and he tells me he has half of Tallaght down to see him play. He asked me, had I any advice.'

Macker gave Noctor a few tips, and when Macker stood up in the dressing room Heffernan beckoned him across the floor.

'We're standing there in the dressing room and I'm looking away at something as he's talking. Next thing he hits me a belt in the jaw. Not that hard, but I got a fright. I turned around and he starts laughing.

'"You're fit to play then," he says. "I'm revising the team and you're playing."'

Macker was in an embarrassing position and the puc in the jaw hadn't sweetened him any. He protested earnestly about Martin Noctor and half the population of Tallaght. Finally he persuaded Heffernan to give Noctor the run he had been promised.

Noctor didn't get much rope, and half the population of Tallaght didn't get much value. After fifteen minutes or so, Macker was in and Noctor was out. Dublin were cruising. By now, though, Macker was wound up to a notch beyond even his regular intensity. It would have taken a team of nerveless experts to defuse him.

Instead, he won a ball and felt somebody yank him backwards by the jersey. He dropped the defender with a punch. Bobby

Doyle and Jimmy Keaveney were over to the ref with a couple of violins and salty tears in their big, sad eyes to explain that Macker had just recovered from a broken jaw, that he was just out of hospital, poor man.

Macker was gone, though. Three months. He wouldn't even get to play in the All-Ireland semi-final.

Yet during the run towards the final, Heffernan had begun to stick Macker into the 'A' team in the games at training. Surely Heffernan wasn't thinking of . . .

But he was.

Doyle had played in the semi-final and, by his own admission, 'wasn't great', but he felt that he hadn't been too bad either. He'd had anaemia that year and was finding the training a little bit tougher than usual.

'It didn't come as a big surprise to be dropped, but I didn't think I'd be dropped for Paddy Gogarty. I went to Kevin Heffernan that week and said that this was wrong. Paddy Gogarty was a different player. He'd shoot from anywhere, which was great when it came off but wasn't the game we were playing. Obviously Paddy felt differently. I went to Heffernan and he made it clear that players didn't pick the team.'

Gogarty, an almost impeccable point-scorer, concedes the point about differing styles but doesn't concede anything else.

'I was a different sort of player to Bobby. I know that. Bobby played a running game. I played quite a bit of the 1975 season and I thought I deserved a shot at a place in the final.'

The selection made things awkward between Doyle and Gogarty, who were two of the more outspoken members of the squad. The team's diplomats worked overtime to hold things together.

After the team was announced that Sunday, Doyle went home. 'Almost as soon as I got in, the doorbell went. Hickey, O'Toole, McCarthy, Ryder. They all called to the house. It was as if there had been a death.'

Gogarty was also approached. 'It would have been put to me at the time during All-Ireland week that I should go and have a word with Bobby. Sort of explain to him why I was in the team ahead of him.

'There is no doubt that what happened was unfair on me,' he says. 'I was picked in that position because I was playing well. I was asked to speak to Bobby Doyle and almost apologize to Bobby for getting picked in his place. The Vincent's fellas were very influential. It was said to me, "You might have a word with Bobby."'

At that stage St Vincent's accounted for a huge part of the panel. Of the starting fifteen, Doyle, Keaveney, Mullins, O'Driscoll and Hanahoe were all from the club, while the subs' bench held Davey Billings, Leslie Deegan, Brendan Pocock, Fran Ryder and Norman Bernard. The team wasn't overtly cliqueish, but for anyone who looked it was clear where the balance of power lay.

'That was the Vincent's thing,' says Gogarty. 'There was a Vincent's group within the group. It was as if Vincent's were an organic group and they were all damaged if one of them was damaged. I went down to Bobby that morning. I was advised to go down and to say hello to him and have a brief chat. I was dropped hundreds of times and nobody ever came to say "Hello". Nobody was ever sent!'

'I went to Paddy on the Tuesday and wished him the best of luck,' Doyle recalls. 'It was sticking in my craw, but it wasn't Paddy's fault that he was picked. Heffernan said, two weeks prior to announcing the team, that there were three of us contesting for two positions. John McCarthy, Paddy Gogarty and myself. Two corner forward positions. I knew in my heart, I suppose, I was out because I was up the other end of the field and he was playing the pair of them on what we recognized as the first team. Fuck. It wasn't rocket science but you keep telling yourself lies.'

As it happened, on the day, Doyle was introduced before half-time in a tactical switch, with midfielder Bernard Brogan coming off. Doyle didn't prosper. Kerry were dominant at midfield and even Gogarty, who had started the final well with two early points, faded as the supply of possession evaporated.

For his part, McCarthy recalls, 'I didn't believe I should have been picked. I hadn't been playing. I felt I needed three or four games. I was a bit shocked. We were all close and we were all feeling sorry for Bobby. Training was bad. It was very hard on Paddy. He was playing well. I was the one, I firmly believe, that should have been left out. I was only training to keep part of the group. I was brutal in the final. In hindsight I thought it was wrong that the focus was on Paddy. Paddy was right to be playing.'

When the men who picked the Dublin team look back on that week, they aren't inclined to backtrack.

'Listen,' says Heffernan, 'it was Bobby himself who was upset. When it came to an All-Ireland, nobody else gives a shite, once they are on the team. Bobby, ah listen, I won't say anything more.'

'Bobby could be awkward,' says Lorcan Redmond. 'He was a good player. He did a job for us that nobody else could do. He opened defences, he created space. He was the one who understood.'

'He had that engine,' says Heffernan.

'He put himself out of the scoring range by doing the job he did,' says Lorcan Redmond. 'There was nobody else we could have asked to do that job. Being in Vincent's and being so close to Kevin, he understood it exactly. As was said at the time, though, when it came to picking the team it was always horses for courses. If a guy was right, he got in. It wasn't popularity we were looking for. Paddy Gogarty was a better point-scorer but he wouldn't do the other job. Horses for courses.'

'We were stuffed that day,' Gogarty says. 'It turned on the goal but, generally speaking, we were stuffed.'

There were no showers to be had in Croke Park after the match. A man from the GAA offered to hose them down. No bonfires burned in Dublin, no open-top buses were needed. They'd let Kerry out of the bag.

Mickey Ned O'Sullivan remembers nothing of the All-Ireland final weekend of 1975, the weekend which began the greatest rivalry in the history of Gaelic football. He can't even recall where the team stayed. He remembers waking up in the Richmond

Hospital at nine o'clock on the Sunday night, having drifted in and out of consciousness for some hours.

The nurse looked at him and told him that Kerry had won, and he recalls that the news put an end to a nagging but not unpleasant thought in his head that the game was still going on and that he might be going back on to play at any minute. He wondered briefly who had collected the cup.

Anybody who has seen the incident at any time in the last thirty years won't need a description. Anybody who hasn't should be told that Mickey Ned O'Sullivan was a good deal smaller than either Sean Doherty or Alan Larkin of Dublin, and when he was propelled by one into the high arm of the other it looked as if his blond head would come off his slender shoulders.

The Doc is contrite but offers context. Football is more complex than it looks.

The seventeen minutes of football before Mickey Ned was injured contained a Kerry goal and many other things which were distressing to Dublin.

'You had Mickey Ned coming up the middle at a hundred miles an hour and nobody doing anything about it. He always carried it further than anyone else, and you never knew as a full back whether to go to him or to stand your ground. If you went, he'd flick it over your head. If you stayed, he'd go for the back of the net.'

During a break in play the Dublin defence had a council meeting. The Doc had some questions for the half back line. What's going on out there, why is this fella being accommodated? He's coming in here unaccompanied every time. Don't be leaving it to us, lads, he's coming from a long way out.

If Mickey Ned remembers nothing of the incident, the Doc carries it in his head in slow-motion detail like the Zapruder film of the Kennedy assassination.

'The time I went to him I knew I was leaving Seanie Walsh standing behind me. A flick of the ball from Mickey Ned was going to mean a goal. When I'm within a yard or two of Mickey Ned, he has the power to make me look like an idiot by passing it over my head.'

Alan Larkin was closing in on Mickey Ned from behind and to

the side. Everyone was moving at top speed. Mickey Ned had a
problem with overcarrying the ball. For a period, Kerry had moved
him back to defence in an attempt to cure him. No use.

'We all knew that to pull up would be to lose the ball,' says the
Doc. 'It was unfortunate, but he could have laid the ball off. He
insisted on all these runs. They are just split-second decisions.
When you do it, your timing has to be right. You have to do it.
Make sure you connect with the ball or the man. On that particular occasion either one of us could have been on a stretcher. It
happened it was him.'

The Doc had one look at Mickey Ned and he knew that Mickey
Ned wouldn't be getting up under his own steam. He was gone,
real gone.

Mickey Ned lay on the wet Croke Park turf. One memory
swims up through the murk to him. Lying there, the sky fading to
black and the voices over his head saying 'Stand back, stand back'.
He could feel himself struggling to breathe. Then the lights went
out and somebody flicked the sound off.

The odd thing is that there was no reaction on the pitch. Even
from the referee. RTE had a few things to say about it and the
Hogan Stand howled with outrage, but down on the field there
were no complaints. The Kerry players just got on with things.

'When these things happen and there's a bunch of players around
and a match going on, you don't feel how bad it is sometimes,'
says Doc. 'As for me? I knew I was going out to hit him. Not to
put him away or put him out of the game, but I had to stop him.
I had to stop him from coming in, I had to make him think again
before coming back in. I never thought he'd be on a stretcher. I
just wanted to give him the message. "Mickey Ned, you'll have
to change your options, you can't be coming in this way."

'I saw it afterwards on television. If Mickey Ned had left the
ground when he saw me coming, if only he'd taken that jump to
burst past me. Lads buckle themselves up and get in the air when
there's a heavy challenge coming so that, when they get hit, they
fly away. I think he knew Larkin was there and he was hell bent
on coming through. It happened.'

Kerry went on and finished the job which they had started with John Egan's third-minute goal. Pat Spillane, just nineteen years old and from the Kenmare satellite village of Templenoe, lifted the Cup instead of Mickey Ned.

'I've no regret,' says Mickey Ned. 'Yerra, you have to be philosophical. It didn't happen. I was disappointed to miss the end of the game. When I was in and out of it, I still thought the game was on. I came around and there was no game. A complete anticlimax but I got out the next day. That's life.'

Decades later, their best hindsight won't alter the scoreline. Dublin lost.

Bobby Doyle played the entire second half. They still lost. Players put forward other reasons for finding themselves planted on the seat of their pants in the middle of the canvas. Many say that Heffernan's anxiety over Kerry seeped into their training schedule. A banner on Hill 16 on the day of the final said 'Took a Dive in '55, Still Alive in '75'. Heffernan wasn't the only one thinking of what had happened twenty years previously.

Others say that they didn't think enough about 1955 and they came to Croke Park taking the young Kerry side for granted.

Overtraining is the most common complaint. Several players remember being relieved, at the last session before the final, that they had survived it all.

John McCarthy recalls a conversation in the week before the game.

Tony Hanahoe came to him in Parnell Park with a question. 'Macker, how do you feel?'

'Fine,' said Macker.

'Macker. I'm fucking asking you how you feel. Now, how do you really feel?'

'I'm wrecked, Tony.'

'I know.'

When they finished training for the 1975 All-Ireland, David Hickey turned to Anton O'Toole and said, 'Well, Tooler, that's it. We made it.'

There was no victory rostrum available, however, and they just headed for the Nissen huts and the tea and biscuits.

The Kerry team had about one razor between them. They were on average twenty-two and a half years old. They were an outfit composed entirely of bachelors, and largely of students. They seized the day and the future.

Kerry won the minor All-Ireland the same afternoon with young fellows like Seanie Walsh, Jack O'Shea and Charlie Nelligan in their ranks. After the minor game, Nelligan went and sat on the Kerry senior bench as substitute goalie. A week later in Tipperary town, a Kerry team composed mainly of the minors and seniors from the previous week beat Dublin in the All-Ireland Under-21 final.

Kerry had put all upstarts to the sword. God was back in his heaven.

On the night of the All-Ireland final, John O'Keeffe flew from Dublin to East Midlands airport. He had started in Loughborough College, in Leicestershire, the previous week. That night he sat alone in a world where nobody knew there was such a thing as an All-Ireland final.

Perhaps he was lucky. Behind him he left younger teammates who were on the cusp of legend. Some of them seemed to have been born to it. Ogie Moran had been a young star in Kerry and for Gormanston College for as long as anybody could remember. 'Ogie was a man at fourteen and I was a boy at seventeen,' is the recollection of his neighbour and friend, Eoin Liston.

Páidí Ó Sé and Pat Spillane had been the kings of football from the day they arrived for their secondary schooling at St Brendan's in Killarney. Famously, because of their footballing prowess the two sixteen-year-olds were given the indulgence of a trip to Dublin for the 1972 final between Offaly and Kery. They missed the train home – or, rather, they never attempted to get it – and the pair spent an hour running around the pitch in a deserted Croke Park, making passes to each other and scoring points and running Micheál O'Hehir commentaries through their heads. They say they wondered if they'd ever be back there for real on a big day. They were bred for it, though; they must have known that this green plot would be their stage.

The weekend set a pattern. The walk in Malahide on the Saturday which ended with a chat as they sat along a wall, looking out to sea. Mass on Sunday with Páidí Ó Sé, a slave to the piseogs needing to see two red-headed women before he could rest easy, the same Páidí Ó Sé who would start early pacing the corridors, bouncing a football as he went. For Páidí the long march started at dawn.

John Egan from Sneem was the coolest of the lot of them. Egan would stay away from the dressing room altogether before the game, just sitting out in the stand, chatting and watching the minor game. He'd breeze in, ten minutes before they were due on the pitch, stick his gear on and go out again. Walking out with the delirious fury of an All-Ireland crowd breaking over his head, he tapped Páidí Ó Sé on the shoulder with a question. 'So Páidí, what are we doing tonight if we win?'

What did they do? They did what was traditional. They drank. They threw themselves into a world which they had hardly known existed.

'It was way beyond anything we'd come across,' Paudie O'Mahoney says. 'We were trained for everything except that. There was nobody to talk to about it. We were a crowd of young bachelors who liked an odd drink, and here we were, confronted with lunacy. Six drinks there on the table for you before you sat down. Another six on the table as soon as you sat down. People reaching in over your shoulder, leaving down pints. You learned to drink. It was beyond reality. It wasn't nice it was so excessive. Looking back, it was something we didn't need. Teams now are protected from that. We should have been.'

In the All-Ireland final O'Mahoney wasn't required to pick the ball from his net. He become the only All-Ireland winning keeper not to concede a goal right the way through a championship campaign. He'd saved a penalty from Jimmy Barry Murphy in the Munster final and another from Dessie Kearins of Sligo in the

All-Ireland semi-final. He has mixed feelings about the air he took in when he was at the summit of his career.

'I remember the Dublin team coming off the field. They were gracious. When we met the next day at the reception, they showed the game again. I felt sorry for them. There was a lot of Kerry fans laughing and cheering the Dublin mistakes. I thought it was unfair.'

They came back to Kerry after the 1975 final, to Killarney on the Monday train.

'We were drunk, most of us. It was sad. I was from Killarney and I had no interest at all in going out to my own road. There were bonfires out there and they were waiting for me. I didn't know there were bonfires because nobody ever came into my house and told me I was a good guy until the green and gold won the All-Ireland. I stayed in town and went into a pub, here in the town. The following morning I was told there had been a hundred people waiting for me on my own road. There's a couple of ways of looking at that. You could be selfish, but it upset me. I didn't like it. Having said that, none of them ever did anything for me. I did it for myself.'

They went around the local schools the following day and then to Tralee for more drinking and parading. Ali fought Frazier that night, and the bachelors were mercifully eclipsed for a few hours. They grabbed their breath and their sleep before resuming the battle against sobriety in the morning.

They were making it up as they went along now, freewheeling. Mickey Ned had been released from hospital, but his fate was almost forgotten by the county board. On Wednesday night the team were due to visit Kenmare.

'We had to do it ourselves. Mickey Ned wasn't even thought about. We went down to Kenmare and made a big night for Mickey Ned out of our own funds. The county board didn't put up a penny.'

And the local politics of football being the politics of the unforgiving, the Kenmare seniors made a point of training that night. As the town celebrated, they turned their backs and gritted their teeth.

★

One footnote from the year. Johnny Bunyan, the vanishing full forward.

Johnny grew up in Ballydonoghue, as small a rural village as can be imagined. He was nourished on tales of Eddie Dowling and Gus Cremins and Dee O'Connor, men from the little village who had left big footprints. He dreamed of being a footballer like them.

He made it. Sort of. He played minor with Kerry in 1967. That year he got work on Tarbert Island, building the new ESB power station. He fell in with a crowd of lads from Ballyduff. Nobody had warned him. Ballyduff was heretic country. In Kerry, where everyone worshipped at the broad and welcoming church of football, Ballyduff was in thrall to hurling.

Out of curiosity Johnny took a hurley in his hand for the first time in his life and taught himself to play. Casual dabbling at first. Recreational use of the ash. He was headed for the Kerry Under-21 footballers and playing away with Ballydonoghue. Still he liked the feel of hurley on sliotar, and after a short while he was going back to Ballyduff in the evenings to hurl. It was a guilty pleasure.

Football could be heartbreaking. He was with the Kerry seniors for the league of 1969–70. Doing well. Johnny was big and strong and could clear space for others in and around the square. In the spring of 1970 it came time for Kerry to travel to the States as All-Ireland champions. There were twenty-three on the panel and the travelling party was to be twenty-one. Johnny and Jim Coughlan, a lad from mid Kerry, were told to stay home.

He was in love with hurling by now and abandoned the football altogether for a while. He made an effort with football again in 1972, and his divisional team, Shannon Rangers, won the championship. Ballyduff won the hurling championship and Johnny had a medal from each to jingle. That football championship ignited his interest a bit and he played hard for a while in the championships.

When O'Dwyer came along in 1975, he wanted Johnny Bunyan in there. Johnny said, 'Why not?' although after a few training sessions in Killarney his body was able to tell him exactly why not.

He loved the fun of it, though. Every evening he'd drive in with Timmy Kennelly and Jimmy Deenihan and Ogie Moran in the car, laughing their heads off. Three big men and Ogie. One evening they suffered a puncture and it was more than their lives were worth to be late to Killarney. They fixed the wheel in a manner that made Formula One pitmen look like sloths. Ogie got the spare from the boot while they loosened the nuts. They didn't bother with the jack. Jimmy, Timmy and Johnny bent down and lifted the car sweet and clear. Ogie took off one wheel, stuck on the other and they were off again. Zoom.

Johnny came on as a sub in the game against Tipperary, replacing Ger O'Driscoll. He did well. He started against Cork and Sligo, taking the full forward spot off Ray Prendiville. Against Sligo, the full back was a fella called Johnny Brennan. Brennan had a skelp off Mikey Sheehy early on and Johnny decided he'd have a little slant off Brennan as payback. He ran at him with the ball. Bam!

Coming home on the train, Mikey Sheehy sat with Johnny, buying him beers. 'I have to mark my guardian angel.' Good times.

That golden summer stretched on into September. Johnny loved the rhythms of it, but the training killed him. Especially O'Dwyer's final flourish every evening. 'He'd give us the 440 at the end. Around the pitch. You know Fitzgerald Stadium, the size of it. It's not a cabbage haggard! I used to take my boots off for that. I'd be so tired, the boots were too heavy to bring around on my feet!' Johnny Bunyan laughs and wonders aloud whether the GPA would like to campaign to get him some arrears for past hardships.

Ogie Moran was a good friend. Ogie's luck that summer had gone in the other direction to Johnny's. He'd started against Tipperary but had been taken off. Johnny had been brought on and had kept his place for the next two afternoons out. Ogie had been a sub for those games.

They supported each other. Every night after training they'd drop Deenihan and Kennelly in Listowel, and then Johnny would drop Ogie off in Ballybunion. On the Tuesday of match week they had a little tradition, a little superstition. Ogie would be getting out of the car and he'd turn to Johnny and say the same thing. 'Johnny, I'll be down for the paper first thing in the morning to see the team. I look for my name first and I'll look for yours after.'

Johnny Bunyan would laugh and say to his friend, 'Ogie boy, I'll be doing the same thing!'

When the team for the final was announced, they were both surprised. Johnny Bunyan was dropped. Mikey Sheehy was moved from centre forward to full forward. Ogie Moran was starting at centre forward. Ogie would go on to win eight All-Ireland medals wearing the Kerry number eleven jersey. Johnny's time was at an end.

'I was disappointed,' says Johnny, 'but I was happy for Ogie. He was a friend and a north Kerryman.'

On the day of the final, Johnny's younger brother Robert captained the Kerry minors to the All-Ireland title. A lesser man than Johnny would have watched the feast and fed himself on self-pity. Johnny danced.

'It was a great achievement for us as a family and a big achievement for Ballydonoghue. That's how I've always looked at it.'

Mindful of his missed trip in previous times, Johnny Bunyan went to America the following spring with Kerry. Then he came back home and devoted himself to the hurling.

He won six county hurling titles with Ballyduff and enjoyed every minute of every game. He left behind the greatest football team in history and hurled till his heart was content.

They went to Athleague one day to play Roscommon in a winter league game. He remembers a Roscommon official giving them a coarse brush on the way in. They had to clear sheep out of the dressing room and sweep up before they could use it. 'We won that day and came home happy as children.'

Another time Kerry couldn't get a field in the entire county to train in. Johnny was doing a little farming back in Causeway, and when they got around to asking he had a look. He found a flat field and he got two spotlights off a lad in Listowel. Johnny tied one light to a tree and the other to a pole and they togged out all winter, sitting up on bales of hay and happy with their lot.

'I loved the hurling. I thought it a far better game. I played on Ger Henderson and Sean Stack and Mick Jacob. I felt it an honour to mark those guys. Winning an All-Ireland and getting a medal would be the ultimate for any Kerryman, but when I was hurling we drew with Kilkenny in a National League game inside in Tralee. For me that was the equal of the All-Ireland.'

And that was Johnny Bunyan, gone out the gate and never a moment's regret.

9

Psychopaths, in the best possible sense.

Páidí Ó Sé

Late in the seventies, looking for some small good thing to kick-start his jaded team, Kevin Heffernan moved Dublin's training sessions from Parnell Park to the Trinity Grounds, a few miles further out of town in Santry. The new venue had wide spaces and nice pitches, good training rooms and a place to park the cars.

One thing wasn't the same, though. The room available for team meetings was too luxurious. Soft chairs and lots of breathing space and windows through which a man's gaze could escape and his thoughts with them.

The players knew that things had changed. The smithy in which they had been forged was Parnell Park. The field itself and the little room, essentially a shed with a corrugated-iron roof and wooden floors and not enough space for a comfort zone. An entire panel of senior footballers and their three mentors would shoehorn themselves in there and talk softly about hard things. Unless talking softly wasn't enough.

Then, talking done, they emerged, blinking, into the world of mortgages and jobs and families. They went into an adjacent shed, where Christy Thompson would have made tea in a large kettle. The tea would have stewed for about three hours. They'd have Club Goldgrains and Marietta and then point the cars for home.

Heffernan had wanted an arena in which honesty always prevailed. In his playing days, the walks over Howth Head with his colleagues had created a forum for talking and thinking about the game. The Room would do the same.

'If I said to a half-back that he was holding the ball too long, I didn't want him to just nod at me. I wanted him to say that yes, he was holding the ball perhaps but the corner forward is hiding behind his man and not showing and then I wanted to be able to hear from the corner forward was he hiding in there because he was afraid or because the passes were bad. I wanted that honesty.'

He got that and more.

There was a leavening of banter, of course. Keaveney was the lightning rod because Keaveney was Keaveney, impervious to insult or injury.

'In fairness to James,' Hanahoe would say, 'he had a marvellous game last Sunday. He covered every inch of that fourteen-yard box.'

'Lads, lads, lads,' Paddy Cullen would add, 'don't be feeding Jimmy those low balls down around his knees. He can't get down that far.'

Keaveney relished it all.

'Fuck off, you,' he'd flash at Cullen. 'I took you from playing soccer in McNaughton's on a Saturday afternoon.'

And he'd be off, pointing his finger around the room.

'I got you on the team and you on the team. And you. So shut up now. Right!'

The slagging was a necessity, a little release of pressure through the valve of humour. Everyone knew what was coming. Some feared those meetings. Some thrived on them. Everyone was marked by them.

Sometimes Heffernan's focus would be microscopic. Paddy Cullen remembers long debates about kick-outs.

'Mullins would say to me, "You can't kick the ball any further than forty yards. Do you want me on the forty-yard line?" But we worked out strategies in the room. Pat O'Neill would drift in for a short one and I'd knock it into the space behind him and Hickey would run in and take it. I picked up Hickey quite a lot. He wouldn't say that, though.

'I'd be told to give an odd one into the middle. Find Mullins if I could. The players began to get the drift of it, but Heffernan was always the teacher. He'd go over and over this again in the room. He'd light up the Sweet Afton and let it roll.'

Other nights, the discussions were more general, but the scattergun could be just as wounding.

'They were vicious, those meetings,' says Bobby Doyle. 'Fiercely honest. They weren't meant as hurtful. There were things spoken about in there that will stay in there. They were honest to the point where it was painful. I won't ever be breathing a word about them. Very tough sessions.'

Tommy Drumm was introduced to The Room in 1976. He was passing through Trinity College at the time. He had a fine record as a soccer player and a Gaelic footballer, and his demeanour commended him even then as a future Dublin captain. But The Room terrified him.

'I'm quite shy. I was never comfortable speaking to a group anyway. Now I was in Parnell Park, sitting in a little room filled with household names. I realized everybody had to talk. Heffernan started off with Hickey. "Davey, what are you going to do?"

'"Don't mind what I'm going to do, Kevin. We're going to beat the shite out of these bogtrotters. We have the best forwards in the game, the defence aren't great, their passing is shite, but if they give me the ball anywhere, even the shite passes, I'll fight for them and I'll pass it to Jimmy within a yard either side. Don't waste time on anxiety. We are going to win this game."'

And Tommy Drumm is thinking now that he is in trouble. Deep trouble.

'He passes it on to Robbie, very reasoned, very analytical. Then Macker spoke from the heart. Moran very serious and intense, a natural in that room. Bobby spoke clearly and quietly. Hanahoe then. Hanahoe would talk for Ireland. Always boxing metaphors. Nowhere to hide, jackets coming off gentlemen. Really eloquent. They were good at it and I was shitting myself. You had to say something coherent and you had to sound as if you understood everything. That space will live on in my mind forever.'

Bobby Doyle was a good friend of Keaveney's. If Keaveney was to point the finger at Doyle and say, 'I got you on the team,' Doyle wouldn't have demurred.

Doyle had left St Vincent's after a row over an Under-16 final and had missed playing minor and Under-21 football at even club level. He'd played soccer with Malahide United instead. Then he saw an advertisement pinned up somewhere for players to go with St Vincent's on a trip to Toronto. It was enough to spark his interest again. He saved for the trip and went. He played well and got into the St Vincent's senior squad in 1971. He suspected that Keaveney might have put a word in to ease the way. They became close.

Every evening after training, Keaveney would drop Doyle back up to his house in Coolock and along the way the pair might divert for a pint in order to dissect the evening's events. Being a satellite of Keaveney's was a pleasant station in life. The team, although fierce about its unity, had several loose subdivisions. The older players, survivors from the mid-sixties, clung together socially. The players from St Vincent's – 'The Club' – were by far the largest club grouping and formed an internal cabinet. Doyle, a St Vincent's man but a loner by inclination, found easy acceptance in the lee of Keaveney's friendship.

One fine summer's evening, Bobby Doyle was especially apprehensive about the shed session which lay ahead. The forwards had played poorly on Sunday, a situation which delighted those defenders who felt that they led persecuted lives. Heffernan was surely going to perform some surgery on a few egos.

Duly they crammed into the little hut. Like the other players, Doyle had learned to gauge Heffernan's mood by watching his style of smoking. When he was animated and talking Heffernan might light a cigarette and let it burn down to his fingers without pausing to take a drag. When he was anxious he took drags in quick succession. Tonight, the cigarette was never far from his lips as the meeting got going.

Heffernan picked on Jimmy Keaveney first.

This was bad news. Keaveney had some immunity in The Room. He was a Vincent's man. He was a friend of Heffernan's. He was a bona fide genius with a football. Furthermore, he hadn't played too badly on Sunday. Doyle glanced around. Drawn faces among the forwards. If Jimmy Keaveney was getting this class of a bollocking, there was far worse in reserve for the other forwards.

It never came. The assault on Keaveney continued, building to a crescendo.

'What are you going to do, Jimmy? Decide. Because you did nothing for us on Sunday. Nothing, Jimmy.'

'Yes, Kevin.'

'You're swanning around here all right and you think you can swan around out there.'

'Yes, Kevin.'

Doyle was sweating now. Across the room John McCarthy's face was ghostlike. Jesus, who's next?

The buck started and stopped with Keaveney, though. He carried the can for the entire forward line. Doyle felt some guilty relief that his friend had taken the hits. He couldn't wait to get to Keaveney's car for the drive home. Keaveney took his time, but when they left Parnell Park there was nothing said in the car for a while.

Finally Doyle, still shaken, was unable to maintain the silence. 'Jaysus, Jimmy, I thought that was a bit hard, back there.'

Keaveney smiled and nodded to himself. 'Ah it was all right, he told me beforehand he was going to do it! Scare the shite out of yiz!'

Whether the criticism of Keaveney was a pre-planned piece of theatre or whether Keaveney was covering some understandable hurt by suggesting that he was in on the ruse is beside the point. Heffernan's choice of target was the salient thing. If Keaveney was vulnerable, then nobody was safe. If Keaveney was covering up embarrassment, it was more revealing.

'You see, Jimmy was considered unimpeachable,' says Jim Brogan. 'He was from The Club! If you said "The Club" in that group, everyone knew who you were talking about. If it was a ready-up that night or even if it wasn't, it had its effect. It was The Club. They weren't an inner group in terms of being clannish. They were just an entity.'

The Club were hated and respected in almost equal measure.

Through the fifties and sixties, St Vincent's not only dominated the game within the county but backboned all Dublin teams. In 1953 Dublin had won a National League final against Cavan with fourteen Vincent's men on the field. They wore their club jerseys that day. St Vincent's dominance and influence were absolute, as was the belief of the club's members that what was good for St Vincent's was good for Dublin.

There's a St Vincent's story which pre-dates the seventies but which says much about the ethos of the club. St Vincent's were playing St Joseph's one Sunday and were winning well with just a few minutes left, when the St Vincent's forward (and, later, Dublin manager) Mickey Whelan received a bad blow to the mouth – a gusher-of-blood job.

The referee had seen the incident clearly and moved quickly to send Whelan's assailant off. Kevin Heffernan was the St Vincent's manager that day, and he interceded on behalf of the St Joseph's player. 'No, leave him on. We don't want him sent off.'

The referee, daunted by Heffernan's presence, nodded and doled out a booking. Play resumed. The St Joseph's player in question didn't make it to the full-time whistle. As he was carried off, the message was as clear as if it had been written in the sky above the field. St Vincent's were tough.

Tough and reared in a culture of winning.

'They were very hard to beat,' says Bernard Brogan. 'I remember in Kinvara Avenue once day, playing against them for Oliver Plunkett's, and we were two goals clear with a couple of minutes to go and the excitement for us was unbearable. We were going to beat Vincent's. And they beat us by a goal in the end. I can remember being stunned by it, but they always absolutely expected to win and they brought that into the Dublin dressing room.'

'They certainly gave us the spine,' says Robbie Kelleher, a Scoil Uí Chonaill player at the time. 'I remember as a club player going out to play Vincent's and you were shivering in your boots. They brought that into the team. They are what Dublin lacks in the years since St Vincent's went down the ranks. They haven't produced those three or four fellas a year for Dublin, and we haven't the same qualities in the team. I think there is an element of truth in that, even though there were times when it used to annoy me. I remember when Hanahoe was in charge, Vincent's would train at one end of Parnell Park and the Dubs would be up the other end with Donal Colfer. It used to drive me mad. Tony and Keaveney and the lads would be down the other end. Laws unto themselves!'

St Vincent's runs in the county championship were always long and dramatic. On one occasion, after a change of chairman in St Vincent's, the club withdrew its nine players from Dublin training for a short period in the run-up to a key club match. Dublin training sessions were decimated. In 1976, when St Vincent's won the All-Ireland club championship, the players would train in the St Vincent's grounds in Raheny with the club from 6 p.m. to 7.15 and then leap into their cars and drive to Parnell Park to be on the pitch for Dublin training at 7.30.

'There was some of them who'd kick their own mother to win a match!' says John McCarthy, who over the years faced St Vincent's in the colours of Na Fianna, Garda and Ballymun Kickhams. 'They always played great football after a row. I think they knew. If there was a row they were always pumped afterwards and they kept control afterwards. They'd really play. You'd be thinking about getting stuck in and looking for retribution. They'd be hammering you. Beating them to me was the Holy Grail. I never beat them in the championship. Ever. It wasn't till I played for Ballymun Kickhams that we even won a league match. I hated them, but I loved the guys. They were great for Dublin, the backbone to lots of great Dublin teams, and they had such influence in The Room.'

One night, when it came his turn to speak, Bobby Doyle said, 'I have nothing to say.'

Heffernan said levelly, 'I have no interest in strong, silent men, Bobby.'

The discussion proceded as planned.

Heffernan used The Room as an instrument through which he calibrated the intensity of the team. Some sunny evenings, when the birds were singing and the mood was light, they'd dance into the shed, expecting to be detained for five minutes. An hour and a half later, only the bravest man would dare to take a peek at his watch. Other evenings, leaden with woes, they trained like men with a death sentence hanging over them. And Heffernan would keep them for a few quick minutes of housekeeping chat, and they'd be gone out the door, all weight lifted from their shoulders.

Sometimes the meetings were a prelude to something else. In 1975 they played Louth in the Leinster championship. They won by four points but conceded four goals along the way. The post-mortem was surprisingly short.

Heffernan threw out the view that the forwards had played well at the weekend. Hickey took Heffernan's bait without seeing the hook.

Yes, he said, the forwards had played well against Louth, but that was out of necessity. Every time they'd looked down the field, there was a ball being picked out of the Dublin net. They'd had to play well just to stay ahead of what was going in down the far end.

There were a few uneasy glances around the room. Hickey was a unique presence, radiating a golden confidence that was an essential part of the team's swagger, but as the 1975 championship progressed and goals continued to be leaked (this was seven in two games) defenders were starting to fret a little.

Then there was the calibre of some of the men Hickey was criticizing. Sean Doherty and Gay O'Driscoll in particular would have been further up the social ladder than Hickey. They were also, as Páidí Ó Sé has put it, 'psychopaths, in the best possible sense'.

Hickey was maligning made guys.

Heffernan drew the meeting to a quick close and proposed a game out on the field. They trooped back out. For sixty angry minutes there were elbows and shoulders flying about the place. Hickey took most of the punishment, but no forward was spared. The next game that summer was the Leinster final against Kildare. No goals conceded. Three scored.

★

Heffernan certainly couldn't be accused of pioneering the squad rotation system. Men spent entire careers sitting on the Dublin bench, waiting for the call.

In The Room they were as integral a part of the group dynamic as anyone.

After 1975, Heffernan purged the half-back line. Georgie Wilson, Alan Larkin and Paddy Reilly went from being stars to being extras. Larkin took it the best and battled on longest. Reilly took it the worst and was occasionally heard to utter sedition when he had the right audience. Georgie was somewhere in between.

One night Georgie stood up and pointed out that there were fifteen guys who played and ten guys who didn't play and, for all the talk of the group, well, it just didn't add up. Fifteen playing and ten not playing.

There was a shocked silence. You couldn't break the spell like that. You just couldn't.

Jim Brogan was a substitute for most of the era. He remembers that during one of the All-Ireland finals against Kerry he spent twenty minutes warming up on the sideline and then Kerry scored a goal. He was told to sit back into the dugout. A friend commented that Brogan had done more running than anybody who had actually played.

What kept him going through the years?

'I don't know. You continued because you were there and participated in training sessions and were told there was a possibility you would be playing. For some games, if you were picked at number sixteen or seventeen, you assumed it had some significance. For eight or nine years, every decision I made in life was influenced by football and the commitment to the team and the group. The Room was important for that.

'I liked the guys. You were exposed to this extraordinary gang of people. You would be frustrated but there were times when you would say, isn't it great to have such a wonderful experience with such a wonderful group of guys. Over time that becomes something I appreciate even more. In your early thirties you might sit down and say, my whole life is gone for football and I played in very few matches. But with perspective I am happy.'

In the kiln some of them were made into men. And some of them almost cracked. Sometimes they were invited to look around The Room and wondered who would be the Judas. Who would betray the team on Sunday? John McCarthy, the beat Garda in a room full of doctors, solicitors, engineers, economists and business-men, was dubious about the value of it all.

'I hated it. It put a fella under terrible pressure. Just because you didn't want to speak didn't mean that you wouldn't do it on the field. I would have preferred to say nothing. Some fellas were bullshitters, they could read The Room and say what Heffernan wanted to hear. The pressure in there nearly cracked me up.'

If McCarthy hated The Room, there were others who thought nothing of it. Kevin Moran joined the panel in 1976. Heffernan liked him from the moment he saw him. Tousle-haired and bull-shouldered and riding a motorbike which he insisted wasn't a Honda 50 but a Honda 90, Moran met the world on his terms always.

One night in the run-in to the All-Ireland semi-final that year, Heffernan was doing his usual run-down of job descriptions. He'd start with Cullen and tell him to put the kick-outs wide, to keep in touch with the full-back line always, and so on and so on. Understand? Yup. On then to Gay O'Driscoll. Stay close and play from the front. Sacrifice your game to take his away from him. Understand?

So it went, with each player nodding his assent, till Heffernan turned to Moran. The new centre half-back listened to the long and detailed list of requirements Heffernan had for him.

'Understand?' said Heffernan finally.

'No, I don't,' said Moran, 'I don't see what you're saying at all.'

Everyone looked up. Heffernan had that twinkle. They could see that Moran had just risen another six notches in Heffernan's estimation.

'I thought it was brilliant having those meetings,' says Moran. 'I've been in soccer a long time and I've never seen it done.

Generally in a dressing room if you throw something out and ask, has anybody anything to say, you hear the greatest silence you've ever come across. Nobody ever says anything. That never happened. On certain occasions, I remember the All-Ireland of 1976, he went around the team, each individual, asking them, what are you going to do? What are you going to do? It was awesome stuff.'

There was the remoteness of Heffernan as he conducted the meetings as an intellectual exercise. There was Hanahoe, lieutenant and liaison. There were the marquee personalities like Paddy Cullen, Jimmy Keaveney, Gay O'Driscoll and Sean Doherty. The quiet, reticent thinkers like Robbie Kelleher. A small, likeable, wryly cynical group of friends made up of David Hickey, Anton O'Toole, Paddy Reilly and John McCarthy. The talkers. Alan Larkin would dissect games with academic abstraction. Paddy Gogarty would argue his case like a Rottweiler. There were men like O'Neill and Mullins whose frightening intensity on the pitch translated sometimes to The Room.

The issues they discussed ranged far beyond football. Men came to The Room with problems at home, at work, in their heads. Together they solved the problems. Everything personal got left in The Room. That was the deal, the trust upon which everything rested.

It holds to this day. The Room terrified them and bonded them. The person you were was fully exposed before you went out into the heat of a championship battle. On the pitch and in life afterwards they never had doubts about each other. The roles they took in The Room have stayed with them. The group dynamic has never changed. When they holiday as a group or get together for golf twice a year, they fall into the same easy positions with respect to one another.

The Room, the intensity of it, became for a while a moveable feast, to be replicated before games and at half-time. You filed in, found your spot and waited for Heffernan's verdict.

'I do remember one occasion,' says Tony Hanahoe, 'when we were playing Wexford. We weren't doing badly, but perhaps not doing as well as we thought. Kevin said, "There's a fella up there in the corner back position and he must have come straight from the ploughing championships, he's so slow. And still we haven't yet exploited him. In fact," he said, "give him a few handy balls when ye go back out in case they take him off." '

Everybody remembers the meeting on the day before the All-Ireland of 1976. Heffernan pushing the intensity up higher and higher, men in tears, men angry. What are you going to do? And what are *you* going to do? When it reached the right pitch, he got up and left them to it. They spoke for another hour and a half and left knowing, knowing absolutely, that they would win.

Several players remember a night when Alan Larkin dug a hole for himself and couldn't stop. Larkin, analytical by nature, sometimes found that, to compensate for nervousness, his contributions dragged on, staled by conditions, rationales and sub-clauses. This particular night they knew it was bad because Heffernan was chain-smoking so hard that he was in danger of inhaling his fingers.

Finally he could wait no longer. He was an eagle swooping on a lamb.

'Can I stop you there, Alan?'

'Yes, Kevin?'

'What fucking match are you talking about?'

Pause.

'Because it's not the fucking match I was watching.'

They settled back into the world Heffernan had created and watched Alan Larkin get pumped full of lead. They knew they'd all be walking out of there in a while anyway, that the wounds were temporary and that it all mattered only so long as they chose to believe in the magic of The Room.

Still, nobody wanted to trade places with Alan Larkin that night.

10

We were cocky little hoors. We needed to have our asses kicked.

Mikey Sheehy

One morning after their defeat in 1975, Kevin Heffernan gathered his beaten team together in the Na Fianna grounds. He invited them to spill some home truths on to the table. They did.

It was felt that fellas had gone soft. There had been a degree of complacency about playing a young team, and about playing in a second All-Ireland in as many years. Three or four lads who had given up smoking in 1974 had gone back on the fags for 1975. They put it all out on the table and renewed themselves.

By the time the opening game of the 1975–6 league season had come about, the Dubs, several of whom had been playing inter-county football since the mid-sixties, had resolved that there would be no retirements. From now on they would be as obsessed with Kerry as their manager was. They opened the league by travelling to Cork and winning.

Bobby Doyle wasn't there, though. Having been dropped for an All-Ireland final, Doyle had made up his mind that he wasn't going back to play Gaelic football any more. He was gone. Being dropped had broken his heart. So he quit.

There were seven boys and one girl in the Doyle family growing up in Coolock, and Jim Doyle would bring a handful of his children to Croke Park and throw them over the stile any time there was a game on.

They were a close family, and the GAA absorbed their energies perfectly. Bobby remembers that when older brothers finished with their boots, they would be passed on to him. He asked Jim one day if he couldn't get a new pair of boots and Jim said that it wasn't the boot that made the player, it was what was in the boot. The answer satisfied.

When they'd grown and Bobby was making it, Jim travelled with a crew of friends to see Dublin wherever they played. For him, to have a son playing in blue was a wonder and a joy.

So being dropped was a personal trauma which was amplified by the way it raged in the papers every day. Doyle Dropped! Doyle Loses Out! The whispered discussions and many of the louder rows in Parnell Park were about the same subject. Everywhere Bobby Doyle went, he was the guy who had been dropped.

He had no stomach for the week at the Listowel Races which the team had promised itself, win, lose or draw in the All-Ireland final. He worked the week after the All-Ireland, pulling cables as usual for the ESB. On the Wednesday he walked into a travel agency and booked a holiday. For one.

The Dublin management were ringing the house, checking on Doyle's availability for that first league match in Cork. Nobody knew quite what to tell them. Bobby got back early on the Sunday morning of the game, and his sister and her boyfriend were waiting at the airport to bring him to Cork. He said no. He wouldn't be going out for football any more.

That night Keaveney and Hickey arrived back off the train from Cork and went straight to Coolock to check out where their friend had been.

He said what he had been telling anyone who asked. He wasn't going out any more.

And Hickey thought for a minute and then spoke tenderly: 'You're a fucking idiot, Doyler. He drops you and you let it annoy you to that extent. Don't be a fucking fool.'

Hickey always did know the perfect thing to say. Bobby Doyle came back and nothing was ever said about his brief absence.

Kerry wintered well. As a crowd of bachelors, why not? Kerry's metabolism was always different from that of their great rivals. Where the Dubs trained with remorseless regularity Tuesdays,

Thursdays and Saturdays, week in and week out, Kerry came together only when the evenings got longer in the spring. Then they burned themselves into the Killarney turf.

That winter, as befits a conquering army, there was drink available anywhere they went. And women. For some it was embarrassing. For others it was nirvana. For the few who were geographically removed from the epicentre of celebration it was just rumour and yarns.

Paudie O'Mahoney in Killarney wasn't sure what had hit his life.

'We weren't used to that shit at all. We were starting off in careers and jobs. Certain players took advantage and certain players didn't. We didn't know where we were.'

After Christmas they started thinking about training. It would be weeks before O'Dwyer would summon them, but already they knew what cruel and unusual punishments he would visit upon their young heads and Buddha bellies.

The smart ones trained on their own. John O'Keeffe found a gym in Tralee. Mickey Ned did weights in a little room in the school in Ballyvourney. Pat Spillane went to a hill near his house, sixty yards from top to bottom. He attached a ten-pound weight to each ankle and exploded up that hill and down that hill for an hour every day. On Banna Strand the Tralee boys would be out running, and in Ventry Páidí Ó Sé would start the business, as he puts it, of 'getting yourself arranged for Dwyer'. They each had their own routine, their own method of getting arranged. Páidí would be out over the hills and into Dunquin and to Slea Head. Two and a half to three hours of stamina running. Getting arranged for Dwyer.

Still, when they came back with their guts tightened and their faces keen, they knew in their hearts that something was wrong. The hunger that had whetted them the previous year was missing. They were champions and the rest of the country would have to catch up. Wrong.

'We were wined and dined all winter,' says Jimmy Deenihan 'and we never left it behind us.'

'We were cocky little hoors,' says Mikey Sheehy. 'We needed to have our asses kicked.'

The Munster final of 1976 arrived in two instalments, both played in Páirc Uí Chaoimh, the new coliseum by the Lee. The first game was a draw and the baptism of Páirc Uí Chaoimh was a disaster. The only mitigation was that nobody died. Some ten thousand people on top of the capacity forced themselves into the ground. They poured on to the pitch and stood in dense masses all the way around the perimeter as the game was being played.

Pat Spillane remembers being assaulted with an umbrella. Paudie O'Mahoney in the Kerry goal was subjected to a non-stop barrage of invective. Mikey Sheehy remembers an undercurrent of nastiness which he felt every time he went to take a free. Brendan Lynch and Kevin Kehilly had a scuffle on the sideline early on. Supporters came into the field, filling the area around them.

The crowd was ugly, and the game wasn't much better. After a winter of happy larking the young Kerry team were startled by the challenge they met and by the circumstances they found themselves in. The game was a draw, but a moral victory for Cork.

A fortnight later Páirc Uí Chaoimh managed to get itself right. The drama which followed deserved an orderly stage.

'It wasn't until half-time in the replay against Cork before we even realized that we could actually get beaten,' says Jimmy Deenihan. They went into that half-time break three points down. The second half was one of the greatest displays of football ever seen. And controversial, too.

Fast forward through the tape: Pat Spillane scores a goal early on. Cork pours back. After a Cork wide Paudie O'Mahony has a brainstorm: the short kick-out! Jimmy Deenihan, marking Jimmy Barry Murphy, is walking out with his back to the goal, waiting for a kick-out to fly over his head.

'Then I heard the crowd. I turned around. Jimmy Barry had the ball. He was on the fourteen-yard line. He was bearing down on goals. He was scoring.'

'I nearly got killed,' Paudie says. 'Literally fucking shot. I went for a short ball to Ger Keeffe and caught my toe in the ground. It went to Jimmy Barry Murphy. With John Egan he was the greatest forward I ever saw. Of all people to kick it to.'

Cork turned the screws. They went seven points clear. They were six clear with twelve minutes left. Five clear with ten left. Tick tick tick. Four ahead with eight minutes left.

And then things got exciting. Kerry brought Seanie Walsh in from the bench to full forward. Another outing as Super-Sub, the role he made his own that summer.

Mikey Sheehy had a short free and, instead of popping it over the bar, he gambled. He chipped it to Walsh, whose shot beat Billy Morgan, only to be stopped by Brian Murphy on the goal line. Murphy had cleared before an umpire reached forward and lifted a green flag to indicate a Kerry goal.

'We got a handy goal off the Dubious Goals Committee that day,' says Mikey Sheehy. 'Brian Murphy was too experienced to have taken that ball behind the line.'

'It wasn't a goal,' says Seanie Walsh. 'We got out of jail. Maybe if you look back, Brian was over the line, but Mikey kicked a twenty-one-yard free. There was no way I was fourteen yards away from him. The pass to me couldn't have been legal.'

Their escape wasn't complete yet. There was more improbability to come. Cork swept down the field in a fury. Sean Murphy popped a ball into the heart of Kerry's defence. Declan Barron soared and fisted the ball into the net from the edge of the square.

Amazingly, the referee, John Moloney, blew for a free kick to Kerry. Barron was deemed to have been in the small square.

'I was the corner back,' says Jimmy Deenihan. 'Declan Barron could jump so high. His body was in the air and he took off for the ball outside the square. It was a perfect goal. It should have been allowed.'

But it wasn't. Pat Spillane equalized. Mikey Sheehy had a free to win the game. He struck it sweetly and it was sailing over the crossbar when John Moloney blew the whistle to end the game. Kerry players and supporters thought they had won, but Moloney cancelled the point. Many Cork people thought Cork had won because the scoreboard said they had.

The game went to extra time. Kerry went for a short break to the dressing rooms. Cork just stayed on the field, waiting for extra time like prisoners about to receive a lethal injection.

Kerry won by four points in the end. Paudie O'Mahony made a stunning save from Jimmy Barry Murphy to preserve the margin. Afterwards, Paudie was sitting on the bench in the dressing room ordering the madness in his head when more madness broke out.

'This guy, a gambler, a fella who'd played a lot of football, he came into the dressing room and he caught me by the throat and twisted it around and said, "You're a fucking lucky man that you survived. I had ten grand on that."'

'I said, "Fuck you, I don't give a damn about your ten grand." I just wanted to win. There was serious money on those games. I was aware of one or two big bets.'

In Dublin there were no high rollers. Quite the opposite. The team subsisted. The county board counted the pennies. Stephen Rooney and Georgie Wilson thumbed in and out from Balbriggan. On occasion Brian Mullins and Fran Ryder did the same from Limerick. Outside, it was booming. Clubs were springing up all over the suburbs. In Parnell Park there weren't two pennies to be rubbed together.

The players chafed sometimes.

John McCarthy often had to make an early exit from training for Garda duty. Although one of the fittest on the squad, he had a propensity to part company with his dinner unless he had eaten at least five hours before he went training. So, leaving Parnell Park in a hurry after a heavy session and with a night's work ahead of him, he was often hungry.

One night he was blindsided in the evening race for one of the dozen bottles of milk which the county board would provide. He went and got changed and, as the remainder of the team went to their post-session meeting, Macker realized that the tea room was empty. He stuck his head in.

Too much for a hungry man. He helped himself to a couple of Marietta biscuits and as an afterthought lifted the large jug of milk and took a sip. At that moment Jim King, the county secretary, walked in. He exploded.

'What are you doing? You're a disgrace. You don't give a damn about anyone.'

Macker responded that King was a disgrace.

There was a shouting match before Macker remembered work. He drove out of Parnell Park like a lunatic. The next night, when Macker came back down training, there were two crates of milk.

Macker felt like Spartacus. He had freed the slaves.

'This was a big concession. We'd won an All-Ireland at this stage. We were being given a drink of milk each. The Dublin county board would have folded rather than give us a sandwich.'

Kevin Hefferman was convinced that his side would fold unless they found a new half-back line by the summer of 1976. Providing he could find the right parts, such a job would require ruthless excisions. With teams you can't make an omelette without breaking egos.

By September he would have what he wanted. Not a lot was said along the way, but the players detected that their manager was depressed by how much running with the ball Ogie Moran, Mickey Ned O'Sullivan and Pat Spillane had been allowed to do in 1975. Heffernan had decided that his half-back line was an organ on the brink of failure.

The players who would be made redundant could argue that they had been picked for different reasons. The old half-back line was designed for a more old-fashioned form of combat. Alan Larkin was a fine fielder and offered the traditional sturdy presence at centre back. Outside him, Paddy Reilly and Georgie Wilson, two north county wits, played it fast and loose. They pumped the ball long and early into the full-forward line when they won it. They never stapled themselves to the shoulders of the men they were marking.

Then Kerry had come along and run riot, looting goal chances and ransacking the area.

Heffernan began rummaging through the county. The new

half-back line came together slowly but it fitted as perfectly as three pieces of a child's jigsaw.

At Easter 1973, in a Corn na Casca game, Pat O'Neill shipped a bad blow to the kidney. O'Neill lived by the sword and died by the sword and didn't think too much about the wounds between times. Later, when the pains came, he figured he was spending too much time just sitting and studying his medical books.

Time passed. The pain stayed. He was mildly concerned, but no more than that. Then one evening he noticed that his ankle had begun swelling as if he was suffering cardiac failure. He went downstairs to his mother, who was a nurse (and 'a fairly austere one at that'), and told her that he thought he had some sort of pitting oedema. She pressed her finger into the red flesh of her son's ankle and it was soft and mushy. Her finger left an impression half an inch deep.

'Yes,' she said, 'you sure as hell have.'

The blow in the Corn na Casca game had left O'Neill with renal vein thrombosis. He had a clot in his kidney vein which was giving him the symptoms of nephrotic syndrome. Basically he was urinating away all his own protein.

There's never a good time to begin flushing all your protein down the urinal, but this was a particularly bad time. Kevin Heffernan had taken over the county team and had brought along some sharp and pungent ideas. O'Neill was also preparing for final medical exams. A treacherous pair of kidneys was the last thing he needed. The hospital diagnosed nephritis, or inflammation of the kidneys, and put him on a course of steroids.

'That would be the right treatment. The following weekend, though, I got a bad cold. You sometimes get that on high-dose steroids. I got sicker and sicker. I went out, trying to go to town to meet the UCD fellas. Bad idea. I woke up in the middle of the night and I could hardly breathe. There was a hand basin in the room. I thought I was coughing up phlegm. As daybreak came I realized it was blood I had been coughing up.'

Pulmonary embolus. Two words you never want to see in a sentence with your own name.

They gave an urgent new dimension to the original diagnosis. O'Neill was quickly admitted to the Intensive Care Unit, where his condition declined sharply.

One night Joe O'Neill came home and asked his mother how his brother Pat was.

She was shockingly frank: 'You'd better go in now to see him because they don't expect him to be there in the morning.'

That was it. He touched the gates of death and then he turned back. They found the clot in the vein which was giving the secondary complications. When he was finally released from hospital, he was on several medications. Anticoagulants, steroids, etc. His weight ballooned. He sat and studied for his finals and as the evenings grew sweeter he pined for the football.

One night UCD were playing the Gardaí in a league game up in the Phoenix Park. It was early summer and the College were short in numbers. O'Neill went into goals to help out. He was still on steroids and anticoagulants, and he knew that if he got a decent belt on the head he would most likely suffer a brain haemorrhage.

He survived. Indeed, he was happy with his evening's work, until he met his mother at home. The O'Neills lived in Castleknock, just outside the Park gates. Pat's face was still red from exercise when he reached the front door.

'Where were you?'

'Down at the match.'

'Did you play?'

'No.'

Joe intervened. 'He did, he played. He went in goals and he was fine.'

That evening O'Neill weighed things up. Playing football while on the medications had been a foolish thing to do. As a medical student he knew better. So he threw the medications in the bin and went back to playing football.

By 1975 he was strong enough and fit enough to be challenging for a place again, and in the All-Ireland final he came on as a sub in midfield, where Bernard Brogan was struggling against the rampant Pat McCarthy.

The taste of All-Ireland final action was fine, but O'Neill had an intense desire to be more than a bit player in the movement which Heffernan had started. He'd risked his health to come back playing football. He'd come some of the way, but not as far as he wanted. So he took an extreme measure to get his place in the half-back line.

In the league final of 1976 Dublin played Derry and Heffernan tried a half-back line composed of Brendan Pocock, Pat O'Neill and Kevin Synott. O'Neill was the old hand in the crew. He got taken for six points by Mickey Lynch. Dublin won, but O'Neill was in a black mood all evening.

He had just moved to Crumlin Hospital and was working in Casualty on the orthopaedic side. It was a nightmare. He was worked to the bone. The weekend of the league final had been catastrophic for a man who understood his circadian rhythms. He'd worked all night Friday and gone straight to training in Parnell Park. Then he'd gone to bed for the afternoon, slept seven hours and gone back to bed at midnight, wide awake all night.

He sensed that the chance was gone. He was out of the team for the start of the Leinster championship. He was recently married, with a child. Football was going badly. He gave up work and concentrated on football.

'I said, I'll just take the summer off. Not such a great idea for a fella that was just married with a kid and needing money. I used to do an odd locum thing, four hours in Casualty in Crumlin or the Mater. Otherwise I concentrated on football on the basis of having been exhausted on the first Sunday in May. I went back and did some post-graduate work in the autumn.'

He nailed the place down, and in doing so added a bit more steel to the Dublin defence. They called him Nailer, and the name suited.

In the All-Ireland semi-final against Galway, he was involved in an incident that his friends enjoy relating. It was a torrid, bitter game in which Brian Mullins, in the middle of his final exams, got his jaw broken. Tommy Naughton of Galway was cutting up to give trouble. As a minor, O'Neill had been sent off in an All-Ireland semi-final on the word of an umpire. This time he was more careful.

The first anybody knew was when they saw Naughton and O'Neill both lying prone on the grass. Lorcan Redmond was first to reach O'Neill with the medical kit. Without lifting his head O'Neill asked, had the ref, Frank Halbert, seen anything? Redmond looked around and advised that it didn't seem like he had.

The punchline came later when they saw the highlights on television and heard Micheál O'Hehir announce that there had been an accidental clash of heads.

Ogie Moran was a schoolboy star with Gormanston in Meath. He played senior championship football in Kerry at the age of sixteen and his schooldays ended with him inspiring Gormanston to an All-Ireland Colleges win. From the time he was swaddled in nappies Ogie had the right stuff.

He has a clear memory of his Gormanston school team going to Dublin in the early seventies to play against Drimnagh Castle School in Parnell Park. When the teams came out, Ogie, already a Kerry minor (as he would be for three years), heard the chant go up: Moran! Moran! Moran! A modest young man, Ogie was both embarrassed and gratified.

The match had been in progress for a few minutes when Ogie realized that any time the tousle-haired midfielder from Drimnagh Castle won the ball, he provoked a massive cheer and more outbreaks of chanting. Moran! Moran! Moran!

Kerry's greatest centre-forward had just met Dublin's greatest centre-back.

When Kevin Moran was twelve going on thirteen, he had been a member of Rialto Gaels. When he was sent to school in Drimnagh Castle, he decided that for social reasons he might as well join An Caislean, the club associated with the school.

He played a game with An Caislean before his transfer registration was through. There was a very typical GAA-type objection. And so the GAA banned him for a year, and he went playing soccer with a schoolboy team called Rangers.

Moran played Gaelic games in school, but when he went to UCD it was soccer he orientated towards. Pat O'Neill and John O'Keeffe and others were in the college at the same time, plotting Sigerson campaigns, but Kevin Moran was a soccer player.

He went to the 1974 All-Ireland final with some mates, but he didn't see Dublin in the flesh again till he played for them. In 1975 he went to New York for the summer, played some Gaelic football to help get himself a job. He watched the All-Ireland final in a cinema somewhere, and when he came back he decided he'd play a bit of Gaelic football with Good Counsel 'for the crack'. Good Counsel played on Sundays. His soccer commitments were Saturdays. Hunky-dory.

One afternoon Lorcan Redmond and Donal Colfer went to see Good Counsel play Civil Service in a county championship match. Moran ran the game. He was invited to play a challenge game in Tralee against Kerry. He turned up at the train station on that Sunday morning and travelled south with a group of strangers whose faces he vaguely recognized.

He was nineteen but he was his own man. At school he'd developed a belief contrary to that of most coaches, that solo running was a good thing. He could run as fast soloing a ball as he could without the ball. He'd bounce the ball a few yards in front of himself and fly after it. Once he'd done that once, he'd hear the sideline getting on the case of his opposing player. 'Who's picking him up? Whose man is that?' The forward always stayed close to Moran after that.

So in Tralee he had a few solo runs. He scored a couple of points. Played it on his terms. His big brother Brendan had travelled down all the way to see the debut.

'Did you enjoy that?' asked Brendan.

'Yeah!'

'I hope you did, because that will be your last time. You'd solo run up your own arse, wouldn't you?'

But his style was never an issue. He was in.

His character made him a part of the team even before he had his feet under the table. Heffernan hadn't many favourites over the years, but the ones who all players mention are Brian Mullins, Mick Holden and Kevin Moran. One hundred and twenty per cent guys.

Moran recalls the tightness of the group into which he had to break that summer. They played a league semi-final against Galway in Croke Park and it was Moran's first time there as a Dub. He always liked to sit in the corner of the dressing room. He went in, claimed a spot and sat down. Bobby Doyle came over and told him to get up. That corner was Doyle's.

'I'm thinking, these fuckers even have their own spots in the Croke Park dressing rooms! Jesus.'

Moran moved up a space from Doyle so that he was sitting beside him. Paddy Reilly arrived in. 'Get out, sunshine, that's where I sit.'

Moran stood up with his gear in hand and looked around for some place to squeeze himself into. He saw Brian Mullins approach him and wondered to himself, 'What now, am I standing where he likes to stand?'

Mullins came over and grabbed Moran by the hair on the nape of his neck. It hurt. Mullins said, 'Come over here, sit down beside me, I'll look after you.'

And that's where Moran started and stayed. Thirty years later, if you ask him which moment is his favourite memory of the old times, he'll recall Mullins taking him by the nape and offering protection.

Soon they were shoving up again to make room for another newcomer.

Pat Spillane reckons that Tommy Drumm was the most difficult direct opponent he ever marked. Drumm was almost lost to Gaelic football as well. He'd played Gaelic football for his club Whitehall Colmcilles and mixed Gaelic and soccer in school at St Aidan's in Whitehall. By the time he got to Trinity College he had been playing soccer with the St Kevin's club for a while, and his cousin Frank had already introduced him to the college soccer scene. There was a bond there, so he played soccer.

Early in 1976 he was coming home from college on the bus when Chris Grady, who lived down the road, said to him right out of the blue that the paper had it that Tommy Drumm of Whitehall was in the Dublin panel for Sunday.

Tommy Drumm is the most gentle and articulate of men, but on this occasion disbelief overwhelmed courtesy. 'Fuck off,' he said, 'you're winding me up.'

Home. No paper in the Drumm household. A sprint down to his Uncle Bill's. Have ye a paper in the house? There it was in small print. The Ceoltas Ceolteori Éireann Tournament. Dublin playing Derry. There was a team list which was supplemented by a roll-call of about twenty-five subs. T. Drumm was the last name on the list.

Heffernan started him at left half-back that Sunday; he'd noticed Drumm playing Under-21 football the previous year. This was quite a feat of perception. Dublin got to the All-Ireland final, but Drumm had played the Leinster final and the All-Ireland semi-final only. He was full forward for the semi-final, scored a goal and got taken off. He was dropped for the final.

In the Dublin set-up Tommy Drumm knew many faces but was friendly with just one guy, Kevin Moran. Their bond was unusual. They had played soccer for the Irish Universities against England (and won). Moran was full back. Drumm was centre half.

'I'd played against him in school. From my point of view I had somebody beside me I was comfortable with. I'd seen him break through. When I got in there, I was just thinking of my own survival. I got a lot of comfort out of him being there too.'

O'Neill, Moran and Drumm played together as a half-back line for the first time in the All-Ireland semi-final against Galway that summer.

The jigsaw was complete.

I've waited twenty-one years for this.

Kevin Heffernan

In folklore and in highlights reels, the defining moment of the 1976 All-Ireland final came after just twenty seconds, when Brian Mullins slipped a handpass to Kevin Moran, who was roaring up the centre of the field like a fire engine cutting through sluggish traffic.

Moran played a one-two pass, using Bernard Brogan as the wall from which he caught the rebound. And then, before he overdosed on sheer exuberance, he hammered the ball just wide of the Kerry post.

The most famous miss in All-Ireland history. The most famous solo run in All-Ireland history. Yet it was Dublin's first score of the game which revealed the genius that lay at the heart of the machine.

Picture it. Jimmy Keaveney, taking a little pass from David Hickey, finds himself in a position perhaps forty yards from goal. He can score from here but he glances up and decides instead on something a little more aesthetically pleasing. He floats a sublime drop kick to the edge of the square. Like a genie Tony Hanahoe suddenly materializes. He pops the ball over the bar.

There, in one movement, were the basics of Heffernan's plan. Wing forwards who fell back and foraged. Keaveney pulling the full back away from the square. Hanahoe drifting away from the centre back and popping up in the most unlikely of places. A great prairie of space down the middle. The discipline to create that space and the imagination to use it.

The habits became so ingrained that many years later, when Keaveney was asked to gather up some remnants of the 1976–7 team to play a charity game in Armagh city, he noticed that, although they were grey and paunched now, everybody moved the same as they always had when they were together on a football pitch again.

That score from 1976 can be watched again and again just for the enjoyment of seeing Keaveney's drop kick. You'll never get used to how casually he played the ball. Sean Doherty says that Moran's solo run had set him on fire, fists clenched, roaring at his colleagues, 'We're on the way, boys!' Seconds later, Keaveney was turning up his nose to a handy point in favour of something a player might try to show off during a kickabout.

In his newspaper column Myles na gCopaleen once created a character called the Dubbalin Man who, having recounted the long and heartbreaking story of his day's sufferings, would conclude with news of the relatively trivial capper to his day: 'I wouldn't mind but . . .' When he tells the story of heading to Meagher's in Fairview to meet his wife and daughter after the 1977 All-Ireland final, only to find the pair of them decked out in Armagh colours 'because Dublin have won a couple of them already and we thought it would be nice for Armagh to get one', Jimmy Keaveney is straight out of Myles na gCopaleen

When he talks about his career, though, he is a different man. He went for a drink in 1966 with Danny Norton of the furniture suppliers T. & D. Norton's. The two men talked football, got drunk – and Jimmy has been working for the firm ever since. He is a natural salesman. By the time Corporate Express bought out the business, Jimmy had a decent shareholding. Good things happen to smart people.

Robbie Kelleher reckons that the Dublin team of the seventies was short on top-quality footballers. Cullen, Moran, Mullins, Hickey and Keaveney. Of those, the only pure genius was Keaveney. If there is one iconic image from the Dublin team of the seventies, it is Keaveney about to release the ball with that low, stabbing, kicking style of his and that number fourteen on his back.

When Dublin met Kerry, the most fascinating and most cerebral duel was that which took place between Keaveney and John O'Keeffe. O'Keeffe was a god among full backs, even though when Mick O'Dwyer first moved him there from midfield in 1975 he had assumed it was the beginning of the end of his inter-county career. Keaveney and O'Keeffe had met often before their paths began crossing on All-Ireland final days.

In the Dublin county final of 1972 between St Vincent's and UCD, Heffernan had chosen Keaveney to play at midfield on O'Keeffe. The reasoning was impeccable as usual. 'Kevin told me not to contest any high balls with him, just to stay on him and punch everything and annoy him all day. That's what I did. I just fisted every high ball away. We won, but I had to apologize to him when the game was over. He was better than that, but I had to bring him down!'

For Dublin, Keaveney's presence and style dictated the forward patterns. John O'Keeffe can scarcely remember contesting a single high ball with Keaveney in the years they marked each other. What came into the full forward's sphere of operation was quality ball, hit four or five yards either side of him.

'Jimmy looked overweight,' says O'Keeffe, 'but he was deceptively quick, he had that ten-yard burst. Mullins and the boys knew it. They knew how to play him. I rarely if ever had to field a high ball. They all came in fast and low and he had a girth which made it difficult to get around.

'He was a two-sided player who could kick very accurately. He was a head-up footballer, with vision. I would have loved to have played a little looser and gone for balls from different places. There were times when he'd take me for little dummy runs to take me away from the play. I had so much respect for him I had no choice but to go with him. Little gaps would open up. Somebody else would take the scores. Jimmy didn't score very much off me, but he opened it up for the others and he laid ball off to them always.'

So O'Keeffe did the job of a bodyguard and sacrificed his game for the greater good. He learned quickly that it was a job that demanded discipline above all else. In a league game in Killarney, Dublin had a fifty and Keaveney was ambling out to take it. O'Keeffe decided not to take the walk with him. Mullins, noticing that Keaveney was unescorted for once, just tapped the ball to Keaveney, who casually turned, flicked his eyes around like a fox looking for stray chickens and then settled for sliding the ball over the bar.

And then there was the dead-ball kicking. Keaveney taught himself on the roads around Whitehall, kicking a baldy tennis ball. He joined St Vincent's when he was thirteen and he kicked frees from the start of his playing career with the club. Practice, when he bothered, was six perfunctory kicks at training on the day before a big game.

Bobby Doyle remembers the All-Ireland semi-final of 1978 against Down. Dublin put together a good move which finished with Doyle flying through the air and handpassing the ball into the net. The referee called play back and gave Dublin a penalty. Doyle's heart was jangling.

Keaveney stood and waited for the ball to be handed to him. His penalty was tipped around the post.

'And Jimmy just turned, waddled out for the fifty, put it down and stuck it over the bar. He never gave a second thought to any of it. It all seemed so easy to him.'

Dublin's wing forwards were encouraged always to run at defences. They would either reach the citadel or be fouled in the attempt. Being fouled was an end in itself.

Whenever he got brought down, the scoreboard in Anton O'Toole's head would flick over automatically. 'It never struck me that Jimmy wouldn't score. It didn't strike Jimmy, either. I'd be lying there, counting my limbs to check they were still there and Jimmy would say, "Get up outta that and go and get me another free."'

Dublin had a problem with penalty-taking until Heffernan decided that the job was Keaveney's. By the time of the 1976 All-Ireland final, Keaveney figured that goalkeepers had cottoned on to the fact that, following Heffernan's orders, Keaveney hit the ball to the goalie's left every time. He noticed that keepers were leaving their position and moving left before he kicked the ball at all. He usually struck it hard enough that it made no difference, but with an All-Ireland coming up he was concerned. Paudie O'Mahoney was a master at saving penalty kicks.

A couple of weeks before the All-Ireland final, Jimmy received a phone call from his old friend, Billy Morgan. Billy had been over in Killarney and had watched the Kerry forwards taking penalties on Paudie O'Mahoney. They were hitting them to Paudie's left all the time. Paudie was diving to his left all the time.

'He's committing himself just as the kicker is coming up,' said Morgan. 'Just thought I'd let you know in case ye get a penalty.'

Mick O'Dwyer was famously intolerant of injuries. There's a story, perhaps apocryphal, of John O'Keeffe being concussed in the first half of the 1979 All-Ireland final. At half-time the medic took a look at the player and announced to O'Dwyer's consternation that his full back would have to come off.

'Leave him on sure,' said O'Dwyer, 'he'll run it off.'

'Mick, he can't remember a thing about the first half,' said the doc.

'Sure, can't he see it tonight on the television,' came the reply.

O'Keeffe played eleven minutes of the second half before coming off.

'He thought fellas were hypochondriacs,' says Ger O'Keeffe. 'He thought that about Deenihan and I in 1976. He blames us for losing the 1976 final because we played injured. Sure, he picked us injured! We trained on an injury, which was worse!'

Paudie O'Mahoney was in the hypochondriac camp late that summer. He was playing in an East Kerry championship semi-final when he got a kick in the back of the lower leg. He felt his Achilles tendon was weak afterwards and went to a doctor.

The doctor said, 'You'd better tell O'Dwyer.'

'Now 1976 was the driest summer in a long time. Hard ground. I told Dwyer and he said, "You'll train like the rest of them." Now O'Dwyer was always finding an excuse to get rid of me, I don't know why. I suppose I used to challenge him. Anyway, I felt like shit before the final. I knew my leg was weak. I used to go straight to bed every night after training. It wasn't the kicking leg. Dr Con Murphy told me I was in serious trouble. Dwyer told me to train on.'

Sixteen minutes into the final, not long after John McCarthy had scored a goal for Dublin, Paudie made a save.

'Next thing, I thought somebody from the crowd had thrown a knife at me. Literally a knife. I looked down to see the knife in my leg, and there was nothing. I couldn't walk. I couldn't stand. I got up and put down the ball to kick it out. I couldn't go back or lift my legs to kick it.

'I called them in. Up to that, no county ever had a sub jersey goalie. Dwyer tore the jersey off my back and it came across very badly on the television. They brought in the sub goalie's jersey after that!'

Paudie was carried off by stretcher and had an operation the next week. He was replaced in the goal by young Charlie Nelligan, thus beginning a great rivalry which was stoked always by O'Dwyer's facility for playing his men off one against another.

(Nelligan was relatively easy-going about the competition for the goalie jersey. He saw himself as the apprentice. O'Mahoney, though, was driven to distraction.

'I hated being number sixteen. If you're on the sideline you'd love your man to break his leg. You would. Charlie was such a good guy, though. We're great friends. We never had any rows, but Dwyer told me so many lies I could make a book of them.')

The second half had scarcely started when John McCarthy was fouled and Dublin were awarded a penalty.

'Keaveney was quite happy about taking the penalty then, I'd say,' says Paudie. 'Taking it on me might have been a bit different. I know he would have been afraid of me. I'd been practising all summer.'

Charlie Nelligan was nineteen and had seen a newspaper head-line the previous week with his name in it. If O'Mahoney was unfit, Charlie would start. He went to Mick O'Dwyer and asked about the headline.

O'Dwyer was reassurance itself. 'Yerra, that's only paper talk. Pay no heed.'

So on the day Charlie was in the dugout chatting to Ger O'Driscoll, and suddenly there were county board officials pulling and dragging at him. Ger O'Driscoll was pulling the legs of Charlie's tracksuit off.

'I should have been alerted to the fact that Paudie was injured. I wasn't tuned in at all. I was thrown in front of the Hill after about twenty minutes and they were saying lovely nice things down to me. In the second half, the first chore was to take the ball out of the net after the penalty. With a penalty you're not supposed to save them. If you do, you're a hero. I knew it would go high. If you look back at that time on the Canal End side where the penalty spot was, it was little bit raised off the ground. It was a great penalty.'

It was a great penalty, perhaps the greatest ever struck in an All-Ireland final. It caused Jimmy Keaveney an uncharacteristic moment of worry, though.

'Billy has given me the tip-off about Paudie. Lo and behold we get a penalty but Paudie O'Mahoney is gone off injured. Heffernan or no Heffernan, I'd decided to stick it the other way if Paudie was in goal. Now Charlie Nelligan was in there. Had he been practising going to his left as well? They hadn't got the phone-a-friend option or I'd have taken a break to ring Billy. I'm looking at Charlie and I don't know what's in his head so I decided to stick it the usual way. He might save it but it'll keep Kevin happy at least, says I.'

That was Keaveney, ambling through the smoke of battle, processing the odds. Enjoying the day.

Dublin won, beating Kerry in championship football for the first time since 1934.

'In 1976 I felt so bad when we'd lost,' says John O'Keeffe. 'Jimmy was terrific. No gloating. No glorifying. I'd rate him so highly in victory or defeat. We always swapped jerseys and hugged. A gentleman and a true Dub. That was why he was so popular.

I see him less and less as the years roll on, and I regret that because the memories are so vivid and the respect is so great for him.'

Kevin Moran, just twenty years of age and the blithest spirit on the pitch, looked around him in bemusement.

'In 1976 Kerry meant nothing to me. I remember afterwards Kevin Heffernan grabbed me and said, "I've waited twenty-one years for this." I'd always had the attitude that what happened in another generation happened, and the one doesn't have any influence on the other. For supporters and for Kevin, that was key. It was Kerry. There was all the history. I understood it then.'

Kerry never led during the game, but they pressed hard in the second half and for a while it looked as if their young legs would get them to the line first. When Dublin's need was greatest, however, they produced the third goal. A picture of a pass from Tommy Drumm, a flick from Anton O'Toole, and Brian Mullins on the edge of the square slid the ball between Charlie Nelligan's legs.

Kerry had introduced Sean Walsh for one last reprise of his Super-Sub role. He came on just as Keaveney scored his penalty. Inauspicious, but then it was a day when nothing worked.

O'Dwyer had gambled that Ogie Moran would be able to burn Pat O'Neill for pace at wing forward. Instead, the first few balls which came between them came in high. O'Neill knew Ogie well from UCD, where they both played. He jumped and pinched each one away in succession, on one occasion driving Ogie out over the sideline in the process.

And the Kerry midfield struggled. The previous September, Pat McCarthy had been the game's most influential player and his marker, Bernard Brogan, was substituted. This time their situations were reversed.

That winter and spring Brogan, an engineer, had been working in the power station in Tarbert. He had struck up a friendship with Jimmy Deenihan, and the two men would train together on the dunes of Ballybunion and on a hill behind the school in Tarbert.

One weekend Deenihan had brought Brogan to the carnival in Finuge. He introduced Brogan to a girl called Maria. Inadvertently, Deenihan had made a contribution to the future of Dublin football:

Bernard and Maria got married and produced the future Dublin footballers Alan and Bernard Brogan.

When Sean Walsh was coming off the field in Croke Park after the 1976 final, Jim Brogan, Dublin's perennial sub, swapped jerseys with Kerry's Super-Sub, Sean Walsh.

That night Jim and Bernard Brogan hit the Oliver Plunkett's pub, the Breffni on the Navan Road. Maria Keane-Stack was inserted into the colours of her county and 'paraded around the pub up on lads' shoulders in Seanie Walsh's Kerry jersey'.

For Dublin, winning was a validation. That summer the team had decided to train itself on a few Wednesday nights, and most afternoons the student contingent had hit the beach in Portmarnock and played ball. Most of all it was a renewal of the principles of 1974 and a partial wiping of a slate which had the All-Irelands of 1955 and 1975 chalked on it.

For Mick O'Dwyer the setback came as no surprise. He'd seen it coming down the line.

'Cork took the divil out of us. That knocked a lot out of us. Then one evening in the week before the final, I remember it well, they rang and asked if I'd mind cancelling training. Nothing to do but cancel it. I knew at the time it was curtains, though. The year before, there was none of that. There was no point in saying anything to them at that stage. They'd won in 1975 and they were so young, everyone sat back.'

The players hadn't rung to get training cancelled because they were fatigued. Ger O'Keeffe had finagled an invitation from Beamish and Crawford for the Kerry panel to attend a reception at the Tralee Races. They all turned up, looking dapper, and things went swimmingly. They'd been at the races most days, but today the drink was free.

'I remember in Tralee,' says Jimmy Deenihan, 'we were in there with our blazers, having a great time. We had a great Tralee Races. We were the flavour of the month.'

'It was a fierce piss-up,' says Ger O'Keeffe. 'That showed immaturity. Any team wins an All-Ireland that young, it'll come out.'

If Kevin Heffernan was satisfied that the All-Ireland represented payback after twenty-one years, Bobby Doyle's wait had been shorter.

Doyle's dropping in 1975 and his subsequent defection was never spoken about between the player and his manager. He came back to the panel and normal service resumed.

Not long after his return, Doyle went to Heffernan and suggested that he would like to start a course in weights because he felt that that he was being pushed off the ball very easily.

'I said, I can't win the ball like Dave Hickey can. I needed two catches at it before I could get it. Davey just drove into it.'

Heffernan said no, definitely no, but it was in Doyle's mind that he had to get stronger. Without telling anybody, he joined the Grafton Health Studio. He picked the gym because of its southside location. Heffernan had his spies on the lookout for Jimmy Keaveney taking a pint. They would hardly be alert to Bobby Doyle doing some weights across the Liffey.

'I did eight months in there. I'd swear I was the only northsider in there. I felt I could take a knock after that. I played the best football of my career in 1976. It made a difference to my body. I could see it in myself and I could feel it.'

The year 1976 was a special one for Doyle. St Vincent's won the All-Ireland club championship that spring, beating mighty Nemo in the semi-final down at the Mardyke along the way. Doyle sailed through the spring and summer on a new wave of confidence.

Then, before the final, he got a hamstring injury. For a week beforehand he trained by himself, jogging slowly around Parnell Park with just his hamstring and his misery for comfort.

On the day before the All-Ireland final he still wasn't right. He asked for twenty-four hours.

On All-Ireland final morning, the Doyles' doorbell rang early. Heffernan was on the porch with a football under each arm.

While people passed up Adare Road to early Mass, Bobby Doyle underwent a fitness test outside his own house. Kevin Heffernan kicked the balls this way and that. Doyle chased in desperation.

'That'll do,' said Heffernan at last.

That afternoon in Croke Park, just before the match started, Doyle went for a little warm-up sprint. He felt a twinge. He went over to Heffernan, mindful that the manager had once told him that he'd drop his own mother if he thought it would win him a game.

'This thing is nagging me a bit, Kevin.'

Heffernan looked at him evenly.

'Do you want to play or not?'

He got no answer beyond the sight of Bobby Doyle scampering out on to the field without risking a backward glance.

12

Is that it?

David Hickey

In Kerry the loss of the 1976 All-Ireland final was hard to digest. There was some grumbling and some rumblings about O'Dwyer, and some more outpourings of anguish about the style of football which Kerry were playing. In defeat, O'Dwyer's abandonment of catch-and-kick was seen as a reproach to tradition. The manager commented that things were hard enough without having thirty-one-and-a-half counties against his team.

In 1975 Jimmy Deenihan had commented innocently, and correctly, that Kerry had more natural footballers than Dublin had. A year later the comment was fashioned into a stick to beat him with.

'Never cast aspersions on the alligator's mother until you have crossed the river,' Con Houlihan chided gently.

'I was right when I made the comment last year,' said Deenihan.

In any case, O'Dwyer's job was fundamentally different from Heffernan's, and it is doubtful if either man would have had the patience for the other's task. Heffernan moderated a group who were mature when success came to them, and often their journey felt like an abstract, intellectual exercise. O'Dwyer harnessed the explosive talents of a cohort of young men, most of whom had known no other form of adult life before they hit the big time in 1975. It was a wonder of intuition and man-management that he kept them fresh and interested for so long.

On the night they lost the 1976 final, things looked black. The team endured one of those sour but necessary receptions in their hotel for supporters, family and hangers-on. They braced themselves for the ordeal of their homecoming the next evening.

It was a big night for one young lad on the fringe of the Kerry panel.

Jack O'Shea knew where everyone sat in the pantheon. He had watched them all. Ned Fitzgerald (father of Maurice) was a local hero in south Kerry since his playing days in the fifties. Ger Driscoll. Gerry O'Mahony, another fine local player, could have made it but went to London when he was young. Michael Casey from Portmagee (father of Dublin's Paul Casey) was a local icon.

They say in south Kerry that you have to be three times better than a player from any other end of the county to get noticed by the selectors. You might not believe it till you look through the list of players that finger of land has produced. Jack Murphy, who was the hero of the 1926 drawn final against Kildare, fell ill before the replay and was buried in Cahirciveen five days after Kerry won the title. The list starts there. Jerome O'Shea, Mick O'Connell, Mick O'Dwyer, Maurice Fitzgerald, John Egan, Jack O'Shea . . .

Jacko always considered that he was lucky enough to be living opposite the football field in Cahirciveen. He could keep an eye out the window for a footballer arriving. Every chance he got, he was in the field. He remembers going down to the field as a young fella, and there'd be fifteen or twenty like him them there and one ball between them. You earned your kicks.

He wasn't fortunate enough to have a football in the house, but one or two footballs would be kept locally. If you wanted to play, you had to go into Connie Byrne's shop across from the field and sign for the ball, and thereafter the ball was your responsibility. You brought the ball back when you were done.

Eugene Ring lived up the street. He'd keep an eye on the field and the young lads who were playing in it. In Cahirciveen the field was the leisure centre and youth club rolled into one.

Once or twice a week two men would arrive at the field and play football with each other. Jacko didn't have to be told more than once that the men were Mick O'Connell and Mick O'Dwyer. He was mesmerized by them.

He watched them every time they came to the field. Soon he got into a routine of fetching the footballs for them. When the two Mickos were there, young Jacko was there, too. When a match was played, he would stand behind the goals. The ball would go over the bar and there'd be a contest between the boys to catch it and kick it back. Curly-haired Jack O'Shea won the lion's share.

The legends began to notice. Mick O'Connell would turn to him occasionally and, standing four or five yards away, kick the ball at him, teaching him to catch it away from his body.

He remembers the first time he ever saw a Kerry team, when he was nine or ten years old. Brother Keating came home from Zambia and Jacko was good friends with Brother Keating's nephews, the Musgrave boys. The Musgraves had an uncle who worked in Zambia, *and* they had a car.

Father Keating promised the boys the treat of a trip to see Kerry training. In far-off Tralee.

This was 1967, in the countdown to a Munster final. On the way through Killorglin, Brother Keating stopped the car and went into a sporting goods shop and bought a brand-new size-four brown leather lace football. From a missionary this was a display of impossible affluence.

Brother Keating had the shop pump the ball up. It was a wonder of the world. Smell that leather, boys!

They brought the perfect new ball to Tralee. They had a simple plan. They'd get all the autographs of the gods of green and gold. The ball would be invaluable.

It was easy to get inside the wire. Training wasn't a spectacle to be consumed unless you were a young boy with your jaw hanging open. The Kerry players were doing a little backs-and-forwards play. The Cahirciveen boys slipped between the huge clattering bodies, proffering the ball and a pen to each in turn.

They were boys, but they were Kerry boys and therefore cuter than boys would generally be. The game plan was to leave the two Mickos till the end. Their autographs could be secured in Cahirciveen during any given summer week. The other gods occupied different planets.

At last they had harvested all the signatures bar those of the two Mickos. They brought the ball to Mick O'Dwyer. He signed and gave his trademark grin. The game of backs-and-forwards was done with now. They approached the great O'Connell, the game's most reluctant icon.

'And of course, Mick O'Connell being Mick O'Connell, he just took the ball off us, put it down on the ground and sailed it over the bar. He said, "That's my autograph now."'

Perhaps it was the political disadvantage of being a boy from south Kerry, or perhaps it was a stroke of selectorial genius, but for the Kerry minor team of 1975 Jacko was picked at full forward. He was surprised. He'd played on Neilly Donovan and Seanie Walsh, the two selected midfielders, and had done well on them. Oh well . . .

Being a young lad of equable disposition, he was content enough. They made him free-taker. In the Munster final he scored 1–7 of Kerry's 3–7 and nobody was inclined to complain about young O'Shea being out of position.

They won the minor All-Ireland of 1975 and celebrated in the shadow of the seniors that night. He'd always felt he had a chance of making it, but that night he felt as good as Mick O'Connell ever could have done.

'I hadn't the age or the sense to know what lay ahead. I was at the top of the tree, enjoying myself. My ambitions were to play football but that night was the first night I ever took a drink.'

Jacko was just a month over the age for minor in 1976. He was at risk, what with all that youth to use up. For the next couple of months after the minor win he travelled everywhere on cloud nine and got plenty more tastes of alcohol.

The problem with being young and gifted is that you don't know enough, soon enough. He wasn't worried about the next day or the day after. His strategy had to be long term. Like everyone else in the county, he had trouble imagining a vacancy on the Kerry seniors for another four or five years at best. And he had the Under-21s to get on with; he played full forward there and they'd already won an All-Ireland the week after the minor success. This was living!

Through 1976 he was being brought into Killarney for trial games. It was a tradition of Kerry football that before big matches, no matter how immutable the first team was, there would be a trial game. Páidí Lynch and Pat McCarthy were the first-choice midfielders, and though he did well against them in trial games he wasn't in full agreement with those around the county who suggested that it was already time for him to be brought into the senior squad.

He was busy living life. Mick O'Dwyer, meanwhile, was busy measuring his team against Heffernan's. In the spring and summer of 1976 he had come to realize that the compliment had been reciprocated. Heffernan had reconfigured his own side in response to O'Dwyer's dashing half-forward line.

O'Dwyer had the acuity to know that Dublin suddenly looked balanced and settled. He looked at his own hand of cards. He had youth. He had natural talents. He had a system. He needed a stronger midfield, and the full-forward position worried him.

Kerry had been thoroughly beaten at midfield in September. More galling was the fact that Dublin's sprightly midfield looked as if they could repeat the trick every autumn for a decade. Mullins leaped for everything and caught most things. Brogan ran like a young colt. They were the perfect balance.

O'Dwyer felt he'd have to gamble on youth yet again. The young lad from the field in Cahirciveen would have his moment if he could shape up.

After the 1976 final, Jacko went to the team function and mooched about the place, catching a little of the downbeat atmosphere. He'd had a few drinks when John O'Keeffe and Jim Deenihan approached him. There was an edge to them. He remembers Johnno backing him up till he was pressed against a pillar. Fingers were jabbed in his face. They lectured him sternly on talent, and how he was wasting his.

'They said if I got my act together I'd be in the panel. Johnno kept saying, "We need you, we need you now to get yourself sorted out. C'mon, get it together. Sort yourself out."'

He nodded. He thought they were mad.

A week later he got called in for his first senior game. Against Meath in Navan in the League. He wasn't supposed to start, but one of the cars broke down on the way to the game, leaving Kerry short. He started at midfield. Two weeks later they played Dublin in Tralee. He got to mark Brian Mullins. Meath and Mullins. Two soft baby steps for a novice.

Mullins was the icon. Jacko had the greatest respect for him, almost a fascination.

'He was tough but he was fair. He was the great leader of that team. I thought about it all week, having to play on him.'

Young O'Shea got an improbable start in both halves of the game, catching the throw-up each time and kicking it over the bar.

It took nerve. When he'd done it once at the start of the match, he felt the shadow of Mullins on his shoulder.

'I think you should be at home in school, son,' said Mullins.

From early 1977 he went off the drink. Not that he'd been drinking too much, but he wasn't giving football everything he could have given it and he realized that he had found himself perhaps in the right place at the right time.

'Once I stopped the drinking, football meant everything to me then.'

Kerry gained Jacko. Dublin lost Heffo.

On a Friday evening a fortnight or so after the All-Ireland of 1976, Heffernan gathered his team into a room in the Gresham Hotel on O'Connell Street. They assumed that they were being called together for some general housekeeping announcements and a few pleasant beers. Instead, Heffernan announced to the room that he was packing it in. No reasons given.

They all remember it differently but in the same way. Paddy Cullen stood up and stared around in disbelief. Many shouted, 'No, no,' as if there was a tragedy unfolding before their eyes.

Tony Hanahoe can see David Hickey standing there 'in a pair of white trousers, looking like F. Scott Fitzgerald'. Sean Doherty recalls a tear running down Hickey's cheek.

Hickey, famously, uttered three words: 'Is that it?'

He felt hugely hurt by the abandonment. He wasn't alone.

'We were all surprised that Kevin walked away,' says Lorcan Redmond. 'He had his own reasons, but there was huge disappointment. There were tears shed when he walked out. Our meeting was over and there were tears shed. Big men, strong guys, crying. Huge disappointment. Kevin probably doesn't know that. It came as a shock. I've never spoken about it to him.'

Decades later, Hickey still feels that Heffernan was wrong to leave without explaining the circumstances. 'I think he left for the theatrical value of it. He gave no explanation. Just left us there. I think it was a betrayal of Lorcan and Donal and the boys.

'I hate what he did. I hate the walkout in 1976, which was so calculated and cynical. I don't want to be seen as the guy who'll go to his grave bitching about Heffernan. Or when Kevin is being buried, they'll be saying there was only one guy who couldn't see, and that guy was David Hickey! I think, though, that in 1976 he saw us as being washed up and he decided to disassociate himself in case he got blamed or people said he wasn't as great as he was supposed to be.'

Heffernan is familiar with the arguments. Tired of them almost.

'In 1976 there was a lot going on. There was a fear in my mind of staleness. We'd been on the go for a few years. Perhaps they needed a new voice. There were issues in my working life. I just thought it was time to step away.'

Some of the players say that the reason for his departure is obvious. Beating Kerry was an obsession which Kevin Heffernan carried for twenty-one years. They had done it and with style.

Pressed again on the matter now, he laughs but leaves it. 'It's neither here nor there. I'm not going to comment. You can feck off. It's water under the bridge.'

Did you ever regret it?

'Not at all.'

Was it hard to look from the sidelines?

'It was great, once we won.'

Did fellas ring to get you back?

'Arra listen, listen would you leave it go would you. It's a thing of nothing. I'm not saying more. No more.'

Whatever his reasons, he was gone. The shell-shocked team regrouped and decided among themselves on a replacement. There was only one choice. Hanahoe.

Some say that when Tony Hanahoe returns to the GAA hinterlands from which he sprang, he carries the air of a benign Law Lord visiting once again the pinched mining town of his birth. It is a testament to his contribution to Dublin football in general, and to the team of the seventies in particular, that this is said with affection rather than rancour.

One of four boys, he grew up in Clontarf, a genteel Dublin suburb with ecumenical sporting tastes. Clontarf indulged rugby, soccer, golf and cricket, while nearby Marino subsisted on a plain diet of Gaelic games and Gaelic games only. Hanahoe's father was a UCD man who played a little soccer before settling for the twilight of the fairways. The Hanahoe boys, meanwhile, spent most of their time on the sands of Dollymount beach, improvising their own nascent sporting lives.

Young Tony's destiny was sealed by happenstance. The Hanahoes' neighbours were the McHughs, an enthusiastic GAA family. Young Tony was encouraged to sample their faith and dabbled a little on behalf of a short-lived club in Clontarf called St Anthony's.

He took what for the Hanahoes was an unusual route educationally, that is, he was dispatched to Scoil Mhuire on Griffith Avenue and then further to St Joseph's CBS in Fairview. His three brothers had all attended Rockwell College, a boarding school in Roscrea. Tony Hanahoe stood apart at an early age.

Perhaps he arrived in Griffith Avenue with dreams punctuated by the patter of running spikes or the whickering of shuttlecocks, but at Scoil Mhuire he played football and hurling. He represented the school, and that achievement marked him out. He played also for St Vincent's, where he traced the steps of the divinities who had gone before him.

'You played for the school and that distinction made you a hero in your world. You had gladiatorial status. Special buses took us off to the park on a Saturday or other days when we had games. There were school songs. We won a lot.'

True to his roots, he was catholic in his interests. When he was a little older he set his sights on becoming a bullfighter and would put together what money a student could muster to visit La Monumental in Barcelona, there to study the *corridas*. He outgrew that fancy, or life steered him elsewhere. He retained a love for horse racing, as befits the boy who would call into O'Leary's shop at the Clontarf end of Fairview Strand every morning for a racing newspaper with which to extract sufficient knowledge to underpin the odd five-shilling bet in the bookmaker's on the road behind.

Boxers were his most constant heroes, and when Ali ducked between the ropes he took up residence in Hanahoe's youthful consciousness. In another life Hanahoe could have been a character of Damon Runyon's, following the fights and trading horse tips in Toots Shor's. He learned off the names of every winner of the Grand National and the Gold Cup. He followed the fortunes of Lester Piggott and Scobie Breasley with gentle piety.

Always he stood apart, and yet of that tight seventies team he is the one whose loyalty can never be questioned. He draws them together and keeps them honest to the cause.

One day, as men, Jimmy Keaveney, Bobby Doyle and Hanahoe played a game in the Phoenix Park for St Vincent's. They were beaten by Civil Service and afterwards the three Dubs repaired to Bongo Ryan's of Parkgate Street for drinks and an inquest. Naturally the chat got around to Kevin Heffernan. The players who voyaged around Heffernan spent large portions of their lives discussing him and second-guessing him.

'We weren't necessarily giving out or complaining,' says Doyle. 'It's just that Kevin Heffernan was what we talked about lots of the time. I'm not able to hold my drink at the best of times and back then I was even worse. I was giving my views a bit loudly perhaps and, next thing, I saw Tony tearing a drip mat apart and taking an expensive pen from his pocket.'

A minute later the note on the drip mat got passed to Doyle. Precise handwriting.

'The guys behind you are very interested. Please keep your voice down.'

That was typical of Hanahoe.

'And it's funny,' says Doyle. 'I still think the world of him. He's so entertaining. He has such a range of friends. Tony could elongate a little story like the one I've just told to the length of a pint. He's a unique character and you never know what's going on in there or when you have him.'

The Dubs had him, though, heart and soul.

'Kevin was a man that made up his mind about things,' Hanahoe says. 'His reasons for stepping down are known only to him. There are various suspicions, but as far as the script is concerned it was for personal reasons. It's an unanswered question. He stepped down and that was it.

'I didn't get time to think about too much. It was put to me that this was the way it would be. I think Kevin may even have suggested me. It all happened very quickly. I had no time to think about it. It was a strong feeling that the successor had to be from the group. In truth, an outsider would never have worked. An outsider wouldn't have had the support and trust.'

Jimmy Gray, who was going away for a week's holiday, had to sell the suits on the notion that the county football team was now selecting its own manager.

Hanahoe knew that the fact that Dublin had beaten Kerry convincingly a couple of weeks previously wasn't lost on Kerry. Much would be made of it among the Pharisees who presided over the integrity of Kerry's football mission. In Kerry they would be demanding revenge. They would be demanding that it be extracted with some style, too.

Hanahoe saw many very ambitious and ruthless men on the far side of the fence that divided the two teams and he realized that he was taking a job which could go desperately wrong. What if the men in the room with him were washed up? What if Kerry came back and repeated the ambush stunt of 1975?

He told himself that it was a challenge he was going to take.

'I thought more about loyalty to colleagues than failure or success.' That was Hanahoe's way. On the field he played as a decoy, a device Heffernan had conceived to unhinge opposition defences. He would drift away from his post at centre forward, leaving a big hole for Bernard Brogan and Brian Mullins to gallop through.

'I may indeed have unhinged the opposition's defence, but it was a lonely time doing it. Half the time, I think some of my own fellows forgot about me, too. There were one or two in the early days when it was quite comical. It worked so well that I would be left standing on the opposition square on my own with the opposition goalkeeper having a heart attack. But nobody could see me.

'If I were to do it all again, I'd try to play a more conventional role. Too many lonely hours.'

Moving into management involved a lot more lonely hours. He spent a lot of time wondering if people were wondering why he didn't drop himself. The meetings in The Room went the same way as they always had, and Hanahoe stayed as a team player in the players' meetings.

'It wasn't always easy to deal with teammates who were sometimes aggrieved. We got through it, though.'

Players remember the handling of one such grievance as revealing the essential quality of Hanahoe.

Paddy Reilly had been dropped in 1975, along with his half-back colleagues, and though he stayed close to a place on the team the demotion went hard on him. Other players could see the justification. Dublin had conceded 12–45 on the way to losing the 1975 All-Ireland, while Kerry had conceded no goals at all. Following reconstruction work, the Dublin defence had conceded just 1–45 in the five games which led to winning the All-Ireland final of 1976. Statistics are no comfort to a wounded player, however.

In 1976 Paddy Reilly had been picked for the Leinster final against Meath but had to pull out when an old cartilage problem recurred. He was broken-hearted.

'I always thought that the selectors had something against me after that, they thought I had funked it. It took me two months to get over it.'

'I knew I was under pressure anyway, because when you were going out of the loop Heffernan ignored you. He never told you. Never warned you. It's the one thing I've always held against them. I went to Heffernan one night in the dressing room. I said, "You have the right to pick whoever you want, but I deserve better from you. I'm here all the time. You bottled it."'

When Hanahoe took over the team, it was reasonable of some players to hope that all previous bets were off and that Hanahoe would be offering amnesties to the subs. As it happened, the Dublin team that started the 1977 All-Ireland final was the same as that which started in 1976. Reilly broached the issue one night with Hanahoe in the Green Isle Hotel and was politely rebuffed.

The issue was eating away at him, though. Bobby Doyle won't talk about the fight with Paddy Reilly, but it comes up in so many conversations that it is hardly a secret. In short, Reilly and Doyle fell to it one night in Meagher's.

There are differing versions of the row. Paddy Reilly thinks that it was mainly drink talking at the end of a long day. Others say it was a discussion over Hanahoe's conservative team selections, which got out of hand when Reilly was challenged to say exactly which team member he felt he should be playing instead of.

Anyway, it spilled out into Ballybough, and Reilly recalls that he and Doyle didn't speak for a year afterwards.

A lot sooner than that, they had both received admonitory phone calls from Hanahoe.

Each man was contrite. Reilly emphasized the context. Doyle noted that he had been defending Hanahoe's team selections.

Hanahoe was curt. 'Please don't. I don't need you defending me. The team is bigger than any need to defend me.'

Hanahoe's moral authority came from that belief, and in 1977 it earned him ownership of the greatest victory of the era. Player, manager, captain and trainer.

The transition had been painful, but by then the team was so mature that Robbie Kelleher reckons, half jokingly, that his mother could have run it. She didn't, though. It was Hanahoe to whom the team turned.

13

We had fun. Christ, we had horses fun!

Mikey Sheehy

When the Kerry team went for dinner after a training session, everyone wanted to sit at a table with Páidí Ó Sé. If you were to compose a list of things you had to do before you died, having a pint in Kerry with Páidí Ó Sé would be one of them – unless you were dead already.

Páidí's life is one long unfolding drama. He plays it for comedy, a trick which conceals both his untamed wildness and his quietly whirring brain. There are two million Páidí stories, a million of which Páidí has forgotten or denies and a million others upon which his reputation rests.

The pictures which crowd the interior walls of his white stucco bar, a few miles out on the road from Dingle, are evidence of a hurly-burly social life. Páidí with Bono, with Tom Cruise, with Dolly Parton, with just about every recognizable Irish face there is. Zelig was less outgoing.

He was the favourite of all favourites with O'Dwyer. They referred to each other as Dwyer and Sé. The lads felt that they shared two versions of the one brain, that O'Dwyer used Páidí to say the things he wouldn't say to fellas. O'Dwyer was a psychological shadow-boxer, teasing players with suggestions about how others were playing, beguiling them at one minute with his enthusiasm, confusing them the next with his apparent indifference.

Páidí was battering-ram blunt and what needed to be said got said. And when it was out on the table they'd catch Dwyer and Sé exchanging fleeting glances. There was an understanding which remained wordless but quietly perfect.

Páidí's laughter was the theme music to Kerry's journey, and there were those who saw the laughter and heard the yarns and came to their own conclusions. The lads looked on and grinned. Nothing about Páidí ever surprised them and anyone who bought Páidí as a fool was advised to keep the receipt.

His football brain was impeccable, and politically he had a dancer's feet – when he was focused. Years later he would become the most successful of the group in terms of inter-county management, yet when Páidí was in the running for the Kerry job he found himself in difficulty.

Many blazers saw the wild man. Many thought they saw a fool. Páidí sought the counsel of his old friend, Charlie Haughey. At the time he was running neck and neck for the job with Seamus Mac Gearailt. If anyone was ahead, it was Mac Gearailt. Haughey advised Páidí to offer Mac Gearailt everything but the title of manager. It worked.

By the time Páidí's first term as Kerry manager had expired, he had brought the 1997 All-Ireland title back to Kerry, the first since the O'Dwyer era. Páidí opted to stay on in the job, and when he submitted his name to the county board for ratification, he was a shoo in.

'I got something like 112 votes out of 116 for the re-appointment. Charlie asked me, did I get the names of the four who didn't vote for me. I said that I did. He said, "Make one a selector and make sure you go to the dinner-dance in the clubs of the other three." Some man!'

And he laughs heartily, eyeing you all the time as he does so. He tells stories that would make you cry with tears.

Himself and The Horse were confederates. One day the pair of them, Páidí and Tim Kennelly, missed the train back to Kerry after a league match in Dublin. They stood in the station, laughing and looking at each other, realizing they both had work to go to the next day but, being young, realizing too that work would always be there.

They dandered out of Heuston Station and across the river and into the Phoenix Park, chatting about what to do. Ryan's of Parkgate Street beckoned, but that would eliminate Monday from their lives altogether.

They spotted a chip van a little way up the road in the Park and walked towards it. It had been a long day and they hadn't just missed the train, they were missing the feed the players would be enjoying on the train. The chip van was empty, though. Then one or other of the boys had a brainwave.

They climbed into the chip van. Put on the white coats. Turned the key, which was still in the ignition, and drove off. Garda and farmer heading south in a chip van. They drove to Portlaoise, where they abandoned the borrowed vehicle. Páidí knew enough gardaí in Portlaoise to procure a lift to Limerick, where he was stationed.

Another lift was procured onwards to Listowel for Kennelly.

The sense of fun which the Kerry team basked in radiated from Páidí like warmth from a fire. He was captain one year, and for the Munster final he had planned a speech for the dressing room beforehand. Meanwhile, Charlie Nelligan and Tommy Doyle had planned something else: a Cork player was making his debut that day and they'd concocted an unnerving little physical welcome for him.

Páidí's speech had to come first, though. O'Dwyer stepped aside and Páidí began to fulminate. He is a passionate man at the best of times, but in a Munster final dressing room his language fizzed and burned like Catherine wheels and Roman candles. He punctuated each sentence with a strenuous bounce of the ball. It was mesmeric and stirring, and at the height of his speech Páidí bounced the ball so hard that it smashed the fluorescent light.

It would have taken a brave man to laugh. Páidí finished the speech as if nothing had happened. With his last word the tension overwhelmed them and they burst for the door. Nelligan and Timmy Doyle hit the door first, the need for laughter exploding in their chests.

Nelligan flung the door open and got pushed out into the

corridor by the rest of the Kerry panel. The players burst past towards the sunshine, letting out war whoops as they went. Nelligan and Doyle found themselves in the corridor alone – apart from, as luck would have it, the Cork player they planned to wind up. They took one look and dissolved into laughter.

'I'd say that had a worse effect on the poor devil than anything we had cooked up for him beforehand!'

Within the team there was a group to whom O'Dwyer would give special attention sometimes. He called them The Heavies. Sometimes he called them The Fatties. They included Páidí, Seanie Walsh, Timmy Kennelly and, when he arrived on the scene like the last chunky piece of a jigsaw, Eoin Liston.

These men, along with Páidí Lynch and Ogie Moran and on occasion Ger O'Keeffe, were the key members of the Rat Pack.

'We were the fellas,' says Páidí, 'who were supposed to have spent a lot of time up on the high stool. We hung around together.'

Were David Attenborough to make a documentary about the habits of the Rat Pack, the money shots would come in the week after the Munster final every year. That was their time.

Páidí had an old caravan across the road from where his pub now stands. After a Munster final the Rat Pack would do a week in it. Like a religious retreat, only with different sacraments and rituals.

'We'd be in the caravan,' says Páidí. 'Ah Jesus. How we lived through it. Some times in there I don't remember at all. There was one morning – I don't know how it became so overcrowded, there may have been a few more people in there – but Ogie woke up in a bed somewhere between Bomber, Timmy Kennelly and Sean Walsh. The word was, he nearly died a cot death.'

They'd meet in Dingle on a Monday afternoon and put the boot to the floor straight away. Year after year after year. They'd hit The Bothar in Cuas. Johnny Frank's in Ballydavid. Báns. Páidí's own shop. Start on Sunday after the match, hit Dingle on Monday and go flat out till Thursday.

'Then,' says Páidí, 'you'd pull it in a little.'

'Páidí Sé was the Taoiseach and I was the Tánaiste,' says Liston.

'I would be able to read him and know what was going on in his head. Believe me, there was a fair bit of black magic in that head.'

They'd locate the caravan at three or four in the morning. Beatrice Ó Sé, Páidí's mother, would have the sandwiches up a table, reeks of sandwiches covered in foil.

'Next thing up in the morning,' says Liston, 'she'd have steaks on for us. Spoiled rotten we were. We always felt she was delighted to see us. A heart of gold. We had massive fun back there. Football means a lot in Kerry but it means an awful lot back there. It was always the best place to go. Magical. I often gave New Year's Eve to it as well. Ringing in the New Year all over the world, and there I'd be sweeping Páidí Sé's old bar, below in Krugers. Which I remind him often about.'

Dublin and Kerry met in the National League final of 1977. The teams were playing each other quite regularly now. Two challenge games a year, one, maybe two league games and a major championship match. By 1977 Dublin and Kerry were so far ahead of all contenders that they organized their calendars around those meetings only.

Kerry won the League final and left town, mildly contented but wary. Brian Mullins had missed the match. Perhaps they'd just won a race against a one-legged man.

A couple of days later, Dublin and most of the Kerry team flew to Chicago for the first leg of the annual All-Stars trip.

Chicago was still cold that April; the winds licking in off Lake Michigan confined the tourists to warm spots, like saloon bars. That early part of the trip is well remembered. Dublin played the All-Stars on an artificial surface, which caused a few injury problems. Jimmy Keaveney had an accidental collision with John O'Keeffe. A genuine accident.

'John hasn't a bad bone in his body. He came out to punch a ball, it bounced funny on the AstroTurf and he hit me in the nose. Broke it!'

Pat O'Neill, the medical professional, remembers the consultation.

'Jimmy got a right splatter. Everyone was looking at him. He was a horror show. This nose with all the snots and the blood hanging out and the tip of it over at his ear. He consulted with me. Jimmy was given the option: hospital, or I could have a look at it. You could see his mind working. Hospital meant no drinking for the night. I probably meant pain.'

Jimmy considered the offer.

'Fuck off, Nailer. Fuck off.'

'Well it's the hospital then, James. We'll see you tomorrow hopefully.'

'I don't fancy the hospital, Nailer.'

'Well, we can go to the emergency room or you can sit back here and we'll try to put it back in. It mightn't be perfect but you're no oil painting to start with.'

'All right,' Keaveney relented. Then changed his mind. 'No. Fuck it, Nailer, you're not touching me.'

This went on for some minutes, Keaveney covered in blood looking at O'Neill like a cow considering the outside of an abattoir.

'Could you not give me something?'

'Yeah. A Panadol, but it'll still be broken in the morning.'

Finally Keaveney said yes. They jumped him before he could change his mind. While the others held him down, O'Neill straddled his chest, got a grip on the hideous, deformed nose.

'I made the elementary mistake that I was astraddle him when I got the wrench on the nose.'

When O'Neill wrenched the nose, Keaveney jerked his knee up in an involuntary spasm of agony. He caught O'Neill perfectly in the groin. Now the two men were roaring. Keaveney's face looked like a half-made pizza. O'Neill was rolling around the floor, doubled up.

Happy days! The players referred to the incident for a long time afterwards as the time that Keaveney went to America for his nose job.

Keaveney treated the injury as a sailor would treat shore leave. He figured no more playing, and three weeks of touring and splurging. Maybe he'd never now be a matinee idol, but it had been worth it.

They spent the night of Kevin Moran's twenty-first birthday touring the bars of Rush Street. Somebody produced a cake with those candles which refuse to go out. In 1977 they were a novelty and a bafflement. The All-Ireland champions blew at the candles with the drunken intent of men who thought they were putting out the Chicago fire.

Next morning they had to move on to San Francisco. The flight was booked unhelpfully for pre-dawn. A tiny thing happened that morning which would change the course of Gaelic football history.

The Dubs, having packed before they hit the town with Moran the night before, were at the airport first. It was so early that the check-ins hadn't yet opened, so they stood in line, looking forward to what sleep they would be able to snatch on the flight westwards. Paddy Cullen was always the spokesperson for the players and that morning he had them lined up in as orderly a fashion as men in their condition could hope to achieve.

Just as the check-in was being manned, Paddy noticed something.

'Ger Power and somebody else, I don't think it was John O'Keeffe, I don't think John would do that, strolled past us all and checked in at the top of the queue. We'd been there for an hour. I was mad. I followed them up to the desk. I let them know what I thought of them. There was a row, but the girl at the desk said she'd started checking them in and so she'd have to finish.'

Cullen was seething. When the teams got to San Francisco, they were scheduled to play an unofficial seven-a-side tournament at a local high school. Cullen saw his chance.

'I asked Hanahoe, could I play out the pitch, see if I could get a cut at Power. We met on the pitch a few times. Nobody was broken up but there was a fair bit of animosity out there.

'I just felt he was one of the guys who would have been a little bit arrogant. He's a fine lad, but let's just say I'd rather have a drink with John Egan or Mikey Sheehy or a few of the lads.'

The incident was forgotten about by all but the main participants. The tour continued without much incident, apart from the usual Jimmy Keaveney postscript.

In San Francisco, Keaveney was still wondering about his nose, which was quite sore despite the tender ministrations of Pat O'Neill. In a bar one night O'Neill got Keaveney to take a drag of a cigarette and exhale through his nose. Smoke came down both nostrils. Like a magician O'Neill stepped back to admire his work: '*Et voilà!*'

The last game of the tour was in New York. Keaveney had a friend in the city who he stayed with. In holiday mode now, he didn't even go near the team hotel in case some training would break out. Come the morning of the match, he recalls that he had been on the beer for three weeks. He wandered down to the team hotel to wish the boys good luck and was collared by Hanahoe.

'Jim, you're playing today.'

Jimmy pointed to his trump card. 'Jaysus, Tony, I'd love to, but what about the nose?'

Hanahoe listed off a long casualty list. Jimmy had no choice.

'Up to bloody Gaelic Park. Billy Morgan was playing in goal for the All-Stars. I was minding my own business but we got a penalty. I mishit it so bad, Billy never had to move. I remember though seeing Morgan's shoulders going as he was bending down to place the ball for the kick-out. He was breaking his heart laughing. The Yanks knew no better. They thought it was great stuff.'

That was the way of it. There was muck and sand everywhere, the usual Gaelic Park deal. They skipped into the showers afterwards and there were drunks urinating in there. The players turned around and came back out again and straight on to the coach to Kennedy and home.

Stinking. And Paddy Cullen still brooding about Ger Power.

14

Twenty-nine minutes still remaining in this game. Hallelujah!

Micheál O'Hehir, commentating on 1977 All-Ireland semi-final

It was the crescendo. For two years Kerry and Dublin had floated around each other, picking their punches and sticking gloved fists into the soft underbellies where each hid their flaws. Now they roared and rumbled.

It was the hallelujah game. This time they got it right.

First, Dublin had overtrained and overbelieved. Cocky heads and tired legs undid them.

A year later, Kerry came back to town, feeling young and golden. They went home with their ears boxed.

Third time round there was no impertinence, no foolishness, no concealment, no hubris. They jumped the ropes and touched gloves, carrying exactly the right amount of respect for each other.

They left everything on Croke Park's green plot that day. When it ended with a theatrical wave of a referee's arms, there was a second of silence as lungs filled and brains computed. And on the grass, breathless men shook hands and gripped hard and looked each other in the eye, and between them they knew who had won and who had lost the big one.

By 1977 their rivalry had enough context and backstory to make it epic. They were personalities and they were young gods. They fitted neatly into the parts the storyline demanded. From the cool disdain their managers kept for each other to the differences in style and personality which distinguished the teams. It was the day of thunder that the decade yearned for. The game was a semi-final,

but it stepped outside the confines of the championship and became
an event in itself, crackling with static electricity.

Picture a perfect summer. A government fell and, despite that
or because of it, there was light in the air as if a war had ended.
The country was full of blue skies and buzzing people. For once
the living was easy.

'One long gorgeous summer,' says Pat O'Neill. 'Training
seemed easy and pleasurable. The city had this atmosphere that I
don't remember before. Dublin was humming. There seemed to
be money around as well. Plenty of money for all the activities. It
started turning a bit. It just evolved so slowly and happily.'

Robbie Kelleher got married eight days before the semi-final,
and for the three weeks before that he was in California, training
on his own in Golden Gate Park, a world away from the shed and
the evening dash for the Mariettas and milk.

He flew back at the start of All-Ireland semi-final week. Robbie
and Florence were in JFK when news went around that Elvis was
dead. That was Tuesday. On Wednesday he was in Parnell Park
having a private training session, with Lorcan Redmond acting as
drill sergeant.

'It was a different sort of summer. We all seemed relaxed and
happy. I don't know how I got three weeks in California, but I
don't think it would have happened if Kevin had been in charge.'

Kerry and Dublin dutifully tip their hats to their other rivals of
that era, and in paying their respects mention that there were no
laggards, just eager rivals who snapped at their heels, great teams
who were unlucky to get jammed in the doorway.

Yes, but . . . Kerry and Dublin hopped and skipped through their
provincial campaigns that summer. Ger O'Keeffe was captain of
Kerry and on the day of the Munster final in Killarney, when
Kerry had beaten Cork by fifteen points, Ger went up to accept
the trophy, but already Kerry had come to see Munster finals as
meaningless.

'I remember there was just one player with me on the podium.
Paudie Mahoney. We were in college together, we were in board-

ing school together, and we worked together as county engineers, and Paudie was that type of guy. That was how the Munster final was seen.'

The day was 21 August 1977. For once two teams came into the game relaxed and happy. Looking back, Robbie Kelleher thinks that what they all remember of the game is what they saw on television later. 'It was too quick to take anything in.'

They have scraps of recollection, though.

The beginning. A dry day and a louring sky. Ger O'Keeffe had won the toss. Kerry were defending the Canal goal. Jack O'Shea stooped for a loose ball. David Hickey materialized and, in one of those moments which set the tone for a team, stole it and passed it. Bobby Doyle with a sweet foot pass put his friend Jimmy Keaveney clean through. John O'Keeffe was some distance away, caught flat-footed for once.

'I had all the time in the world,' Keaveney says. 'Deenihan was coming in from the side, but I looked up and I could see Paudie Mahoney and I just decided to put it a little away from him and I stubbed it wide of the post. I couldn't believe it. You didn't get away from Johnno much in those games.'

Keaveney lay on the ground and wondered if another chance that good would come. Paudie O'Mahoney fetched the ball for the first kick-out of the day.

Before the game, Paudie O'Mahoney was anxious. He was an anxious kind of player, sensitive, a worrier and inclined to take things to heart. He could see a flaw in the team Mick O'Dwyer had put together. He went to O'Dwyer with a complaint.

That summer O'Dwyer was starting two midfielders he'd sprung from the blue. Páidí Ó Sé and Jacko. This was their first time in Croke Park as a tandem. Nothing seemed really settled. After two games Paudie didn't know what altitude the pair liked to operate at. They didn't know what distances they could expect him to kick. He was worried – but then Paudie was always worried. O'Dwyer told him to just cheer up.

'Christ, Anton O'Toole won several of our kick-outs that day,' Paudie recalls. 'Mullins, too. I said to Dwyer at one stage I feel like going home, this is a joke. You have a player there on the sideline and he's the best catcher in Kerry, put Pat McCarthy on. Give it five minutes, he said. We were destroyed in midfield. We did very well to survive. I kept calling the sideline through the second half. Can I talk to Dwyer? He used to send a selector around. The next thing, Dublin got two goals in the next five minutes. Dwyer brought Pat in when the goals were gone in. Nothing against Jacko, it was just that he wasn't Jacko yet.'

It was Jacko's first senior championship and, although he knew the fibre of the Dublin midfield from his home debut for Kerry in that year's league, he knew too that the difference in intensity would be immense. Here he was, in Croke Park, stepping into a grown-up's rivalry, and expected to influence it. He was eighteen and a half years old.

He had a game plan, though. To be competing against Mullins wasn't realistic. He'd let Páidí Ó Sé handle that battle and he'd stay running. He'd let Bernard Brogan do the same. They'd mark each other for kick-outs and then set off again.

So, early on, Jacko is getting the tempo into his legs. Paudie O'Mahoney, still fretting, places the ball for a kick-out. Jacko watches him. Paudie makes his slightly stooped run and floats it. It's hanging up there like a silver moon. Jacko is maybe fifty-five yards out. He has a line on the ball and a conviction that, once he gets there, it will be his.

Dead cert for a circus catch that would set the Hogan Stand crowd into a growl of that basso hollering. G'wan ya boy, make a name for yourself.

He goes for it, pace quickening like a lion closing on prey, swoosh he's gone, off into the air with his splayed hands above his curly head ready for their appointment with the ball. Perfect.

And bang! A body strikes him from behind, hits him fairly, but squarely and traumatically. Suddenly Jacko is grasping for nothing. His feet cycling the air. He flies four or five yards and hits the turf. Brian Mullins leaps over him, going forward with the ball.

'You have to get bigger,' Jacko says to himself before he gets up. 'You have to get bigger.'

Kerry toughed out the first half. *In extremis* strange things happen. Few teams could handle Bobby Doyle ('I loved to see a corner back coming with a fat arse and big thighs!'), but Kerry could.

(Dessie Brennan of Laois once contained Doyle by twisting a wodge of Doyle's shirt around his fist and holding him in place for an entire half. When the second half started, Brennan went to grab the same swath of cloth. Doyle demurred and asked of Dessie if they mightn't actually play football in the second half. 'I'll be done with ya in just over half an hour,' said Dessie, 'and sure you can do what you like then.')

Ger O'Keeffe, who once placed behind John Treacy in a cross-country race, had been a prominent schoolboy athlete. He seemed made for the job of tailing Doyle around the plains of Croke Park. He tracked Doyle everywhere that day. Bobby Doyle ended up with a point in his credit ledger. Ger O'Keeffe ended up with one, too.

'You start looking at the bench when the corner back has scored the same as you have,' says Doyle.

'My point! It straggled over or, as I like to say, just missed the top corner of the net,' says O'Keeffe.

So Doyle was neutralized. So too was David Hickey. Mick O'Dwyer still hadn't figured out that Ogie Moran was a lucky charm when playing at centre forward, so Ogie began the day marking Hickey and performed superbly. It was that sort of game, swirling and unpredictable.

Seanie Walsh got an old-style full forward's goal, catching a fifty, swivelling and scoring. The score sealed the quality of Kerry's first-half performance. By the time they could smell the half-time tea brewing, Kerry were five clear. Dublin pickpocketed a couple of points before half-time but the current of the game was with Kerry.

Hanahoe did the talking in the Dublin dressing room. Nobody sat down; the energy coursing through the room was too great. When Hanahoe stopped for a pause they began roaring at each other and then bang, they were through the door.

Kerry were in a more difficult position. They had been the

better team in the first half. They had never been led. O'Dwyer
asked for the same again. They looked at their manager, the man
who had made them. He needed this one as badly as they did.

Sometimes you don't get what you need. From the throw-in
for the second half Kevin Moran reproduced his favourite parlour
trick. He burst through the Kerry defence, he had the goal at his
mercy, but he shot weakly at Paudie O'Mahoney.

No score, but Croke Park was ablaze.

'People look back,' says Jim Brogan, 'and they say the football
wasn't that great, but the context and the intensity made it different
from any other game. This was two teams at the absolute limit. A
history of this extraordinary rivalry came down to that day, and
for both teams that was the moment they were at their best. It was
the rubber game.'

The ending was like a crazy chase scene, played out purely on
adrenalin and nerve. Dublin took the lead for the first time as the
game went into the final quarter. Kerry flamed back. Dublin
levelled. Kerry were to lead three times and get caught each time.
Dublin led twice and got caught.

SEAN DOHERTY: The last ten minutes of it. That was exciting. It
was batten down the hatches from our end. Everything was
rolling somehow. I just remember John Egan scoring a fabulous
point to put Kerry two ahead again.

GAY O'DRISCOLL: The main thing for me against Kerry was that
when a Kerry half back looked up I had to be in front of John
Egan. When he got the ball, all you could do was foul him.

He was very quiet. I remember that day, it was funny. John was
such a great player but he had no intensity. We lined out. He
came out and shook hands and just said, 'Big crowd today, Gay.'
He won this ball with less than ten minutes left and I hit him
with everything. He just seemed to bounce off the floor, look
up and score.

JOHN EGAN: It was an instinctive thing. Gayo would always give
you a good wallop, in fairness to him. He hit me. I got up. It
was rage more than anything. I said, I'll punish him now.

TOMMY DRUMM: Egan had scored a point. Kerry were rushing out after scoring the point, they had won the game. They believed they had won it. I could see it on their faces. I looked around and we didn't know we were beaten. I couldn't see anything on the faces that said we were beaten, there was just this same look of confidence like Kerry had.

Egan's point had put Kerry two ahead. A glance at the clock showed six minutes remaining.

Brian Mullins hit a lineball to Anton O'Toole, who was playing the game of his life.

ANTON O'TOOLE: I hit what wasn't a great pass. Somebody, John O'Keeffe I think, got a hand to it and it fell to Tony.

DAVID HICKEY: Tony just slipped it to me and I couldn't miss. In that moment the goal just seemed so big.

Hickey couldn't miss. He rounded off most evenings in Parnell Park rifling balls at Paddy Cullen from precisely that distance while Cullen scoffed disdainfully at the chance of Hickey ever getting a clear shot from there. It was the goal which Hickey was destined to score. Dublin were one up.

JIM BROGAN: Of all the games I can remember that time in the dugout, when David got that goal, Lorcan Redmond was there and I remember lifting him right off the ground. It was Manila, Frazier and Muhammad Ali. They slugged each other. Both teams thought they were going to win right to the end. That's what made it so phenomenal.

JOHN O'KEEFFE: I just remember when David Hickey scored we still believed. We went at them again. There was nothing in it and four or five minutes left.

JOHN EGAN: They hit us on the break. They got a superb goal. We went on all-out attack. There was indecision over a free. Ogie Moran went over, put it down and went for the score. Ball dropped short. Sean Doherty went up on his own.

SEAN WALSH: I was sort of standing in front of Sean Doherty. Ogie's kick came in at speed and I never really got off the ground to challenge Sean for it. I just saw him bursting out with the ball a second later.

SEAN DOHERTY: I caught it and fell over Kevin Moran on the way down. If you look at the film, you can see Mullins there, shouting at me to bring it out. You'd think the way people talk about it that it was the only time in my life I'd ever caught a football!

It was time to drive it home. We had the foot on the back of their neck. Kerry were like that. You took the foot off the back of their neck, and next they would be on their knees and next they'd be looking you in the face and you'd have to start again.

JOHN EGAN: Ger Keeffe went for it. He got hit with a wallop. The ball spilled. O'Hehir could see there was a goal coming. On the commentary you can feel that he has a sense of it.

PAT O'NEILL: When I look at it again, Bobby Doyle won a ball at that stage that he had no right to win.

GER O'KEEFFE: Myself and Bobby covered every blade of grass in Croke Park that day. We were contesting a clearance by the Dublin defence at that stage. Bobby was a corner forward and I was supposedly a corner back.

JOHN EGAN: They hit us in a wave. Brogan came straight through the middle.

BERNARD BROGAN: That summer I worked in New Ross for three months or so. They were building an oil rig down there. To finish, we took the rig to France. When it came back it was offshore, so I worked offshore for a period. When I scored the goal O'Hehir said I'd been drilling for oil and now I was drilling for goals. I suppose it was better than saying I was an engineer! The goal was fairly straightforward.

PAT SPILLANE: It was a cracking goal and credit to the Dubs, but I'd say our defence wouldn't think so. We were torn right down the middle.

PAUDIE O'MAHONEY: That last one of the goals was deflected.

It came off Ger Power's fingers. The press never agreed with
me about that. I got bad press over even saying it.

PÁIDÍ Ó SÉ: We were just hit with a goal and then another goal,
and the game was over. You could hardly write the script for it,
it ended so suddenly. I think they put a point on right at the
end, and then it was done.

Dublin won by five points.

For two players in particular that second half was an extraordinary
climax to epic careers. Tony Hanahoe and Jimmy Keaveney had
started off in the Dublin team on the same afternoon in 1964. They
had sat along the sidelines of Croke Park together on hundreds of
afternoons through their youth. School friends, clubmates, Dubs.

The goals that Dublin got that afternoon were a tribute to the
maturity of play of Hanahoe and Keaveney. In each instance Tony
Hanahoe had possession and did the right thing, the selfless thing,
with the ball.

'The seventy-seven victory was the zenith,' he says. 'I remember
it very well. It was the way to win. A bit of aplomb, character and
style.'

And Keaveney? 'My job that day was to take Johnno away from
the square. Usually I played off the square a little bit to this side, a
little bit to that side, but playing off the square. That day I was
asked to take him away.'

And in the outer perimeters of the frame for each goal you can
see Keaveney executing the plan.

First goal: Tommy Drumm drop-kicks a glorious diagonal pass
which leads to John McCarthy's goal. Keaveney is sprinting out
towards centre field with John O'Keeffe in tow as the ball flies in.

Second goal: As Hickey shoots to the net, at the end of a move
which comes down the right centre of midfield, Keaveney jogs
into view from the prairie, way out on the left. He had been
pulling John O'Keeffe out to the side when O'Keeffe fatally got a
hand to the ball and put it in the path of Tony Hanahoe.

Third: Hanahoe feeds Brogan. Brogan shoots. Jimmy Keaveney

comes jogging in from the far right to celebrate. John O'Keeffe is still shadowing him.

There are the dreary sciolists who sit in front of videos to slo-mo through the afternoon, counting the errors and tsk-tsking at every stray pass. They miss the essence of the game. It is not ballet, it is not a thing to be judged on its beauty and contrived aesthetics. 1977 carries the splendour of context, the perfect climax to a sizzling rivalry. It was a passionate helter-skelter game that consumed seventy minutes of an August afternoon but felt no longer than a half-time break. The storyline was jagged but romantic, thrilling and unconventional. It had to end before you knew how it ended.

'When I look at it,' says Gay O'Driscoll, 'I genuinely think it was the greatest game of football ever played. It had everything.'

'I notice,' says Jack O'Shea, 'that a lot of the greatest games of football ever played are ones that Kerry lose!'

'It was exciting, I suppose,' says Mick O'Dwyer, 'but I think the pro-Dublin media made a lot about it!'

The buzz of summer reached its height that afternoon. Pat O'Neill was working in Dr Steevens' Hospital at the time.

'I went down to Meagher's that evening after the game. Everyone was agog. The people were spilling across the Bridge from Ballybough to Clonliffe Road. Technically, they were all drinking in Meagher's. You could hear the hum as you walked towards the crowd. There was a gang of young doctors from Steevens' who had come to see the game. Friends of Dave Hickey's and of mine. From being a Protestant, genteel establishment it had become a bastion of Gaelic games because of us two gurriers who drank and cavorted their way through Steevens' and all the well-heeled Trinity graduates.

'What struck me was how wound up they all were. Paul Byrne, a vascular surgeon who's now down in Limerick, said to me "Pat, that was poetry in motion."

'It struck me for the first time, was it that good?'

At the other end of Clonliffe Road, Robbie Kelleher took his new wife Florence into Tom Kennedy's pub. From the roadway to the bar people stood and applauded them in.

'Luckily Florence was well versed in GAA. My father was there, too. It was a great experience. A perfect day.'

Tony Hanahoe, who had fashioned it all, drove to Garristown in north County Dublin, just looking for the solitude in which to consume a long, slow, quiet pint, some tranquillity to help him absorb it all. He sat and thought the day through and finally got into his car and drove back to carnival town.

Weeks later, Dublin beat Armagh to win their third All-Ireland in four years. Afterwards the players repaired as usual to Listowel, there to enjoy the races, the drink and the adulation.

By the end of that summer Kevin Moran was a national celebrity. The previous year he had won an All-Star at centre back after just two games playing in the position. His strength, his mobility and his aggressive game made him a huge part of Heffernan's team. He was young, rode a motorcycle and was close to graduating as an accountant with Ollie Freaney's company. He was different.

His brother Brendan reminds him of a story sometimes. The 1976 All-Ireland final seemed to come around just weeks after Moran made the Dublin team. The family home suddenly fizzed with excitement.

On the days of big games, Sean Doherty would call to Moran's house to take him on to Croke Park or wherever the team were meeting. On the day of the All-Ireland final Moran was having lunch while he waited for Doherty. Neighbours and friends came in to watch the new star feeding and to wish him luck. A good friend of Brendan Moran's was in the house, too.

'He often said to Brendan afterwards that he couldn't believe the dinner I had before the game. Doc is picking me up at half one. This is quarter to one. The Ma is coming out with the roasts, the boiled spuds, cabbage, carrots, gravy. He said he'd never seen anything like it. And I just sat there and demolished it and the Ma trying to get extra into me. Everyone's looking and then my ma disappeared out to the kitchen and comes back in with a massive trifle. Because I'm playing in the All-Ireland! So I eat most of that, too. Then the bell rings and it's the Doc and I'm gone.

Just carnage left on the table. I didn't know anything better. And me ma would be giving me a little extra because I was playing a game.'

In 1977, while the racing was on, himself and Bobby Doyle stayed in nearby Ballybunion.

Doyle and Moran had become good friends. Doyle had noticed early on that, as a result of a fine underage swimming career, Moran had good upper-body strength.

'I had a good sidestep and body swerve, and when Moran came I used to take him aside on the wing and try to get by him. My belly would be in bits. His arms were unbelievable. You'd go one way and try to get back and he'd hit you. He had arms of steel. We'd spend quarter of an hour at this and he wouldn't go back an inch.'

In Ballybunion in the early autumn of 1977 the work was done and the days were long and dreamy, the evenings were long and frothy.

One balmy night, both friends had some drink aboard and Doyle looked at Moran and the younger man started to cry.

'1977 was a specially happy year and I was very pally with Kevin. He just started to cry. I said, "Come on, come outside." We went out and we were sitting outside on a big kerb. We were well jarred. I said, "What's wrong, Kev?"

'"I'll miss all this."

'"You won't, sure this will go on for a few years yet."

'"No. Manchester United are looking for me."

'"Jaysus, Kev. How much have you had? C'mon. You'll be all right."

'"No. They wanted me to go last year and I wouldn't go."'

Moran and Doyle went walking down on the beach in Ballybunion. Doyle asked his friend, what could he lose? He had the chance of a lifetime. It either worked out or he came home to a long career with the Dubs.

'I remember telling Bobby,' says Moran. 'He was supportive and I spoke to a few of the lads and Kevin afterwards and they were the same. I remember thinking it was over, though. I was actually only going over for a trial. There was every chance of them just saying no, but it was a huge emotional wrench for me. I always felt that all I wanted to do in England was play the once. I wanted to know, could I do it. I told myself then, I'd come back.

'When I was asked first of all, Dave Sexton and myself were in a car coming back from a training session. He said, "I'd like you to sign a two-and-a-half-year contract with Manchester United." My heart actually fell. The words I said back to him were, "You're joking me." I wasn't expecting this.'

He took three weeks to think about it. He went from day to day. One day it was yes, the next day it was no. In the end it wasn't money, contracts or football, just the thought that he'd always ask himself, could he have done it.

'The lads I spoke to said none of the team would begrudge it. The news broke on a Friday. We were training. I was going to tell them on the Saturday. I felt desperate. That broke my heart.

'When I went to United I was still living in Parnell Park for a long, long time. Matches were different, but in training if I was after somebody I'd picture a Kerry shirt on his back and I'd run faster. I told meself I was here to play the one game and go back. I didn't look at it as a job or a living. I lived in Parnell Park and beating Kerry was the biggest thing in life.'

Life never brought him back for good. A long and epic soccer career followed. Manchester United, Sporting Gijon, Blackburn Rovers and Ireland. He ran forever.

And yet . . .

'The only games I would ever watch at home are the 1976 final and the 1977 semi-final. One or other, regularly. Sometimes I watch the first twenty minutes of the Ireland v. England game at Wembley in 1991. The twenty-five minutes before Niall Quinn got the goal. It's worth watching just to see it, but apart from that the only thing I would ever take out and sit down and watch would be 1976 and 1977. Sometimes I'd shed a tear. That'll tell you something.'

Years later, when he was a star with Manchester United, Kevin Moran would fill out one of those vox pop questionnaires for the young readers of *Shoot!* magazine. In answer to the question regarding his favourite holiday destination, he baffled many of his audience by answering simply with one word. Ballybunion.

15

I remember watching Kerry in their semi-final of 1978 and looking at Eoin Liston. I said, Jesus, is that the best they can come up with? How wrong can you be!

Robbie Kelleher

Eoin Liston's father had a bar in Ballybunion. Eoin was lazy and didn't enjoy serving drink and changing barrels. In fact, he hated it.

One day, Mick O'Dwyer asked Ogie Moran, was there any big fellas about in his neck of the woods, and Ogie suggested Liston. When he was contacted, Liston thought quickly. He was raw and slow and the Kerry training sessions were legendarily hard. Then again, while he was away training he wouldn't have to tend bar. He said he'd go.

There's a story they tell about Mick O'Dwyer and Liston and their subsequent friendship. In fact there are many stories, but one in particular makes them laugh. It illustrates O'Dwyer's feral competitiveness and Liston's quiet sufferings all in one go.

Liston hadn't been part of the panel for long when O'Dwyer noticed that the new boy had quick hands and a distinct football intelligence. Liston had no underage career with Kerry and had arrived virtually as a secret weapon. If the excess tonnage could be whittled off, well, O'Dwyer would have for himself exactly what he craved: a tall target-man full forward.

Hey presto! O'Dwyer still affects surprise at the coincidence which led to Liston landing a job as a science teacher in, of all places, Waterville Vocational School. In Waterville, Liston's gentle metabolism came into the orbit of O'Dwyer's awesome industry.

'People always said I was one of Dwyer's pets,' laughs Liston.

'They didn't see the extra stuff that I had to do. I played football, soccer, badminton, squash, handball, everything down there with him. He was like a brother to me. I'd finish school at twenty to four and he'd be waiting over at the golf course for me to finish. Four-ball for nine holes. Eat. Out for a few kicks. Then in for a game of badminton.

'His seniority made him the referee in everything. If he lost, we'd play the point again. I'd often be ten points or so ahead of him and need another two or three, and he'd come back and beat me. He had an Indian sign. We had great fun and great banter together.'

O'Dwyer has similarly warm memories.

'When Bomber was in Waterville he never got peace from me. We had round-robin competitions. Handball, badminton, tennis. A friend called Donal Brosnan would be kicking the ball out between myself and the Bomber, and the two of us going up to win it for hours. The Bomber used to say to me, "You might be able to take them now, but in ten years' time you won't have a hope." He was a lazy guy. We played a lot of golf, too.'

'My first day playing golf with him, I got an idea of what he was like,' remembers Liston. 'My father had dropped me down to Waterville. I was in digs. Micko took me out golfing with Peter Huggert from the Butler Arms. I'd walk out to my ball, two or three times it was plugged. Dwyer'd stand on it for devilment.'

Everything O'Dwyer and Liston did had a competitive element to it. Liston was years younger, but it scarcely mattered. One of Dwyer's favourite tortures was a three-and-a-half-mile run out along the golf course. Up hill and down hill, on sand and soft turf. It had everything as a workout and the finish was perfect, a flat three-hundred-yard sprint towards a white post which served as the finishing line.

A couple of weeks before the 1979 All-Ireland final O'Dwyer had Liston out for a gallop. This particular evening happened to come after a long series of runs where O'Dwyer would tear away on the final sprint and exultantly touch the white pole while Liston struggled along behind, cursing.

So this evening Liston had just about had enough, and when they got to the flat area he decided to surprise O'Dwyer and break early and go flat out, three hundred yards to the post. He could hear the exclamation of surprise from O'Dwyer's lips as he registered the break.

Liston had been saving himself for this. He had huge strides and a reservoir of determination, built up from a series of defeats. He pumped away, feeling the early lead stretching as O'Dwyer bided his time, hoping perhaps that the big man would tire.

He kept going. The white post was getting nearer and nearer. There was still no sign of O'Dwyer's breath on his neck. He was going to win.

Then suddenly Liston's ankle buckled under him. He let out a yelped curse and tumbled to the ground. The player who O'Dwyer had decided would be the pivot of his Kerry team lay, crumpled, on the grass, two weeks before an All-Ireland final.

And almost instantly Liston was aware of the Doppler effect of O'Dwyer's footfalls nearing him and then O'Dwyer leaping over him and his footfalls receding into the distance. He heard the roar, saw the clenched fist.

Then O'Dwyer, a winner once more, jogged back out to where Liston lay and carried him on his shoulders into the Waterville locker room, where he tended to the ankle with cold water and ice.

O'Dwyer was indomitable. Not everybody knew it, though.

After the 1977 semi-final, some people in Kerry felt they had swallowed enough. They felt revulsion in their stomachs. Kerry were playing this new fancy-dan football but getting beaten by the fanciest dans of all. In 1977 they had been beaten at midfield for the second time in succession. Men were spinning in their graves. Dr Jim Brosnan, son of Con, brought the weight of his lineage to the debate when he criticized the team in the weeks after the semi-final. With the floor open, the contributions flowed in. It was agreed that hand-passing was an abomination.

The Kerry team who had come home looking golden in the

blaze of bonfires two years previously were now derided. Years later, when Páidí Ó Sé would describe Kerry supporters as 'the roughest type of fucking animals you could meet', he wasn't being gratuitously unkind. He meant that Kerry is the toughest constituency to play to, that it demands the most and offers the least loyalty. Kerry is La Scala. Appreciative of perfection, riled by earnest mediocrity.

There was a putsch designed to get rid of Gerald McKenna as County Chairman. If McKenna had walked the plank, O'Dwyer would have followed.

'I might have gone anyway,' O'Dwyer says, 'only for the heave that was put on to get rid of Gerald. If he went, I was gone. I felt they were getting at Gerald to get to me, so I went and backed McKenna to the hilt.'

It was close enough, but McKenna survived. O'Dwyer had only set his easel. He was yet to paint his masterpiece.

Kerry went on and won seven All-Irelands after that, establishing themselves without rival as the greatest team in the game's history.

O'Dwyer resumed with new selectors. Liam Higgins was an astute analyst and a good brain and he had fresh ideas about the team. Joe Keohane was a tough idealist. Once Keohane was running for Sinn Féin in north Kerry and he consulted with John B. Keane as to what his chances were. John B. was frank in the roundabout way of Kerrymen: 'Joe, if you get the Jewish vote in Knocknagoshel I think you have a chance.'

Joe didn't care. He was a tough man and felt that Kerry needed a transfusion of the same toughness. He would have his say. Bernie O'Callaghan from Ballybunion came on board, as did Pat O'Shea from Killarney.

Things changed.

Pat Spillane was teaching in Listowel at the time. One evening he and Jim Deenihan were walking along the beach at Ballybunion and they came up to the Castle Hotel to buy a paper.

'We read in the *Evening Press* that we were dropped. Not even told. I went to Dwyer and asked. He's a rogue. He told me he wasn't at that meeting of the selectors.'

Deenihan got a different sense.

'After 1977 a number of us were dropped. Spillane, myself. Paud Mahoney and Ger Power. He thought my injuries were all in the head. I think he'd run out of patience.'

'There was a change of selectors,' says Paudie O'Mahoney. 'It was 3–2 for Charlie [Nelligan] now in goals. I wasn't getting a look-in. I decided I was going to leave, but Dwyer felt I was good for the team because I was a good talker in the dressing room. It was decided to give me every second game in the league and fuck the championship, we'd see what happened. I stayed on.

'He'd be cute as a fox, Dwyer. He'd tell you he was bowing to the powers. Nothing he could do. There were other times he told me to go home and tell the family that I was playing on Sunday. I was coming down from Dublin at the time, and I'd say, fuck this, I'm sick of you telling me lies, I don't want you telling me lies any more. He'd say, "No, no, ring your mam and tell her you're on the team." You'd get the *Irish Press* the next day, and you'd be sixteen. And still you'd go back for more!'

Things began to change quickly for both teams. With Kevin Moran gone to Old Trafford, the centre of the Dublin defence gaped as invitingly as an empty eight-lane highway.

Many were tried, many were found wanting.

A lot of hope was vested that spring in the shape of Andy Roche, one of those players whose life on the fringes was to make him a cause célèbre.

Roche had pedigree. A grandson of Luke O'Toole, the first General Secretary of the GAA, he was a schoolboy prodigy, acknowledged as the best midfielder in the county during his teenage years.

He ran on to the reefs of GAA politics early. Roche played with Whitehall Colmcilles through the juvenile grades and was one of the youngest members of a successful team which won virtually everything as it came through the ranks. When they got to the level of first-year minors, their coach was told that somebody else was taking the squad.

'We were divided geographically between Beaumont and Whitehall. Most of us from Beaumont just left. I was one of the few who joined St Vincent's.'

He did well with St Vincent's and looked set for a glittering senior career. He had one vice, however. Soccer! As a schoolboy he attended St Aidan's CBS, the school that produced Liam Brady. The culture that had nourished Brady threw up a wave of talented youngsters in Whitehall in the years after his move to Arsenal. These kids played hurling and football for Whitehall Colmcilles, and they played soccer for St Kevin's Boys. The Ban had disappeared and a kid could pursue his dreams in whatever language he liked.

One weekend there was a clash in Andy Roche's diary. A cup game for St Kevin's. A championship match for St Vincent's. He weighed up where he was needed most and decided to play soccer. Vincent's would get by without him, no doubt; he'd apologize for his unavoidable absence and everyone would get on with life.

The soccer match was played in Ellenfield, the public park in Whitehall. He doesn't remember at what point he realized that the St Vincent's championship game was about to take place on the pitch right next door, but he remembers Brinsley Lowth, a great monumental slab of a man, walking up and down the sideline of the soccer pitch, holding aloft a St Vincent's jersey, urging him to come off the field and put it on.

His St Vincent's career was over. So, too, for a while, was his Gaelic football career. He went out for the trials for the Dublin minors that year, but St Vincent's held sway on the selection committee. He got exactly a minute on the field at the end of the first afternoon's trials and wasn't asked back.

He was unforgiven. The scale of what he was missing out on didn't become apparent for a while. He went and played soccer for Shelbourne. Did well for three years or so, but the Dubs had changed the landscape of the city. He had a row with Shelbourne during his final exams, and by late 1977 he was back playing football with Whitehall. Kevin Moran's departure to England left a window open. There were many who remembered his underage prowess. He played a challenge game against Down at centre back before Christmas 1977. He was rusty and his timing was shot but these things come back. Don't they? Meanwhile, the landlords withheld the tenancy on the number six jersey.

As usual, Dublin reached the league final that spring. Alan Larkin had been playing through the regular league campaign at centre back as Roche worked on his game. In a challenge against Armagh, Alan Larkin's shin connected most unpleasantly with the knee of an Armagh player. A lot of people in the ground heard the cracking sound which Larkin's shin made.

Roche was brought in for the league semi-final against Laois. Dublin won, but Tom Prendergast gave him a bumpier ride than the scoreline suggested. Still no lease. Jim Brogan played in the final. Roche went back to biding his time.

After that league final other things changed, too.

Kevin Heffernan came back. If there was a touch of the autocrat about the manner of his return, Tony Hanahoe was graciousness itself.

'We won the National League 77–78,' Hanahoe says. 'After the National League Kevin indicated that he would like to be involved again. Genuinely I thought that if he did want to be involved again, he was entitled to be. I'm not sure what way it went down with the players. There was a bit of division, but not between he and I. That's the way it was.'

It was agreed that Heffernan would come back and that Hanahoe would continue to be part of the selection committee. In the meantime Dublin went to America for another All-Star trip. Heffernan stayed at home, pondering the summer ahead.

New York, New York. Dublin were fitting in a game with Kerry to raise funds for Sister Consilio Fitzgerald's rehabilitation centre. Kerry were coming out, and those Kerry players not involved in the All-Stars' trip were going home the next day.

They have two versions of what happened in Gaelic Park on that May Sunday. In one version, the relationship between the two sides tilted irrevocably. In the other, they played a scrappy, dirty game and forgot all about it.

What is agreed upon is that Kerry were nettlesome and muscular that day. Joe Keohane's bonnet was still swarming with bees over the manner of Kerry's defeat in the previous year's All-Ireland semi-final. He was particularly scalded about Tim Kennelly, who had taken a punch from Jimmy Keaveney that day and had lain on the ground afterwards, perhaps hoping for a free.

Keohane believed that retaliation was for getting in first. Time and again he exhorted the Kerry players that there would be no lying down. Kerry would stand up for themselves and they would stand up together. This was a chance to lay down a marker.

'We felt,' says Jimmy Deenihan, 'that Dublin blew us out of it a bit in the previous two years. They were stronger. They intimidated us. There was this perception. Physically they were stronger than us. That was the perception. That had to be dispelled.'

There were other issues, too. Clobber. Fashion. Gah Couture.

'We were mad jealous of them,' says Eoin Liston. 'Mad. They had the suits, they'd been out there for a while and they were heading to Los Angeles and San Francisco. They'd tans and they looked a million dollars. We had these red jumpers. We looked like hicks.'

And there was the weight of history. In 1974, when Paddy Cullen had been out to America as a replacement All-Star, he had written a magazine piece in which he mentioned his disappointment with Gaelic Park as a venue. His criticism didn't sit well with John Kerry O'Donnell, the godfather of Gaelic Park.

'I said that Gaelic Park was a kip. I slated it. It got me into hot water with Kerry O'Donnell. I got sent pictures from which I'd been cut out with a scissors. I was told not to come back to New York. The showers there were disgraceful, we often left in the dirt we were in. Stuff like that was unnecessary. I never felt that welcome there afterwards.'

The day of the challenge game, the skies issued a deluge of Old Testament proportions. The teams felt that the game would surely be cancelled, but Hanahoe, mindful as ever of duty, herded them to Gaelic Park anyway. They arrived in the south Bronx, riding a fleet of taxis which they kept waiting till they ascertained whether there would be a game or not.

There were a few dozen spectators in the ground and the local officials were eager that the game be played even though their pitch was now submerged and the rain was showing no signs of easing. It was agreed between the two teams that the ordeal should be done with as quickly as possible. Play the first half, turn around, play the second half, vanish.

Seamus Aldridge of Kildare was the referee. He threw up the ball for sixty minutes of mayhem.

'The dirtiest fucking match ever,' says Paddy Reilly, who played a lot of his football in Dublin's north county and could thus be said to know his stuff. 'I got banjoed by Tommy Doyle, who then was banjoed by Pat O'Neill, who got a belt off the Bomber. The Bomber got up and got sent off.'

The Bomber corroborates Reilly's account.

'I was captain that day because Ogie was injured and didn't travel. It was lashing rain and we were out there, frustrated and jealous, and playing as if it was an All-Ireland final. They played like it was an exhibition.

'I was marking Jim Brogan. I was on the forty. Tommy Doyle was getting a bit of a hammering. I went to Tommy at half-time and said, "Are you afraid of that fella [Paddy Reilly]?"

'"Fuck off," he says.

'I said, "Jesus, I'll be straight over, you don't have to take that. Just say."

'"Fuck off, Bomber," he says.

'The ball was thrown and I look over and Tommy is flaking with your man. I ran straight over. Jesus I was nearly killed for getting involved. I had boot marks up here. I felt the whole Dublin team was after me. I was sent off.'

And that wasn't even the highlight. At half-time Kerry broke the agreement they had made and bolted for the dressing rooms. Dublin stood in the middle of the pitch like beasts of the field. When it became clear that Kerry weren't coming out again in a hurry somebody was dispatched to get the Dublin dressing room opened. The messenger was told that no key could be found. Kerry re-emerged in time, refreshed and wearing new kit. The pitch was muddier than the Somme. Dublin were livid. They were also purple with the cold.

Suddenly everything which lay beneath the surface of a respectful relationship between the sides began to bubble up.

John McCarthy had always found Jimmy Deenihan very difficult to deal with. Macker always says that he understands how Deenihan ended up in politics. He was too smart for anything else.

'He was an absolute gentleman. I'm sure he still is. There's something about knowing a fella, though, and he knew me. He could get into my head.'

Every year in Croke Park, right before the National Anthem, it would start. Deenihan could niggle a good player to death, as Jimmy Barry Murphy might attest; but with McCarthy he was killing him softly with his compliments.

'Jesus Christ, Johnboy,' Deenihan would say, 'you look like a greyhound. You'll tear me apart today. No doubt about it, John, look at the shape of you. A thoroughbred greyhound.'

And he'd pinch McCarthy's waist.

'Not an ounce of fat on you, boy.'

Macker would turn red.

'How do I answer that? What could I say? Usually I just said, "Ah fuck off, Jimmy." He deflated me straight away every time I went out. He'd just keep talking bullshit. I wished I hated him. It would have suited me better. He was a guy that wasn't malicious. He'd pull and drag, but that was it, He'd come crashing into you. He was all corners and elbows but he'd be helping you up. "Sorry, John, are you all right there, boy?"

'He wasn't malicious but he was good. I could hit any of the rest of them happily, but in my mind the idea of slapping Deenihan was wrong. He'd mess with your head. He'd slap the ball away from you. He'd talk and talk.'

Macker and Deenihan were paired off yet again in New York. When the umpteenth mêlée erupted, Macker remembers eagerly running half the length of the pitch to get involved.

'There was this big guy with a beard whom I had never seen before. I saw him draw a dig. I said, I'll go for him. I went in fast and slipped, and my feet went up in the air. I kicked the Bomber a beauty, entirely unintentionally.'

All of which was in keeping with the near-slapstick nature of the violence as it unfolded. McCarthy got up and was about to pile in when he felt somebody's hand seizing his wrist. Deenihan!

'Jesus Christ, I thought you were fast with the fists, John, but you're like lightning with the boot. Calm down, calm down now like a good man.'

Macker was furious, but Deenihan had a spell over him.

'You'll miss the whole championship, John. This is only a Mickey Mouse match. Calm down.'

Macker started thinking that maybe Deenihan was right. He walked back to his position with Deenihan.

'Next thing, the game is back on and he gives me a shove and he's off the other way, chasing a ball against Pat O'Neill.'

O'Neill got first to the ball where it landed with a plop. He bent to lift it, stood up and and got plonked down into mud. He thinks he still had the ball. Jimmy Deenihan reckons it squirted loose.

O'Neill had a sense of grievance, nourished not just by the afternoon's proceedings but also by the previous year's semi-final.

'I said to myself, I know who this is and this is the chance I'm looking for. Payback for an incident that happened in the 1977 semi-final when I got taken out quietly. I caught him perfectly as I was coming up. Did the job. The rain was running down, there was mud all over his face and suddenly there was blood coming down.

'When I looked again, I realized I had the wrong man. I'd thought it was Páidí. I walked straight off before Aldridge could send me off.'

Deenihan is philosophical about the miscarriage of Wild West justice.

'The ball went spinning. I pulled and connected. Out of frustration he hit me. We were in a bar, down in Midtown, that night. I met Fran Ryder. Pat was there. I was feeling a bit sorry for myself. I was told that Pat was sorry, he thought I was Páidí. I just said, "Fuck it, I'm taking that fella's belts all my life."'

In the moment when Deenihan's nose was sent on its journey towards his ear he wasn't quite so mellow, though. He was in a state of shock. He walked back to his corner to where Macker was standing, gaping in disbelief.

'His nose is spread all over his face,' says Macker. 'It's not just broken, it's over at his ear. He's covered in mud and blood and it's lashing from the heavens. And what does he do? He runs over to me. He says, "Jesus, McCarthy, is my nose broke?"

'"Is it broke, Jimmy? It's all over your face, my friend!"'

Deenihan accepted the inevitable and left the field.

O'Neill meanwhile had walked straight off the field and was standing inside the wire up at the end of Gaelic Park where Lefty Devine used to do his match commentaries. There was a bit of abuse coming over the fence from the crowd.

O'Neill stood and watched the game until a local official came running down the line towards him. He had a Kerry accent with the New York intonation.

'Jesus, come over to the dressing room, the man that's injured says he can't breathe.'

'Would you ever fuck off,' said O'Neill. 'I came out here to play football, not to practise medicine.'

'Well,' came the answer, 'you're doing a bad job of both of them.'

And from the spectators' side of the fencing came a Dublin accent, the owner having heard the exchange. 'Go away and tell Deenihan he's just seen a doctor.'

Deenihan and Pat Spillane both got broken noses that afternoon. They had them repaired in a hospital in the Bronx. It was a small price to pay. Kerry won the game easily and the majority of the Kerry players felt that they had proved a point.

Tony Hanahoe feels that 'no Kerry player needed that game to make a man of him', but Jimmy Deenihan feels it was part of a process of growing up and standing up: 'We came away with confidence.'

David Hickey makes perhaps the most salient point. 'I know they reckon that it was the weekend in New York and that match which changed everything. It's a pity there was no weekend we could have gone on to make us all five years younger!'

16

Anecdotally a lot of things are said. Let me answer you by saying
that in front of 70,000 people when things are going wrong,
there is nothing in the manual.

Tony Hanahoe

Jack O'Shea and Charlie Nelligan roomed together always from the
time they were minors with Kerry till the end of their epic careers.

Each has fond memories of the other's tics and traits. Charlie,
oddly for such a good-humoured man, was nervous before games.
Jacko remembers having to slap his friend across the face in the
dressing room on the morning of the 1977 All-Ireland Under-21
semi-final in Carrick-on-Shannon.

On All-Ireland final weekends, when they were senior players
together, they fell into the comfortable habits of an elderly couple.
On Saturday night Jacko would go out and buy all the papers, and
as Nelligan would be trying to sleep he would browse through
them, looking for something negative written about himself.

As soon as he found something which could be considered
vaguely pejorative he was happy, and so was Nelligan. Jacko had
his motivation. Sleep could follow.

On the morning of an All-Ireland, Nelligan would awaken,
wired with nerves. They would push the two beds together, and
Jacko would take the four pillows and throw them in turn at the
wall as Nelligan dived about on the beds, saving them.

Having thus reassured his friend, Jacko would leave and head
for a game of pitch-and-putt. Usually some subs would tag along,
and the highlight for Jacko would be if they met a gang of Dubliners
at the course. The slagging settled him for the day.

Jacko and Charlie put themselves somewhere in the middle of the spectrum in terms of nerves and general fidgetiness. Páidí Ó Sé, crippled by the piseogs and gripped by the nerves, would be at one end, whipping himself up into a state of religious ecstasy by throw-in. John Egan, at the other extreme, never felt his pulse quicken. The passionate speeches, the banging of tables, the running through doors, the vows to die for the colours and the county, they all left Egan a little bemused. Football was football. You went out and enjoyed it. You came back in again.

Ogie Moran and John Egan were in the old Skylon Hotel in Dublin once and heading out to Mass on a Sunday morning. As they were passing out the hotel door they spotted the Ulster Railway Cup team holding a team meeting in the hotel lounge. The Kerrymen went to Mass and strolled back to the hotel. As they walked in, Egan was surprised to note that the Ulster team were still deep in conversation.

'Ogie,' he said, pointing at the northerners with a look of genuine mystification on his face, 'what could they be talking about all this time?'

Egan was a tonic to them all as the intensity boiled over before games.

Once, coming out on to the field for an All-Ireland final in Croke Park, he tapped Páidí Ó Sé on the shoulder. At that particular moment Ó Sé was almost radioactive with the tension.

'Páidí.'

'What?'

'Where are we going to go this evening?'

On All-Ireland final day, Jacko, who lived in Leixlip and who would have his car with him at the team hotel in Malahide, would always drive to Croke Park for the game, while the rest of the party went on the team bus. Jacko liked to drive, partly through superstition, partly because having John Egan in the car on the way to Croke Park just chilled everyone.

'John used to have a fella coming with him, a fella by the name of Willie. He'd have Willie sitting on his knee. I'd have five in the car and Wille would have to come with us. John would say, "Give us a song on the way in, Willie," and the singing would start up. I never saw Egan nervous.'

Willie Cronin of Gneeveguilla, near Rathmore in Sliabh Luachra, had spent many years in San Francisco, dreaming of home and singing about home. Egan reckoned he slept in a green-and-gold jersey. He was a fine singer and Egan was 'worried for the lads, they'd get so uptight. Willie would have a song and a laugh for them. We had the best of crack going to All-Irelands.'

Much as Dublin feared and respected Egan, those who know him estimate that you saw him at his best in his own environment. He was a Sneem man, or, as he might point out, a Tahilla man (Sneem being the domain of townies), and it was there that he thrived.

In Sneem you can sometimes imagine that the rest of the world is a million miles away, and when you do you can feel that the remoteness suited Egan's character. There they remember him for an exhibition of forward play which he gave in the final of the now-defunct Towns Cup in 1972. Sneem beat Finuge. Egan was marked by Jimmy Deenihan. He turned him inside out.

Sneem always struggled against the seepage of emigration and dipped to Division Three of the Kerry leagues on one occasion. Egan stuck with it, though. For a while he lined out with his brothers, Paddy, Jimmy and his own twin, Jerry. They were magical together until emigration took Paddy away.

The big day in Sneem every year is the seven-a-side competition for the Fr Teahan Cup. The local field down on the graveyard road is known as the Inch, and in this arena Egan has given his greatest performances. They'll always talk about the 1975 semi-final with the cocky townies, Austin Stack's of Tralee. Mikey Sheehy was held by John Shea. Michael Joe Burns got a flurry of Sneem scores in the final minutes. There were several heroes, but the combined posse of Ger O'Keeffe, John O'Keeffe and Ger Power couldn't put the cuffs on John Egan.

Sneem lost the final to a Thomond College team that included Pat Spillane, Brian Mullins and Ogie Moran. They lost to the same opposition in 1976, but in 1977 John, Jerry and Pat Egan were on the field together when Sneem won their own trophy for the first time.

'You'd have to see him in club level,' says Jack O'Shea, shaking his head as he recalls the wonder. 'The brothers were lethal when they got together. They'd get the ball and they'd be working under the one brain. Paddy would have played minor with me. He went to the States. The youngest. I got a great view of the Egans, especially John. He had magic. That was his greatest stage.'

Egan's coolness, his aggressive passivity, his genius, rescued them again and again. When they needed settling he would find the goal; when they needed rescuing he would be there with his hand outstretched.

It became such a commonplace to say that Egan was Kerry's most underrated player that Egan eventually became celebrated for being underrated. They owed him lots by then, but mainly they owed him for 1978, when his intervention saved them from humiliation and gave them time to summon the cavalry.

Dublin, old and sated now, had lingered for the three-in-a-row, the treble being a sort of Holy Grail to teams that rise towards greatness. For the third final in succession Dublin fielded precisely the same fifteen players, and they surprised even themselves by dominating the opening twenty-five minutes to a greater extent than either team had ever bossed any games between them. In hindsight, those opening passages seem slightly surreal. Dublin patiently added point to point, mainly through Jimmy Keaveney frees. The Hill braced itself for ecstasy, as if their favourites were delivering some sort of novel foreplay.

The Dublin forwards began to hear sweet music: Kerry defenders arguing with each other. With each free that Keaveney cashed in, the cost of fouling Dublin away from the square seemed to mount. Some Kerry players were shouting that the fouling had to stop. Others were inclined to the view that if the fouling stopped, the drive-by shootings at goal would increase.

For Eoin Liston, his first All-Ireland final was turning out to be less fun than he had hoped. On the Friday evening, two nights before the game, Ogie Moran had called into the Liston house in

Ballybunion. They'd said good luck to Liston's father and grand-mother, before heading off to Dublin early the next day.

Liston had a pleasant sense of well-being about the weekend. 'I knew we had a great team. It was my second year in there with them, looking at the guys first-hand. I thought this must have been a fantastic Dublin team to be considered in the same breath. I knew we'd run at a wall with our heads if we needed to. We were motivated. Mad for it.'

Now, on the Croke Park pitch there was no wall, just the Dubs flicking the red cape and Kerry charging, only to get a jab from the picador each time.

'They were so calm. I remember Keaveney selling a dummy, pulling it back and popping the ball over for a score. They were all playing out of position, just throwing the ball around. I looked up and it was six points to one. Any ball that came up to my end of the field, Sean Doherty had me cleaned. I ran out to the Hogan Stand at one stage, just to be making a bit of a shape. I got a bad dart in my knee. I tried to run it off. But I knew I'd done a bit of damage. I said, "Jesus, I'd better go off. They'll be wanting fifteen fit men the way this is going. I was trying to call Micko."'

O'Dwyer remembers his prodigy coming to the line. It was no time to start believing in the frailty of his players.

'In 1978 Bomber put up his hand. He said, "I can't move. Pain down my leg and a problem with my neck. I can't stir." Egan got the goal. He could have come off when he came to the line. I wouldn't let him come off. He got better after that pretty quick.'

Dublin were enjoying themselves in a light manner which had Kevin Heffernan worried and everybody else tickled. Both Dublin corner backs had scored points in the course of the journey to Croke Park that summer, and now Gay O'Driscoll and Robbie Kelleher cantered forward whenever they could. *Olé!*

Jimmy Keaveney remembers placing the ball for a fifty and notic-ing with a start that Robbie Kelleher was standing beside him.

'What the fuck are you doing here? Go back,' said Jimmy before calmly beginning his run-up.

Kelleher, the quiet, introspective philosopher of the team, seems an unlikely defendant for charges of showboating. He has stood in the dock, though.

'The Vincent's fellas always blame me for 1978. Maybe they're right! Not so much the famous goal, but the first goal. I think that was the crucial one. I would argue that I was chasing after Mikey Sheehy, he was up the pitch. Maybe. No point in arguing about it now. Maybe we did get carried away with ourselves. What can we do about it now, though?'

David Hickey remembers seeing the first signs of rot. 'Robbie Kelleher and Bobby Doyle arsing around with the ball on the Kerry fifty-yard line. I remember screaming for the ball and in any of the three or four years before that, it would have come in to me without anyone thinking. Now there had to be embellishment.'

The two goals that Kerry scored before half-time scarcely need resketching for anyone who saw them. Dublin, effervescent with confidence, got caught twice. First Bobby Doyle, sanctioned harshly perhaps for overcarrying, conceded a free in what should have been a harmless situation. Only the sight of Robbie Kelleher standing a few yards off him raised alarm bells.

Quick free. Liston, who had wandered to midfield, caught it in the clouds and passed to Jack O'Shea, who flicked it out to Pat Spillane.

'I was wide open,' says John Egan. 'I was hoping Spillane would think about me for once in his life. In fairness, he did.'

Paddy Cullen almost got to the ball before Egan did.

'The only decision I ever wonder about was John Egan's goal in 1978. I got to him and he just turned and he actually closed his eyes and just shoved it up and over me. I saw the ball floating in to him and I left the line immediately. I often wonder back on that. If that goal was stopped . . . It wasn't the next goal that killed us. John Egan's was the one that started the rot. I was just a foot short. I think I had to go, though. It was John Egan, after all. If you ask me who was the best player on that Kerry team, it was John Egan. He did more damage to us than anybody.'

The ball looped into the net. Two half-backs, Pat O'Neill and Tommy Drumm, chased it over the line in despair. Before the kick-out could be taken, Egan heard Pat Spillane asking why he hadn't passed the ball back to him.

Dublin had taken a gamble at centre half-back that day. Heffernan and his selectors had been unable to satisfy themselves as to a replacement for Kevin Moran, so they opted for . . . Kevin Moran.

Unbeknownst to Manchester United, Moran had played in the Leinster championship during the off season. Later on, as United went back for pre-season training, Kevin Heffernan and Tony Hanahoe travelled to Old Trafford for a meeting with Dave Sexton, the Manchester United manager.

'We played it all down,' says Moran. 'This was just some little low-profile thing which meant a lot to us.'

Things weren't quite as smooth back in Dublin, where Moran was still a folk hero. There were strenuous objections by die-hard members of the Dublin county board, and reports of patriots spinning in their graves. Jack Lynch, the Taoiseach of the time, contacted Jimmy Gray in the Dublin county board to express his concern.

Gray insulated Heffernan from it all. Not that it would have made a difference.

Moran played in the All-Ireland semi-final and returned to Old Trafford in one piece.

'The funny thing was that for the final I mentioned it again and Dave Sexton said, "Sure, why don't you go over a week beforehand so you can train with your friends." On the Tuesday before the final I pulled my hamstring in Parnell Park. I should never have played. I couldn't run that day. It took me till January to get it right when I came back.'

Moran played the final at half gait and when Kerry noted how badly the hamstring was inhibiting him they had their first scent of blood. The game would be a sad way for Moran to finish his Gaelic football career.

Late in the game Moran would receive an accidental knock on the head that would require eight stitches. Sunday was a long, long night of drinking and lamenting. He hit the Manchester United dressing room at ten the following morning, looking like a wounded escapee from a home for the bewildered, hamstring flapping and head bandaged.

'The only good fortune was that Dave Sexton and Tommy Kavanagh, one of the reserve-team coaches, were supposed to come over to see this little final. Something happened to their flight and they turned back.'

Just as well.

Mikey Sheehy's goal that day has been analysed and parsed more vigorously than anyone who was there could have imagined.

Justin Nelson was the director of outside broadcasting that day for RTE. He told Cullen that he got criticism internally over the fact that he had opted to zone in on the keeper as the famous incident unfolded. From the time that the referee's whistle first blew, Cullen's developing outrage was irresistibly picturesque. On the other hand, if Nelson had left the open shot, it was argued, everybody would have seen what happened. Instead, viewers just saw Cullen scampering back to his goal as the ball floated mysteriously towards the net.

Whether they could have made sense of it is another matter, though. When Cullen retired and purchased a pub in Ballsbridge, he contacted Nelson and got him to make eight video-grab shots of the incident, which he placed in a frame and hung on the wall.

The goal became a symbol of friendship.

'Paddy and myself. Many is the night we fell out of his pub,' says Mikey Sheehy. 'Oftentimes. We had horses' fun over it. Horses' fun. Great sessions and great memories.'

When Paddy got out of the pub trade in 2006, he gave the pictures to Peter Garvey in the Sunnybank in Glasnevin, unofficial headquarters of the seventies team. Paddy didn't need to look at those frames any more. They were burned into his brain.

The little bit of enmity between Ger Power and Paddy Cullen still lingered from the previous year's American trip. During Dublin's period of dominance, Cullen left his line quickly to clear a ball and suffered a slightly late tackle from Power. As he cleared the ball, Cullen half kicked, half tripped Power and turned back to his goal. It was a flashy piece of retribution. The referee, Seamus Aldridge, didn't notice. Most of the Hogan Stand did.

Cullen was booed for the next while, as if he were the bad guy in a panto. The pay-off came minutes before half-time, when Mikey Sheehy fisted on a long floating ball from Jack O'Shea and Cullen was again out first. He tapped it clear and followed to get rid of it. Power came in to tackle as Cullen flicked the ball to Robbie Kelleher. Cullen and Power jostled without making any real contact. As Power had backed into Cullen, the goalkeeper assumed he had been wronged.

No player on either side believes it ought to have been a free to Kerry.

'Let's be honest. It was no free. You could watch it a thousand times over,' says John Egan.

'He must have been blowing for something else,' says Ger Power.

'No doubt about it, there was no free,' says Mikey Sheehy. 'Paddy came out. Passed the ball to Robbie. The ref blew the whistle. It was as if he was catching up for what he missed a few minutes earlier, maybe. Robbie, being the nice man he is, handed me the ball. Then, I got a rush of blood. I kicked it and didn't even look at the ref. It was probably totally illegal. He had his back to me. No whistle. He didn't know what I did with the ball. He didn't know what happened. I often say to Paddy, I genuinely get fed up of talking about the goal.

'It was very funny, though. In the dressing room at half-time, Dwyer only looked at me, never said anything about it. I know what was going through his head. If I'd missed it, he'd be saying, "Why the hell didn't you put it over the bar?" He'd have been right.'

Kerry went to the half-time break two points clear, having been, as Eoin Liston says, 'annihilated'. After the break, O'Dwyer's gamble on Liston paid off. He scored three goals, two of which he describes as lucky.

'The first goal I got, no doubt Jacko meant to kick for a point. I was standing beside Sean. I remember saying to myself, I'd better get away from this fella just in case anything comes in. I took two or three steps back. And next thing, this ball comes straight into my hand. I just had to turn, to let on to put it in the net one way, and put it in the other. Jacko was definitely going for a point. I wasn't even looking for a ball, next thing, straight into my hands.

'Second goal, Páidí Lynch took a free. I played a one-two with Ger Power. I got goal of the year for that. It was a good goal.

'The last one could have been inside in the square, although I protested that I wasn't. John Egan gave a lovely floated pass across and I boxed it in. The match was over by then. The game was gone on them. You could sense they were broken. They'd been playing so well. They hadn't lost a championship match since September 1975. The breaks went our way.'

O'Dwyer had come back off the ropes in the most spectacular fashion. Kerry won by seventeen points in one of the most bizarre games of football ever played.

'We were let out of jail, really,' says Jimmy Deenihan. 'It was incredible. That game, well, Dublin should have sewn it up. They got too cocky. There were backs having pots at goals. The referee had his back to the ball. If Paddy Cullen stayed where he was, instead of scurrying back. It was extraordinary.'

At one stage, as the game went further and further away from Dublin, Pat O'Neill suggested to Sean Doherty that they might try softening Eoin Liston up a little bit.

'They had a fifty. I said to the Doc to get in front of Eoin and to back in. I'd stay behind. He could back him over me. Doc didn't even acknowledge it. He'd lost it. That's not a criticism, that's a reflection of how the mood was. It was an awful place to be, playing out a game that you have no hope of winning in front of over 70,000 people. To feel your proud team dying in that public way.'

It was a slow, agonizing end, with no privacy. Suddenly age couldn't be defied. Dublin's demise was made more poignant by the knowledge that their old rivals, Kerry, were feeling sprightly as they bounded through the foothills of greatness.

★

The aftermath was both messy and delicate.

Dublin sought to register their dismay without appearing ungracious. There are codes of deportment for losing teams, and grievances must be aired with a sense of humility. The Dublin players believed, though, that it was the referee, Seamus Aldridge, who had prostrated them on the canvas, not Kerry.

Not many days after the final, Tony Hanahoe sat down in the back room of the Clarence Hotel and gave a long interview to *Magill* magazine. He said that he had 'personally objected to the referee' before the semi-final, as he had before the Offaly game. 'It now must be apparent to most people,' he said, 'that there was one common factor in the All-Ireland final which we lost, the game against Offaly in Portlaoise [that year's Leinster semi-final], which we nearly lost, the game in New York against Kerry, which we lost, and the bizarre game against Wexford in the first round of the championship last year. That one common factor was the referee.'

Dublin did indeed have history with Aldridge who, as well as being a top-grade inter-county referee, was also secretary of the Kildare county board. In 1977 David Hickey had sat at the Kildare table at the annual end-of-year All-Star dinner. 'The vilification of us as a team and Hanahoe in particular was so bad that I got up and left,' he says. 'Aldridge was present and never objected. I thought, rightly or wrongly, that from then on there was going to be a problem with this guy.'

That spring, Seamus Aldridge had come to Dr Steevens' Hospital, looking for a familiar face, Pat O'Neill. The doctor had done that which he trained for, he had healed the lame. He repaired the cartilage on Aldridge's knee.

O'Neill told Hanahoe this piece of news after the All-Ireland: 'You know we got him fit again in Steevens'.'

'I know what I would have done with him, Pat,' replied Hanahoe.

'Ah, you know *now*, Tony. You didn't know *then*.'

Hanahoe would claim otherwise. Dublin had objected to Aldridge's appointment before the game. Hanahoe has long believed that Kerry also had problems with the appointment. The Kildare man had a reputation as a fussy referee who punctuated flowing games with plenty of interventions. Ger McKenna confirms this.

'Yes. It is true. As far as I know, neither Kerry nor Dublin wanted Seamus Aldridge. We had nothing against the man personally but that style of refereeing didn't suit us. Dublin felt the same. Nothing to do with Seamus Aldridge, who is a very honourable man. At that time you were asked a few questions in advance as regards your opinions of the proposed referee. That doesn't happen any more. The Games Activities people appointed him anyway. When it came out, we just accepted it.'

Tony Hanahoe's *Magill* interview was wide-ranging and, by today's standards of controversy, quite tame. The Activities Committee didn't feel that way about what they read, however. Hanahoe was called in.

'The interview was thought out and premeditated. It wasn't an overreaction. When I went before the Activities Committee in November, it was very clear to me that Paddy McFlynn had two alternatives written in front of him. One was an apology. The other was suspension. There was no question of him getting the first.

'At the end of the hearing, poor Paddy was nearly apologizing to me, saying, "Well, you know, I have to suspend you now." I remember Jimmy Smyth was the secretary and at one stage Paddy suggested a break so we could have a little word in private, so we broke and Paddy said to me, "I don't understand, Tony, why you said it."

'Jimmy said, "Because he probably meant it, Paddy."

'We went back in. Paddy said, "I have to suspend you for a month. But you can appeal."

'I said, "OK. I appeal."'

Hanahoe walked out and his legally trained mind told him that this was a new situation, a '*trial de novo*'.

Dublin played Kildare the next day and Hanahoe defiantly led out the team. The GAA had a different perspective.

'And the referee said to me, "I didn't expect to see you here today!"'

Dublin believe still that conservative voices at the higher echelons of the GAA were determined to see the matter through in an exemplary fashion. Hanahoe's next outing was before the Management Committee.

'That lasted four and a half hours. When I played against Kildare, they'd added another six months, making it seven months. Our players issued a statement and there were all kinds of revolutionary mutterings about standing down from competitions, etc. It was all quite serious.'

In the end, the six-month sentence was withdrawn. The month's sentence stood. Only Ger McKenna of Kerry and Jimmy Gray of Dublin voted against retaining the original punishment.

The Dublin players never forgave Aldridge. Mikey Sheehy, who has enjoyed so many good times with Paddy Cullen, accepted an invitation a few years ago to appear on an RTE programme about famous sporting incidents.

'They had a set, we were sitting down at a table. Myself, Aldridge and Paddy. I never realized they don't talk. Paddy says to me, "All I want him to do is admit that it wasn't a free." It was tense. Aldridge said nothing.'

Cullen stills bristles at the very thought of it. He is one of the larger-than-life characters in the game, and RTE had hoped for a little light entertainment. A producer approached the table before the show began to get a flavour of just what sort of amusing banter could be expected.

'They came over and said, "Well, lads, what are you going to say?" I said that I wanted to know what the story was. He'd never spoken. Aldridge, the main man, was there. Let's hear from him. It wasn't a free. There was no whistle given to signal he could take the kick. He had his back turned. Mikey could have thrown the ball in for all he knew. Let's hear it all.'

The producer blanched. There was discreet conferencing. Then some beseeching of Cullen. For God's sake, please don't say that. Aldridge stared straight ahead the whole time.

'Your man was sitting at the table. He never said a word to me. When the footage came on, he'd only say that "the goalkeeper

committed a foul". He couldn't muster a bit of humour or humility. The goalkeeper! He couldn't say Paddy or Paddy Cullen.

'So, I had to put the cap on it and be a bit magnanimous. I
would like to have been stronger in the end. Sheehy was just
holding his breath. It was funny. Mikey and I were very uneasy
around him. Aldridge was not very forthcoming.'

Seamus Aldridge told the interviewer that he had been getting
letters and phone calls for ten years after the game.

Cullen said, 'Yeah, and they were expensive as well.'

17

It was like going into World War One and nobody telling you
what your hand grenade was for.

Mick Hickey

Dublin were finished after 1978. The corner men could do nothing
to put the vigour back into their legs. Smelling salts to clear the
head, astringent to heal the wounds. Nothing would work. Still,
they answered the bell and came out for another round.

Typically for a man who thrives on exasperation, Jimmy Keaveney, who had been suspended after an incident in the Leinster
final, was prevented by the Pope from playing in the All-Ireland
final. Nothing personal. Keaveney had been given a three-month
sentence, which was due to expire the night before the final. The
Pope's planned visit to Ireland forced the GAA to bring the game
forward a week. Dublin were still in the black books, following the
previous year's All-Ireland. No amnesty was offered to Keaveney.

Dublin needed a free-taker.

When Belvedere College won the Leinster Schools Senior Cup in
1972 they beat Terenure College in the final with Michael Hickey,
David's brother, taking the penalty kicks. The out-half was a
skinny, red-haired kid called Ollie Campbell. He understudied as
kicker.

The following year, Mick Hickey captained Belvedere and they
lost the schools final to High School. He had left his calling card,
though, as a special athlete.

Mick Hickey had been a Dublin minor in 1971 and 1972, but
when he went to UCD to study pharmacy in 1973 he was lost to

Gaelic football for a while. He came back to the game in January 1976 and, along with his friend Tommy Drumm, he got a call-up to the Dublin senior panel in May of that year.

The Dublin forward line remained unchanged for the All-Ireland finals of 1976, 1977 and 1978. Hickey dug in for the long wait and enjoyed the experience. He loved the training and the camaraderie.

'I loved the sense of us all coming together to do something we all loved. I played two or three league games a year. I was happy enough.'

In 1978 he went back to play a little rugby (he is one of very few players to have won a Sigerson Cup with UCD and also to have played Colours for the college in rugby) and had the luck to tear a cruciate ligament. That was November. He got back for early 1979, and the same old faces were in Parnell Park; but there was a sense that if Dublin were to see September, it would take more than the same old faces to get them there. Mick Hickey was ready.

Dublin didn't exactly cut a swath through the forest that summer. They were struggling against Wicklow when Hickey came on and scored a goal and two points to establish the platform for a rescue. The achievement gave him no sense of security. He was getting to play in each game but was seeing no sign of an offer of a full-time appointment.

When Keaveney got sent off in the Leinster final, however, all eyes turned to the next best kicker in the group. That summer, Hickey and Tommy Drumm would go to Belfield for a couple of hours every day just to practise place-kicking. Just in case. When the chance came, Hickey was determined that everything would be perfect.

Robbie Kelleher broke his leg while playing club football in January of 1979. He recovered speedily but when he came back in May he had lost some pace. He was dropped. He was unhappy. Kelleher was a realist, though. Heffernan seemed bent on inserting new faces into the full-back line. Kelleher became resigned to missing out.

On Friday nights Kelleher was in the habit of meeting an old friend for a drink and a chat. He went out as usual on the Friday night before the semi-final, and when he came home the babysitter had a message.

'She said somebody called Kevin Heffernan had rung and he'd said I was to ring him no matter what time I came in at.'

It was past 1 a.m. Kelleher rang. The familiar voice.

'It's very late to be out, just two nights before an All-Ireland semi-final!'

Kelleher ignored the cut. Heffernan had an agenda, surely.

'You're playing centre forward for Scoil Uí Chonnaill at the moment. Do you kick frees?'

'Yes.'

'Are you good at them?'

'Well, I'm not Keaveney.'

'There's not many that are.'

Dublin were training the next morning out in the Trinity Grounds in Santry. The session was scheduled for noon. Heffernan told Kelleher to get out for around eleven o'clock.

Next morning Kelleher spent an hour kicking frees from different distances. A few went over, a few didn't.

The team did some light training and then, as usual, there was a light match. Kelleher, the corner back, was told to play at full forward, marking Sean Doherty.

'Kevin deliberately blew up a free, about fifty yards out. He said to me, kick that. I put it down and kicked it. It went a little wide. To this day I'm convinced if that had gone over, I would have been kicking the frees in Croke Park the next day. Instead, they picked Mick Hickey.'

Hickey was the obvious choice, but there was a connection missing between himself and Heffernan.

'I suspect he thought I was windy. I had this thing that we would be better if we expressed ourselves a bit rather than insisting on physical domination all the time. Sometimes it's not battle out there, it can be ballet.

'That weekend was a ridiculous thing. Keaveney was off but I didn't know till Saturday afternoon after training that I would be actually playing. I knew he had Robbie trying to take the frees. I had the clear sense he doesn't believe in me. I was twenty-four. You need to make a guy feel he's great. I was picked, but I was deflated. They tried everything else and were left with me.'

Hickey was superb the next day. He scored nine points, including the free that won the semi-final for Dublin.

Mick Hickey's twenty-fifth birthday fell the day before the All-Ireland final. The papers noted that his celebrations were 'on ice'. On the day of the final, he missed two fifties in the opening stages. He got called off after twenty minutes.

'Did they say anything to me as I was coming off the field? Listen, they never said anything when I was being put on. It was my first All-Ireland. Other guys had been around the block for sure, but nobody ever came to me and said this is what we want. Nobody said, don't worry, this is what it will be like. Have no fear. You're marking Mick Spillane, you're twice as good. It was like going into World War One and nobody telling you what your hand grenade was for. I felt very unsupported out there.'

That failure of management style was to set the tone for several mild disillusionments towards the end. Heffernan preferred to let a player work things out for himself.

'Kevin would never have been one to come and say, "Thanks for the dance, it's over,"' says Bobby Doyle. 'You lived in hope. He let you fade away rather than tell you. In my last year we were beaten by Offaly in the Leinster final and I remember him looking around to see who he was going to put on. I was on the bench but I didn't have a jersey. The numbered players were allowed to run on the field at the start; the rest of us had to walk up along the back of the Canal goal and into the dugout. I remember saying to myself, "What am I doing here? Am I a fucking eejit?" Yet still half hoping he'd look at me and tell me to go on.'

Bernard Brogan's inter-county career finished with an injury sustained in a league game with Kildare. He was taken to hospital wearing his jersey and made a gift of it to the nurse on duty. He never heard anything again from Dublin, apart from a terse request to give the jersey back.

'I was never dropped,' he likes to joke. 'Officially I'm still availalable.'

Other players never fully understood Heffernan's instincts regarding players and people. When the time came to change the team, that lack of understanding hurt some. Heffernan had a fondness for the wholehearted player above all else. In 1979 he found Mick Holden, who was a county hurler. Heffernan saw him as a full back before anybody else, including Holden himself, saw it.

At first Holden declined the invitation to play football as he had a hurling commitment with his club, Cuala. In the end Holden was inserted into the Leinster final for his first game of that summer. Holden was a limited player but a character. 'How could anyone not like Mick Holden?' Heffernan says fondly today.

Nobody disliked Mick Holden. He smoked. He arrived carrying quarter-pounders from McDonald's. He'd turn up late, with amusing stories with which to gull Heffernan. He always had the option of returning to his first love, hurling, so everything about playing football had the feel of holiday to him.

Two stories from 1979 illustrate Holden's role as the antithesis of everything the group had believed in through the seventies.

The day before the All-Ireland final, the players trooped upstairs to the big, airy room in Santry. Heffernan gave his team talk, which was, as usual, perfect: cerebral and rousing and motivational. Everything just right.

At the end of it all, he asked if anyone had any trouble sleeping. Rest would be hugely important. If there are problems, there are a couple of sleeping tablets here. One hand went up at the back. Holden. The most laid-back man in the room.

Heffernan's eyebrows shot up but he said nothing.

Next day Holden was asked if the tablets had helped. He laughed.

'Ah no. I got those for me mother.'

One training session stands out as well. The team had got through their drills and were playing their game at the end of the session. Heffernan was refereeing. Suddenly a mustard-coloured Fiat Ritmo screeched into the car park. Heffernan glanced up and went storming off the field. Straight to the Ritmo, out of which Mick Holden jumps.

The players stood, silent as statues.

'What's the fucking excuse?' said Heffernan while he was still ten yards away from the car.

'You won't believe it,' said Holden. 'Jaysus, Kevin, I was coming across town this morning and you know the way there was the bank robbery yesterday?'

'Yeah.' Heffernan nods and by now the steam is coming out of his ears at a slightly lower rate.

'Well, I was stopped by the police. I apparently resemble one of the guys who was in the robbery, so I was detained for questioning.'

Heffernan is shaking his head. Only Holden.

'Really?' he asks.

'Not at all, Kev, but doesn't it sound better than saying that I slept it out?'

Holden was a maverick. He had no respect for anything much. Instead, he had this easy capacity to get along with everyone in the squad. Eventually he would be a wonderful full back. That summer, though, everybody was seeing the end and nobody, apart from Heffernan, was seeing Mick Holden as the start of the beginning.

'I remember in O'Toole Park one day,' says Andy Roche, 'having a blinder against Mick Holden. Poor Mick didn't get a ball off me. I remember walking in with Heffernan and himself and they were a foot or so in front of me and Kevin put his arm around Mick and said, "Jesus, what's wrong with you this morning, Mick?"'

'I got pissed off in 1979,' says Jim Brogan, 'when [Heffernan] replaced the full-back line. It was spun out then, it had come to an end. I would have thought if you weren't considered good enough, then in the light of the experience you had you should be just given your P45 and allowed to walk away. I wasn't told anything. I was told there was a possibility I would be coming in. By then, though, it was unravelling.'

'Kevin and the selectors made a huge mistake by dropping the full-back line,' says Gay O'Driscoll. 'I got injured coming into it. I tore a calf muscle in training before the Offaly match. I was just about ready for the semi-final against Roscommon, but they didn't pick me. For myself, Sean and Robbie this was going to be our swansong. I came in at half-time. I said to Kevin coming off the pitch, put me in the fucking team. He did, he put me in just after half-time.'

By then, however, Heffernan was using a thimble to bail water from the ship. Kerry were younger and fitter and hungrier. Dublin duly lost, and the music ended. Suddenly in the silence it became apparent that the legacy left by the departing team was daunting. Six Leinster titles in succession. Six All-Ireland finals in succession. From the Division Two League final in May of 1974 they appeared in every national final till September 1978: ten on the trot. They'd done it with a side, most of whom couldn't have been sold for scrap in the autumn of 1973.

In sport, endings are always brutal and disfiguring. All the repressed woes come spilling out. Players drifted away. The city came to realize that the team of the seventies would never quite be replaced.

For Dublin, the seventies officially ended on 27 June 1980, when Brian Mullins drove his Fiat 127 into a lamp-post on the Clontarf Road while heading for his home in Portmarnock. A simple accident. Mullins, blinded by the lights of an oncoming car, left the road and almost died at the age of twenty-five.

Mullins remembers the sight of the bone sticking up through his right leg and the pain in his mouth. He had badly damaged his jaw and broken eight teeth.

That he walked again was remarkable. That he came back and played in three more All-Ireland finals told all that anyone needed to know about the extraordinary will at the centre of the Dublin team of the seventies.

Tommy Drumm played in the Leinster Under-21 final in 1975 against Meath. The usual game of dodgems between the two counties. Early on, Drumm got badly hit in a tackle and was left sprawled on the ground. Mullins came over and lifted Drumm up.

'He just said, "Listen, no worries. I'm right behind you." That was the man he was.'

Drumm remembers, in the latter stages of Mullins's two-year recovery from his crash, going up to the Deer Park in Howth outside of training sessions and watching with a grimace as Mullins worked at doing sprints up the long, steep hill beside the golf course.

A couple of years later, when Drumm moved to Qatar for work, it was Mullins who wrote regularly. Others called on the phone, but Mullins sent the thoughtful, witty letters that an emigrant loves.

The 1979 campaign, though it ended in failure, somehow encapsulates Mullins. Take the Leinster final. On that day they could smell the hunger on Offaly's breath. Keaveney had been sent off. Dublin were in seven types of trouble and Mullins was playing like a cornered desperado.

At one moment he stands, frustrated, around the midfield mark, having given away a free for throwing a ball at an Offaly player. Suddenly he notes that Paddy Collins, the referee, has changed his mind about the free and is going to throw the ball up. Instant animation. Zero to sixty in half a second. He leaps, salmon-like, and scoops the ball away one-handed and starts the move which leads to Bernard Brogan's last-minute goal. Dublin win.

In the All-Ireland semi-final he receives a bad eye injury and concussion. In the final, early on he is shaken by two bone-jarring collisions. He drives on.

'At his best,' says Tommy Drumm, 'there was nothing to touch Mullins. I feel a tinge of sadness every time I think of that crash. They are defining moments for Dublin football. Kevin Moran's exit. Brian Mullins's accident. We could have survived one of those things perhaps, but not two.'

If Heffernan had been thinking about transition, he no longer had a rock to build his new team around.

Fate, always waiting around the corner with a stout stick in its hand, put a full stop to the good times.

★

Kerry had no concerns about endings. As Micko had once skipped over the fallen carcass of the Bomber one night in Waterville, so they leapt, whooping, over the slain form of their old adversary.

Brian Mullins declined to speak to Seanie Walsh after the 1979 final.

'I played him negatively,' Seanie says. 'I stopped him from going for balls, got in his way, stood on his toes. My job was to take him out of the game. Brian made it clear that he didn't like it. We didn't speak for maybe two years, and then one night I was in Rosie O'Grady's in New York and Brian was in there. He asked me to go for a pint. We talked and had a good night. I was glad that was put right.'

Apart from the entry in the record books, that minor coolness was the longest-lasting legacy of 1979. Kerry took not a lot of pleasure from their win. Landing punches on a beaten fighter is no fun, especially when you have known the man in his vigorous prime.

Mikey Sheehy scored 2–6 to equal the scoring record for a final which Jimmy Keaveney had set, just two years previously. In all other respects the Dubs were about to be eclipsed.

Sheehy, Ogie Moran, Páidí Ó Sé, Ger Power and Pat Spillane would finish their careers with eight All-Ireland medals apiece. Even on that day in 1979, perhaps such riches seemed unlikely, but they went to their fun, feeling that they could outlast the sea itself.

18

Some fellas don't like living in the past. More fellas would prefer
never to be out of it.

Eoin Liston

Three decades and counting since Mick O'Dwyer gathered a sheaf
of golden youths and dressed them in green and gold.

Half a lifetime? Can it be? Three decades and counting since
the lean, hungry kids of Kerry came to Dublin on that greasy day
in 1975 and set up the greatest era in football. All those springs and
summers since the headless captain himself, Mickey Ned O'Sullivan,
soloed too far for his own good and wound up in hospital. Nah.

Mickey Ned O'Sullivan teaches in Ballyvourney, where once
he was a young star of colleges football. He has at times owned a
teashop and a pub in Kenmare, but now he is starting to take his
ease. He enjoys life in the little nest and he trains the Limerick
senior football team for recreation and challenge.

In 2005 they ran an Iron Man contest in Kenmare. Mickey Ned
O'Sullivan had been eyeing it all year. In January he'd rung two
friends, asked would they take a leg each. Sure, they said.

One pal, he'd been for two or three runs in twenty years. Now
he was being asked to do thirteen and a half miles up the mountains.
When asked, I will, he said. The other has had his hips replaced.
He was being asked to cycle sixty-two miles up hill and down
dale. Sure it'll give me something to work towards, he said.

And Mickey Ned went off to Calcutta for the summer to work
with street kids. He set up sporting projects and wrote another
chapter into the story of a varied life. While he was there he
thought of his two friends and texted for news of their progress.

John O'Keeffe had three months of heavy bike training done. Same old Johnno. He texted Ogie Moran to see how the running was going.

One word came back: 'Bolloxed!'

On the day, Mickey did the swim. Half seven in the morning, two kilometres out across Kenmare Bay. Johnno did the bike stint, sixty miles over the mountains in a young man's time. Ogie finished very well, running within himself as others floundered.

Thirty years and counting? Not, when you're special.

True story. It goes down in a bar on the seashore in Cape Town, many years after apartheid and many years after the seventies. You know the place. No doors or walls, just warm breezes passing through in the African night. There's some slow music on the jukebox and it's wee hours late. On the floor there's a white guy dancing with a black girl.

The guy is a little drunk and he's just fooling around because that's what he does when he has a few taken. The girl, she knows the score too, and as she's no advert for temperance herself she'll have a good time until the music stops.

And then from a high stool a large Afrikaner leans forward. He's built broad and knotty, like the base of a tree; he's more blond-haired and blue-eyed than a stereotype should be, and he knows not where the line is. So he leans forward on to the dance floor and he grabs a large handful of the black girl's ass and squeezes it greedily.

Now another white man steps from the shadows and this man, he taps the Afrikaner on the shoulder and asks him if he might not think about behaving more like a gentleman. Glasses are put down on tables, conversations fizzle and heads turn.

'Wit yew saying, man?' says the Afrikaner slowly. He draws himself up to his full non-bar-stool, non-leaning-assward height, and he is quite immense. 'Yew git a problim, my frind?'

The white man who has stepped forward to press the case for gentlemanly behaviour happens to be one of the planet's leading transplant surgeons, a renowned urologist. He also happens to be

100lb. lighter than the Afrikaner. He looks down at his hands, his instruments. His knuckles aren't for fighting with. His face isn't for pulping.

'Look, my friend,' he says and he sweeps his hand in front of his chest, 'there are twenty-five of us.'

The Afrikaner looks slowly around the bar, where twenty-five large men with sun-reddened faces are holding on to their glasses. He is filled suddenly with awe and respect. Something radiates from this band of brothers. He doesn't even know that he is looking at the Dublin football team of the seventies, but he knows he is looking at something different.

'Alreet,' he says quietly, 'alreet.'

When the football finished, it left holes in a few hearts. For some of the men of the seventies the game was a springboard into life. They had honed themselves on competitiveness. They tore into careers with zest.

For others, life had a different flavour.

For Paudie O'Mahoney, fame and recognition were like being slapped in the face with a shovel. To this day he has problems with it.

'I can't walk down the town here in Killarney – where I have a business with fifteen people working in it – I can't walk out without a pat on the back or some fella asking me about the Kerry team today and the Kerry team tomorrow and the Kerry team of the past. I suppose I would love to be able to walk down the town without being recognized. That's my ambition. I have to hide at functions. Some fella will always want you to make a speech.

'I think at heart most of us would like to be nonentities. We were never prepared for it. For it starting, or for it ending.'

There was a time in his life when Paudie and his brother sat out in a house in Caherdaniel and drank. Dark, lonely drinking. Paudie doesn't own the house any more. The house came to haunt him.

'My brother is dead from drink. He died at forty-nine. He learned his drinking through the GAA, and I became a drinker through it. I abused alcohol because of playing.'

People say to Paudie that surely for a sportsman there's self-control and self-discipline. He doesn't know where to begin in replying.

'The thing would be that my first drink was out of a cup. It was whiskey. I was eighteen, I got Man of the Match in the O'Donoghue Cup final game, here in Killarney. I got sick when I went home. My mother didn't know how I could be sick. I suppose she should have known.'

There were good times, but a river of drink ran through them.

Jimmy Keaveney's father, Seamus, was a small man from Belfast and fiercely republican in outlook. The first drink Jimmy ever had was the year he was in the minor grade in St Vincent's. He was playing ahead on the junior team as well, and Vincent's were listed to play in not one but two Loving Cup finals as the county board looked to clear a grand backlog of fixtures.

Keaveney was asked to play.

'I'd say, with the rate they used to play fixtures in those days, that when the competition had started I would have been twelve years of age. It took that long to play those things off. In those days a Loving Cup was next best to a junior championship, though. We played in the first final. Scoil Uí Chonaill. We won.'

Jimmy had a little motorbike at the time. Gerry Murray said to him that everyone was going to Meagher's.

'I had three bottles of Harp. I went home. "Well done," my da said. "Were you drinking?" Bam! He puts me on me back. "I told you the first drink you'd have was with me on your twenty-first birthday." '

Jimmy was one of the lucky ones. The drink came down on them all like a soft rain, but Jimmy didn't catch a chill.

Páidí Ó Sé remembers the last night of a football trip to New York. They had an early start the next day, but he and Páidí Lynch opted to drink through the night. The pair came back to the hotel at seven o'clock in the morning. They'd packed their cases while still sober, and now they brought them down and into the breakfast room.

The late broadcaster, Mick Dunne, arrived in for his morning repast and was impressed to see the two Páidís up and about.

'You're up early, lads. Fair play to ye.'

By the time the Irish breakfast arrived, the two Páidís' heads had slapped down on to the table, one after the other. Mick O'Dywer came down and found his two players dead to the world and Mick Dunne having his breakfast between them.

'Serious, serious drinking,' says Páidí Ó Sé. 'I don't know how much damage it did, but it was serious.'

Mick O'Dwyer never drank, but those players who did remember something he used to say to them. His mother drank and as a boy it wasn't easy for him.

'He came up from nothing,' says Paudie O'Mahoney, 'and in fairness he kept going after us. That was the mark of him. He said oftentimes he had no shoes and there was drink in the house. When he grew up he never bothered with the drink. It was one of the things I admired about him.'

Some time between 1982 and 1983, John Egan's life became troubled and serious. He was captain of the Kerry team which went to the All-Ireland of 1982 looking for a record fifth title in a row. They lost to a late goal by Offaly.

'That hurt me. It was the difference between failure and being remembered as the captain of the greatest team ever. It's such a public thing. I found it hard. Will you be remembered as the most famous captain of all time or the man who lost the five-in-a-row? There's a huge difference.'

Not long afterwards, Jerry Egan, twin brother of John, died in a drowning accident at a party. He fell into a swimming pool.

Anyone who knows Sneem will have heard of the Casey family. Rowers and wrestlers, the Casey family owned the only pool in Sneem.

The Caseys had a party. Jerry was there. The party went on late and Jerry was sent to Ger O'Connor's shop down the street to get fags and provisions. He was on his way back and he shot around the corner of the house and must have walked into the pool. Everyone assumed he had just gone home. Nobody missed him. He was found in the morning.

Football never seemed the same afterwards for John.

'Everybody drinks, and I drank too much in the end. Family reasons. Hurt. I could tell some stories about it, where it took me. Dark places. Drink was the culture. Football was social. It led me to the bar. Sometimes I think it's a wonder I'm alive.

'I didn't drink until I was twenty-two or -three. I always drank heavily after that. Away on trips, through the winters. It appeared that everyone was doing it. Maybe some of us were heavier at it than others. You'd be in a situation where you thought everyone was doing it.'

John's counterpart in the Dublin number-fifteen jersey did the same job all his life. John McCarthy went into the guards at nineteen. By the age of fifty he was out on retirement. When the lads talk about Macker, they remember his bravery on the field, the fact that he got his jaw broken twice, that he could drink a pint in a second and a half, and that he once did 150 press-ups on the floor of the Drake Pub in Finglas to win a bet, one All-Ireland weekend.

Today he does a little taxi-driving.

'See this place,' he says of the Sunnybank Inn. 'I come in at four, have a few pints. Then a few pints. Breakfast would come around, I'd say fuck the breakfast and stay on the drink. I might do it the next day and the day after. I might stay on the batter that long. Then I mightn't drink for two weeks. Every year I say I'll have four every night. I went off it for nine months. Torture. I just love a good old session for a few days. I've given up on trying to stop. I can't sleep after five or six.'

The old Rat Pack, incorporated in drink and bonded through football, survived, just about. The story is told of Timmy Kennelly deciding once in middle age that he was going to run the Dublin marathon. Timmy was a beloved figure in Listowel, and the good-will followed him down the street as he set off running every day towards Tarbert.

Timmy had long owned his own bar by then. The life of the saloon bar and the life of the athlete proved incompatible. The Dublin marathon remained unconquered.

For many of the players, turning their backs on the crowds and the prolonged adolescence which a dressing room can offer was the toughest part of life.

'Especially our men,' says Mickey Ned. 'Many of them knew nothing else from the time they were in their late teenages. They were the princes of the county. It was a tough one to walk away from. Even tougher when it walked away from you.'

Some lads walked away. Others paid the bill.

'It broke up my marriage,' says Paudie O'Mahoney. 'My wife wasn't that interested in Gaelic football, she was interested in me and my kids. I gave my life to Gaelic football, though. Gaelic football and drink. During the periods that were successful, and afterwards when I was training teams, I was never home before twelve at night. The kids grew up without me. Massive regrets. Huge, painful regrets.'

John Egan and Paudie came through it fighting. When you meet them, they have coffee to drink and they say it will always be that way. The good times had their underworld.

'There was drink everywhere,' says Egan. 'When we were training, we trained, and when we were drinking, we drank. I had great times drinking. I know the crack I had. I know I did a lot of fucking crazy things. That's why I'll never drink again. Drink is a disaster. We were in drink all the time. Out on trips, everywhere was drink. Meeting people, receptions. Drink all round you. In the company of drinkers and you're not drinking – I wouldn't stay there too long.'

There's a video of Kerry in their prolonged pomp; it's called *The Golden Years*. John Egan watches it occasionally. Sometimes his son, a wonderful footballer himself, joins his dad.

'You can't tell a young fella looking at the *Golden Years* video that there's twelve years have passed in that hour and half they see, and that's why you're so big and rough-looking at the end. You're after drinking your way through New York, Chicago, San Francisco and the thirty-two counties of Ireland. You can't explain that.'

Pat Spillane, who grew up in a pub, never had much of an

interest in what the pub sold. The family obsession was with football, and Pat often comments that his mother worked herself to the bones in the bar while her strapping sons slept the days away upstairs, preserving themselves for the field.

'Football, and all that goes with it, fills your life. When you are winning, you can go out and have as much of what is on offer as you want. You are on top of the world. A lot of the Kerry boys never filled that void. We lived hard and trained hard and partied hard. When the fitness went and the good times went, it was a bit sad. And as a team we're not close, either. That's another sadness.'

The boys of those magical summers are everywhere you look, now that they are men.

Jimmy Deenihan in the Dáil, Páidí Ó Sé working for Bord Fáilte, Robbie Kelleher one of the nation's leading economists, Kevin Moran a high-profile soccer agent.

In Tralee there is a row of businesses which starts at the corner with a Supermac's burger joint, which Mick O'Dwyer has a share in. 'Supermick's' they call it. Next door is Charlie Nelligan's coffee shop, and a couple of doors further along is Eoin Liston's building society.

Around the corner past the hotel, Mikey Sheehy is selling financial advice. On the corner, a little way up from Supermick's, Seanie Walsh's auctioneering firm thrives. Tommy Doyle had a pub for a while just along the way. Ogie Moran, who works in business development, isn't far away.

In Tralee the boys are tight with each other. They golf together and lunch together. They are the biggest extant clique of the team.

Ger Power still works for the department of employment in the town and he and John O'Keeffe (teaching in Tralee CBS) have been giving a hand lately with preparing the Kerry hurling team. Eoin Liston trained Kerins O'Rahilly's senior team in the town for seven years ('Until I became a complete bore about it,' he says) and the boys of the golden era are visible everywhere, from the sidelines where they coach or watch their sons or daughters play to attending receptions and performing the functions of local celebrity.

The odd marriage has broken, the odd illness has been struggled through. Adult life intruded some time along the way.

Sport at the highest level played with the purest intensity is a zone where no ironies survive. In their middle years, however, the Kerrymen who won so much for so long have come to appreciate one abiding irony. They won more than Dublin won – but perhaps they lost more, too.

The closeness, the brotherhood, the mutual reliance which has sustained the Dubs and made their cause a lifelong commitment to each other has been denied to Kerry. They say that geography caused it. That the county system of rotating the captaincy left them without a natural leader like Tony Hanahoe. They say that they got so much together at a time when they were so young that they never developed socially as a group.

They came together for summers, and on the pitch they had a magic and a tightness which was special. Afterwards they drove home to a dozen different destinations and mingled with clubmates, brothers, sisters, colleagues. They had no Room. They expressed no dissent and looked for no deep reasons as to why they did what they did. Football was their culture and their heritage, and that brought responsibilities, pressures and rewards. Not necessarily in that order.

Today, they are somewhat riven. Eoin Liston says he has had words with Páidí Ó Sé and where once they were 100 per cent, now perhaps they are only 98 per cent. Páidí says he knows he caused offence not too long ago to Ger Power, and there is coolness there. Before Páidí snaffled the county management job, he commented freely on the performances of past comrades. He knows he hurt Mickey Ned O'Sullivan and Ogie Moran.

And then there is Pat Spillane.

In the beginning and in the end there was Spillane. He had the bloodlines and he had the obsession and there was no amount of football or medals that were ever enough for him. He finished with eight All-Irelands and a well-earned reputation as one of the greatest players ever to play the game.

His athleticism, his extraordinary point-scoring ability and his sheer style epitomized the great Kerry team. Some Dublin players feel that the system they played under denied them the opportunity of full expression. Spillane is the man they point to in order to bolster their argument. Spillane gave everything and got everything out of himself. O'Dwyer handed him the platform and left it at that. He was the essence of Kerry's exuberance.

'He just saw I'd do it and he allowed me to indulge. He never said to me, start roaming or stop roaming. He could see the benefit of it and he left me off. He used to get on about overholding the ball sometimes. And he was right. With Dwyer, though, he told you what you wanted to hear. He'd tell others what he knew you needed to hear.'

Spillane didn't spend much time listening to others. When the end came, he moved neatly into a career as a pundit, writing for the *Sunday World* and later providing expert analysis and eventually hosting RTE's flagship GAA programme, *The Sunday Game*. Spillane is a huge and generous personality for whom talk comes as naturally as football.

His teammates say that Spillane is Spillane. He was always a talker. There was never any harm in him. That's the way Pat is and that's the way he always will be.

They don't always forgive him. On television and in his autobiography he has trespassed on his comrades' toes. Criticisms which Spillane would absorb like weak tackles have left scars on others.

'Don't talk to me about him,' says Ogie Moran. 'I won't be speaking about him.'

'If there was any friction, the cause was because of the breakdown of confidentiality,' says Mickey Ned O'Sullivan. 'There is a sacredness of trust within a group. I find that hard to take. Whatever happened between us all happened in trust. That's the only area where the media and the team diverge. Pat betrayed that. He hasn't been forgiven.'

'His book disappointed me,' says Jack O'Shea. 'He had a fair cut at me. I think Pat is himself and always will be. He'll never change. I was a bit disappointed he said things about his colleagues, though, that didn't need to be said. He has hurt a few lads. You can't change that. I was disappointed.'

'I know that Pat's romancing if he says fellas would get up and leave the pub if he walked in,' says Eoin Liston. 'Fellas think too much of their pint. I know there's fellas though that wouldn't get up and go over and shake his hand. You don't knife lads you soldiered with.'

That there is a schism is surprising, given how long everyone spent in the same dressing room. As Ger O'Keeffe says, 'Pat was always mouthy. He was always Pat. You never minded him.'

Spillane himself is a little bewildered. He criticized Ogie Moran on the television one night and found himself up to his ankles in his first domestic controversy. It's in his nature to regret the hurt but to feel compelled to open the discussion again.

'Ogie never talked to me again. He's a lovely fella. He took the criticism on the television very badly. I met him a couple of months after. I forget about everything. I went to shake hands. He just walked away from me. Life is too short. I'm not bitter about anything. You could abuse me left, right and centre, and you come in the next day and I'll talk to you. I'm a different creature.

'He was the one, really. The rest were a bit cool. Ogie is a lovely man and we won eight All-Ireland medals together but he'd never managed a team in his life when he took over Kerry. He was the wrong choice. He wasn't ready for it. The night I criticized him, it was as a disappointed Kerryman rather than as an analyst. Dara Ó Cinnéide played wing-back in a Munster final, for crying out loud! It was my job.'

Spillane has a thick skin, but the isolation hurts a little.

He tells a story about meeting Timmy Kennelly in a bar, not too long after the book had come out.

'"How's Tim?" He just fucking stared at me. I thought to myself, Jesus, not Timmy as well. Timmy was a rogue like me. I could understand Ogie, but now Timmy.'

Spillane stood at the bar, waiting for his drink, and he could feel Kennelly's eyes on him.

'And then Horse broke his heart laughing. "Had you going there, Spillane," says Tim. "Come here, you fool."'

And Spillane, the black sheep of a dispersed flock, shakes his head and comes close to shedding a tear.

'He was a thundering melted rogue! Was I glad to hear those words. Great man.'

When the football was over, Sean Doherty bought a pub by accident. The lads felt that this vocational mishap suited their old full back well. In the good days when the big matches were coming thick and fast, the Doc would sometimes forsake the drink and the big dinners and they noted that abstinence made him soft and more gentlemanly. These weren't qualities that a Dublin full back should be remembered for.

He bought the pub in 1983. The story started in another pub. He was a little drunk one evening in The Barge, down by the canal. The barman said to him that he'd seen that the Doc's local pub up in Ballyboden was for sale. Leslie Allen's was a darling little shebeen of a place of which the Doc was fond.

'How much is he looking for it?' asked the Doc out of curiosity.

'Well,' said the barman, 'I had a drink in there the other night, he said he wanted £190,000 for it.'

'Hmmm,' said the Doc, assuming that he was now acting in the role of consultant for a group which the barman was putting together. 'If you offered him 210k, would he take it? I'd say he would.'

The barman said he'd be sure to ask.

Doc thought nothing more of the conversation. He was a plumber and had forty men working for him. More than enough to be dealing with. Three weeks later, he strolled into The Barge again and asked for a pint.

Up came a case of champagne on the counter. Now The Barge had the sort of business clientele who would often be celebrating good deals with cases of champagne, and the Doc was curious.

'Who's buying the champagne?'

'You are!'

And the barman drew out a picture of Leslie Allen's.

'They accepted your bid!'

'What?'

'You told me to put £210,000 on it.'

'No.'

'You did so.'

'I didn't,' said the Doc. 'Sure have you any money?'

'No,' said the barman. 'I can borrow ten grand, though.'

'I've nothing either,' said the Doc, 'so let's not worry.'

'Fine.'

By coincidence the Doc was in the right company. John Parley, a banker, was standing beside him. Mick Cronin, an accountant, and Paddy Kelly, a solicitor, were just down the bar.

The sixty seconds when he had been in danger of owning a pub had been curiously satisfying. He turned to Parley.

'What's the chance of a loan of a few quid?'

'Are you serious?'

'Ah, yeah, I suppose I am.'

'Is it a good pub?'

'It's great.'

'Come in Monday morning so we'll draw up the papers. Kelly will be your solicitor.'

The Doc didn't tell the missus till the following Monday evening – 'She said I was for the birds.'

The pub suits him. Doherty's is an ex-footballer's pub with pictures on the walls and the expansive host who likes to talk. The Doc knows every face and he knows every story.

He is at the centre of the best yarn, but David Hickey tells it with a nicer twist.

Hickey played rugby and studied medicine in France in the mid-eighties when the football finished. One evening he was with a group of French colleagues having a few drinks and the television was blaring away in the background.

Something caught the attention of one of his colleagues and they all glanced up. French TV was doing a top ten countdown of the worst, most violent incidents in sport. Ice-hockey sledgings, rabbit punches, high-arm tackles. Every time somebody got slammed or broken up, everyone in the bar would wince and there would issue from the drinkers a collective 'Ooh'.

'And then,' Hickey likes to say, 'I see these people I recognize on the screen. It's only the Doc at number five!'

Opening night. The stories which the Estadio Latino Americano could tell go back to a time before Fidel. The warm November night is unlit and carries the smell, naturally, of cigar smoke and *cabeza del lobo* beer. Those things, and anticipation too. Sixty-four thousand nine hundred and ninety-nine comrades chatter to each other and one other. David Hickey closes his eyes and inhales it all. Beisból reminds him of another life.

Tonight it's Villa Clara v. Industriales, the first game of a season that will lead to the Serie Nacional next March, and, if you allow yourself to dream a little, onwards to the Serie Selectiva. Oil is scarce, so the generator which powers the floodlights lies sleeping until it is time. There is no extra fuel to burn for people who are just sitting and waiting.

With the blaze of light the grass, the sanded lines of the diamond and the gentle rise of the mound take shape with a brilliant familiarity. The slogans of *revolución* mark the perimeters where billboards would normally lurk. This goes to the soul of things, to the mood of a nation. Normally they take a dollar at the turnstiles. Tonight, everyone comes for free.

Industriales, 'The Blues', will win by six runs to two, but when the final inning has been played that matters little to the neutral. It's the feeling of having been close to the soul of Cuba which lasts. The players' deeds are cheered and studied from the bleachers by friends, family people of the same tribe. It's a world without big-money deals and oily agents and lurid distraction. The men who play tonight have jobs to go to tomorrow. Those who cheer them may travel home with them.

Another life. He remembers being taken to the 1963 All-Ireland final by his dad. Seeing those other Blues win and being born then into the faith. At Mass on Sundays he'd pray fervently for the Dubs to win that afternoon. Please God. Please. Even when he was old and in blue himself, he never took it so seriously again.

The best of the football times, he thinks, were right at the beginning when it was pure and innocent. The club in Raheny was run under the steam of one man, Brendan Lee, and the weekend meant being picked up in regular swoops by Brendan as he drove through the suburb, shaking young fellas from their beds to come out and wear the maroon of Raheny.

Paradise. Fixtures in the *Evening Press* on a Wednesday. Petitioning the gods for the rain to hold off on Thursday and Friday, and then off again in the old Volkswagen. The Under-21s played on a Saturday afternoon. The minors played on Sunday morning. The sixteen-and-a-halfs played on Sunday afternoon. If you were lucky, you played all weekend in the same gear. Paradise was the Number 9 pitch in St Anne's Park. Paradise was the black, festering hole of a dressing room. Paradise was dreaming of the big leagues.

Or winter mornings, and lads playing with jerseys over their Mass shirts. Up to the Phoenix Park, galloping on the wind-scoured prairies with footballs from other pitches trespassing and getting chased down as you tried to play your game. Up to Crumlin and the tight pitch behind the Star Cinema. Or Ballyfermot! Playing hurling up there. Two metal goalposts at either end and the high grass out along the sidelines. A ball went out there and you didn't hit it clean and suddenly you were looking for it with the sound of thundering hooves coming behind you. Or Good Counsel in Galtymore Road on a bad day. Sweet Jesus!

He went to France for two years in the early eighties. He practised medicine and played rugby. In 1983 he came home and went looking for a place in blue. He played one practice game in which he tore his knee. He ended up working the line as a medic when Dublin rode to another All-Ireland in September.

Then, to draw the curtains on it all, he walked away and hardly looked back.

'What amazed me was that I'd been with Kevin since the sixties. I was fifteen when I first played for him, and I never got a call as to how the surgery went. I had to organize the surgery myself. I had to limp about the place. Nobody even rang up. I was gone. I had been in the plans a week before. I was gone.'

They say that Hickey was the confident, vigorous heartbeat of the team. They say what happened to his brother Mick in 1979 soured him and put him on the path to revisionism. Yet if Hickey embodied the joyous confident young heart of the team in his prime, he represents its adult brain today.

'We all have regrets. Things could have gone differently. I could have got more from myself. It could have ended better for guys, but as a bunch of people on a journey together it was unmatchable. It was an experience that very few people will ever have. Sometimes I would say it didn't change us, that Kevin just came upon a group of extraordinary people. And sometimes, when you count the friendships and sit down and start telling the stories, especially if you've been away from the group a while, you know that it was something special.'

David Hickey breathes in the Havana air. The city is beautiful. The North Atlantic hits the main street wall, the sea soughing comfortingly as his head fills with music and baseball and fragments of Spanish, the loving tongue. The abandoned people all around him are gracious and forgiving. He has found something here.

'I don't want to be the guy who complains always about Kevin. We had wonderful times. Sometimes it just ended badly for guys. Sometimes it just ends badly. At the end, though, Kevin is a good guy. We had a room full of good guys.'

He remembers his first trip to Havana, that feeling of never wanting it to end. Touching down in Paris on the way home, he felt alone and depressed.

'You know you love Havana when arriving back to Paris makes you depressed.'

In Parnell Park, they all knew their Havana. Leaving was never going to be easy.

The Dubs are older and the Kerrymen are arthritic.

In Kerry they went on for longer and they stretched less and their training habits were different. Kerry hibernated and then crucified themselves from early May onwards.

'Nobody ever really suggested this, that or the other,' says Ger O'Keeffe. 'We looked up to Dwyer. He had graced great football games. Who were we to judge his approach? He had a carte blanche. We ran a lot. Very hard in training. We did a lot of running on the field in Killarney, which was always very hard in the summertime.'

Jimmy Deenihan suffered severe injury in 1980 when he severed a muscle in the leg.

'It was just the intensity of training. We were doing a piggy-back exercise. I had Tim Kennelly on my back. The muscle snapped. I tried to go too far too fast.'

Paudie O'Mahoney remembers being inveigled back to Fitzgerald Stadium after a period away from the team, and vainly trying to set conditions for his return.

'I said to Micko to be careful with me, I wasn't fit. I went back the first night and he gave us twenty-seven rounds of Fitzgerald Stadium. Hard ground. Well fuck me. I said halfway through it, "What the fuck am I doing here. I've been fooled again." I looked over to the stand and there were fellas I knew. I had to grind my teeth and go. That was the way it was. People came to watch us suffer. You wouldn't give in.

'A lot of the guys I played with are busted up. We took cortisone to get through games. After the game you'd be in agony.'

Eoin Liston, whose hamstrings plagued him for years as a player, reckons that it is impossible to audit the extra work the Kerry players did or how they damaged themselves.

'We probably would have a case against him! I have a few doctors doing a survey. I'd be first in,' he says with a laugh. As a hardline Dwyer loyalist, he means only humour.

'You look at the work we had with Micko, if you added up the years the lads were doing with him and then maybe there would be another two or three years' worth of work done on their own. I don't think I left anything on the training pitch, ever. There was no warm-ups, no stretching. Lot of miles in hard ground, running on roads. For every session. Fellas were training on their own. We didn't come back till after Paddy's Day. Nobody has monitored what they did.'

Liston's point is well made. Kerry reached a sort of ecstatic fanaticism when it came to training and competing among themselves. Mikey Sheehy's and Pat Spillane's knees are gone, replaced by transplant surgeons. Seanie Walsh and John O'Keeffe have had hip replacements. Tommy Doyle suffered from chronic Achilles tendonitis for years, having taken many injections to play in big games.

They took too little care of themselves and they rushed back from injuries. Nobody blames Mick O'Dwyer. With five PE teachers in the side, they knew enough to know better. They were immersed in a culture of total commitment.

'Every man in that panel gave everything that was ever asked,' says O'Dwyer. 'If they gave too much, that was the way they were. Nothing was too much for football.'

Nothing.

19

The two most competitive divils ever put on this earth, I'd say.

Pat Spillane

When the evenings stretch and the sun musters some warmth, that's when he likes to set foot in the world again. Winter is for coffee and cigarettes and talk. Spring and summer are for the field and work. He's seventy-six years old now and long past the age where he could have settled for just being an old codger. The same steel clasp of a brain keeps working the same as it ever did. Its owner keeps moving. Stay still and you die.

The pains in his back mess him around some days but Kevin Heffernan never stooped for anyone, and a bit of back pain isn't going to cause him to start now. This year he is in charge of the St Vincent's minor hurling team. Young fellas who need some work. His sleeves are rolled up. Another generation being shaped beneath his lathe.

St Vincent's operate from a large premises with two adjacent pitches, just off the Malahide Road. They are a big club, but not the biggest in the city by a long stretch.

From St Vincent's it is possible to see Croke Park, a mile or two away, looming on the horizon like Ayers Rock. Croke Park and the clubs that dot the surrounding city are supreme testimony to the confidence and well-being of the GAA, a volunteer-based amateur body. In an era of overwhelming cultural homogeneity, the survival and prospering of Gaelic games is a warming phenom-enon. Were you to suggest to Kevin Heffernan that it had anything to do with him, he would give you a short, sharp answer.

Still. The story speaks for itself. In 1934, just 36,143 people came to see Dublin in an All-Ireland football final with Galway. In 1942, just over 37,000 came along to see Dublin and Galway in another All-Ireland final. In the period from 1933 to 1954, these were the worst attendances for any All-Ireland finals. They were the only occasions on which Dublin contested the final. Those Dublin teams were backboned by country men.

On the other hand, when St Vincent's played Garda in a county football final in 1955 (actually delayed till March of 1956 because of a fixture backlog), the game almost billed itself as a battle between city and country, and some 28,887 paying customers turned out to see St Vincent's win.

Heffernan was central to everything in those heady times. If Dublin didn't win big as often as they might have, it is because Heffernan and his colleagues were playing week in and week out, football and hurling. They were remarkable. The St Vincent's footballers went unbeaten in any competition from October 1948 till November 1956, a period in which the club's hurlers also appeared in five county finals, winning three.

The wear and tear can scarcely be imagined. On Easter Sunday of 1956 Heffernan was to be found in Cork, playing for St Vincent's against St Finbarr's. The next day, Easter Monday, he was in the Woolwich Stadium in London, playing football for Dublin. At the start of June, Dublin beat Wicklow in the Leinster champion-ship, before heading to the US the following day with thirteen St Vincent's players for a three-week, three-match tour which began with an emphatic win over Kerry in the Polo Grounds in New York. Little wonder that an exhausted Dublin team were beaten by Wexford in the second round of the Leinster champion-ship, two days after their return.

Heffernan wasn't just the most innovative star of the times, the only one of the group who would make the GAA's team of the millennium. He was also one of the few who saw the bigger picture, the difference which Dublin teams could make to the GAA and the difference which players born and bred in Dublin could make to Dublin teams.

'You played your football and your hurling,' he says, 'and you got on with it, but if you took the time to look, you could see the impact which the policy of Dublin players was having. It made the game attractive to people. Sport is a great thing to give a sense of identity to a place, and Dublin people wanted a sense of identity. They liked the team and they liked the way we played. They cottoned on very quickly that this could stand for them in some way that was attractive, not just for us – it was attractive for the GAA as well.'

'Kevin would always have appreciated the bigger picture,' says Jimmy Gray, whose decision it was to make Heffernan manager of the county team again in 1973 and to give him what he wanted in order to succeed. 'He was involved and interested administratively and would have always seen the direction the game was going in, the trends, what rules changes meant. And he understood what the GAA was to Ireland as a whole, and what level Dublin needed to be at if the GAA was going to survive. He's a very smart man. A bit grumpy sometimes, but a very smart man!'

Today no team fills Croke Park with quite the same regularity or the enthusiasm as the Dublin footballers do. Even though it is more than a decade since the county last won an All-Ireland, it takes a run of just two wins in the summertime to set the city alight with expectation.

The county football team is the prism through which many Dubliners see their own identity. Dublin play with the confidence and swagger of city teams. Dublin feed off the glory moments, goals, big wins, the communion between the crowd on Hill 16 and the players on the field. The Dublin team jersey has become a marketing phenomenon over the past ten years, and on a summer Sunday in the city it is possible to make oneself believe that the sky-blue shirt is the mandatory uniform of the masses.

'Tradition,' he would say to Robbie Kelleher, 'do you understand what tradition is now?' In Dublin, the tradition of Gaelic games burns on. Kevin Heffernan grew up in a time when it was just a flickering pilot light. He played on a team that changed, before the cultural deluge of the sixties washed everything away. Then he stood and looked at the new landscape and created a new team whose legacy rolls on.

In that sense we are all Heffernan's children.

His other children, those who played with him and worked with him, still revere him. Even those who would criticize him tiptoe about the subject, spreading caveats and justifications and contexts like confetti. They loved him. They followed him. They worshipped him. Some of them feared him, but all of them respected him. His word was law.

In 1974 Jimmy Keaveney got a job working for T. & D. Norton's.

One day in 1976 he approached Heffernan after a game to explain something to him. Norton's were launching a photocopying machine in the Silverspring Hotel on Tuesday. Big deal. Lots of clients. Lots of dealers.

'Kevin,' he said in as casual a manner as he could muster, 'I won't be here next Tuesday. We're launching a copy machine in Cork.'

'OK.'

He could see that Heffernan was not enthusiastic about the notion or much interested in the photocopy machine.

A few minutes later, the first question. 'So what time is this launch at?'

'Lunchtime.'

'And when are you going down to Cork?'

'I'll drive down on Monday evening.'

'Monday? How long will it take you to drive down?'

'About four hours.'

'Lunchtime? Four hours? OK. I'll see you in Parnell Park on Tuesday evening so.'

Heffernan turned and left. And Jimmy Keaveney saw him at training on Tuesday evening as usual. Nothing was said about photocopying machines.

His way worked. He held the best cards. Heffernan could peer into the heart of a game and pick out instantly what was necessary and what wasn't. If you weren't necessary, it was crushing. If you hadn't worked it out yourself, it was chastening.

Some players claim that he ruled by fear ('a psychological terrorist', John McCarthy once said) but you'll wonder what weapon he possessed, apart from that power to make you not part of the team.

'That was enough for most fellas,' he says himself, 'it was meant to be that way.'

It was meant to be, and it was. Players he touched, players he picked, players he dropped. None of them are neutral about Kevin Heffernan. None of them walked away with a shrug. None of them ever said it was only football.

Decades later, there is deep respect and affection but not the easy knowledge of intimates.

'After six years, and all that time with him, if you were to ask me what did Kevin Heffernan think of me, I'd have to say that I've no idea. Not a clue,' says Jim Brogan.

And would he like to know?

'I think I'd cut my losses there! I'm coming from a certain perspective here. I was a sub!' He pauses. 'I suppose that says it all.'

Robbie Kelleher played under Heffernan for all his inter-county career, from minor through to retirement. He enjoyed Heffernan and admired him but never got close.

'To this day, if I meet Kevin I'll say, "How is Mary and the family?" Kevin will say, "Great. How are Florence and the family?" "Great." And then there'll be a silence. It's a difficult thing in a way. Other fellas would have been a lot closer and would find mixing with him much easier. That's the nature of me, though, and I think the nature of him.'

John McCarthy was once quoted as saying that he would cross the road if he saw Heffernan coming towards him on the street.

He clarifies.

'What I meant was that there is this awkwardness. He's shy and he's reserved. We'd have nothing to talk about after saying hello. Yet I've often met him in a bookie's office and we could talk about horses for an hour, no problem. It's just that socially he's not an easy fella to know.'

He has affection and respect for them all. The fellas, as he calls them, the lads who played under him and who changed the face of the 1970s. It was all for a cause. Not a moment of it personal. He takes pride in what they did and what they became. He hopes they can look back on those days as fondly as he can look back on his own pomp as a player.

'There was a closeness, a sense of us achieving something together. It was a time of total honesty in the discussions we had, in the way we played on the field. It got to a stage where I could look at a player running out on to the field for training and tell by the way he was carrying himself if there was something bothering him. They were men, mature, intelligent men. They had had choices. We can't go back and change any of it.'

He hopes they understand what drove it. Football. The love of place. The sense of identity. The pursuit of Kerry. The belief that 'beating Kerry in an All-Ireland final was always a double All-Ireland to me'.

When he talks about the seventies, he makes sure always to credit his two selectors and confederates, Lorcan Redmond and Donal Colfer. If he is speaking about the later years, he will offer a genuflection to Tony Hanahoe. They played their parts, but he stands alone.

In the years since the great circus folded, Heffernan's students have served their time preserving the legacy. Brian Mullins, Robbie Kelleher, Sean Doherty, Pat O'Neill, Fran Ryder, Paddy Cullen, Jim and Bernard Brogan, Bobby Doyle, Davey Billings and, of course, Tony Hanahoe have all given their time to various senior management set-ups for the Dublin team. The rest have devoted huge chunks of their lives to clubs, to mentoring senior teams and juvenile teams, passing on what was given to them in such abundance. Tradition.

As a group of people they are phenomenally succesful. When they travelled all together for a holiday in South Africa some years ago, it was commented that there were at least ten of the team who could have afforded to pay for the entire travelling party.

In 2004 he was given the Freedom of the City of Dublin in recognition of his achievements – including his positions as head of Labour Relations at the ESB and Chairman of the Labour Court and of Bord na gCon – and not long afterwards himself and his old adversary, Mick O'Dwyer, were conferred with honorary doctorates from the National University of Ireland.

For Heffernan the fuss was an embarrassment. He was being rewarded, as he saw it, merely for being what he is. Football and hurling had always made their place in his existence, along with family and work. In the games he grew up with he found a part of the unique passion of Irish life. He found games which suited the soul of the people who played them.

'They suited me, anyway,' he says with a laugh, 'and I think they fit our Irish temperament. The pace, the colour, the passion and speed of our games. Would it be a cliché to say that those things are part of what we are?'

Dublin football is a different business now from what it was when Kevin Heffernan picked it up off the floor in 1973. The culture of the GAA flows through the city. On yet another Sky Super Sunday, when all the world is indoors watching the over-hyped soccer pros from over there, it is still possible to stroll out and see men and boys and women reaching for the sky, playing Gaelic football and hurling. They are enjoying the last shred of Irish culture which can attract mass participation. It makes Dublin a different city from Manchester or Birmingham or Liverpool. Not better, perhaps, but different; and different is enough.

Every summer the city's hunger for All-Ireland success is palpable. A little run of wins turns the city electric.

And Heffernan is the emeritus professor, presiding quietly, invisibly, over it all.

O'Dwyer, who started out his Kerry career with suffering because of the geographical isolation of the club he hailed from, will end his days as the central figure in the history of Kerry football. His achievements are so great that the simple fact that he has had to travel thousands of lonely miles just to play is sometimes obscured. He has defied Waterville's isolation and put the little place on the map. You hear the word 'Waterville', you think of Mick O'Dwyer.

The Waterville which O'Dwyer grew up in seems an unlikely source of Kerry football lore. The town's location shaped its destiny in the oddest of ways. Waterville was where the cables came ashore.

The first transatlantic cable was laid by Western Union from Hearts Content in Newfoundland to Valentia Island, in August 1858. Twenty-five years later, Waterville had been picked by the Commercial Cable Company of New York as the landing place for a submarine cable linking North America with Europe.

The submarine cables (six were eventually laid) were a miracle of their age. The lines ran overland from New York City to Canso in Nova Scotia and were then insulated in gutta-percha and laid on the bed of the Atlantic from Canso to Waterville. In Waterville the signal was repeated for strength, and the line ran on under water as far as Weston-super-Mare in south-western England, and then onwards overland to London. At the peak of the cable tele-graph business, Waterville was a significant stop on the boreen which pre-dated the information superhighway.

Waterville had been a picturesque hamlet of some fifty or so houses and a few hotels which catered for the parties that came to fish for salmon and trout in Lough Currane. The Commercial Cable Company brought with it some 350 telegraphists from Eng-land, Scotland and Wales. In turn, the telegraphists brought with them their own games and pursuits, and those diversions rubbed off to give Waterville the culture of a garrison.

The telegraphists brought cricket and croquet to Waterville. Soccer was played, although only in internal leagues among staff. Tennis was popular. There was a nine-hole course in Waterville, and to all intents and purposes the cable people owned it. The local population provided the caddies.

It was a curious, slightly uneasy relationship between the town and the Commercial Cable Company. Such an influx of workers brought money and some prosperity, but no real integration. The staff of the cable company were overwhelmingly male, and yet, from the early 1880s until satellite forced the company out of business in 1962, there were scarcely more than twenty marriages recorded between staff and local women.

The local people played Gaelic football, of course, but even among them the game had yet to acquire the status of a religion as it had in other parts of Kerry. The breeding of foothounds was a popular pastime, and in the O'Dwyer house beagles were valued over footballers. Rowers were valued over footballers, too. South Kerry had a vibrant tradition of regattas, and Micko's maternal grandfather, Bateen Galvin from Scariff Island, was a legendary oarsman.

The O'Dwyers lived in a small house opposite a little field known locally as Melrick's Garden. Every evening the little field teemed with small boys chasing a football. There was a proper football field down by the lake and, as young Micko graduated from the games in the garden, he spent increasingly long chunks of his days down there, perfecting the skills of a game which fascinated him.

In St Finian's National School the teacher was Dan Kennelly, and his enthusiasm was infectious. Every afternoon he'd divide the boys of the school into two teams and then opt to play on one team himself. Micko came to realize after a while that he himself must have attained some skill at the game, because Kennelly always picked himself on the opposite team. The thought spurred him on to more and more practice.

After a few years, a teacher called Sean McCarthy arrived down from Dublin and took the football on to another level again. The GAA still feels the momentum born of Sean McCarthy's early nudging.

In Kerry today, football occupies the same sacred place that it always did. The game has its own philosophers and its own dialectics. Each region brings its own subtleties which, like wine, seem to arise from the landscape. Football in north Kerry is frank and robust and tough. In south Kerry the game is played for beauty, an aesthete's feast.

And Micko, though his work these days is of a missionary nature (coaching Laois after a long stint with Kildare), is still, at seventy years of age, a significant presence in the county. The team he produced is the yardstick by which all teams will be measured in future. Their eight All-Ireland wins were a feat of longevity and creativity that will never be equalled.

Everything Micko says about the current Kerry team and its management is taken out and held up to the light. Is he praising? Is he being critical? Perhaps he's just gassing for the tape. And every team is compared, unfairly and unfavourably, with the boys who strolled through those glorious summers.

Now that they are the men of winter, O'Dwyer's protégés still speak of him with that curious mixture of awe and irreverence they have always held for him.

Paudie O'Mahoney has been sharply critical of O'Dwyer down through the years. Paudie never enjoyed twisting in the wind as O'Dwyer played mind games, and often the pair of them fell to rowing. Paudie could never lay a glove on O'Dwyer, though. The thought of their sparrings makes him laugh now.

'Whenever I was dropped I always thought O'Dwyer was personally attacking me. I knew when he'd be telling me lies. I was sensitive. It was hard like that. He drove us hard, played us, one off the other. Fellas like myself and Tim Kennelly were driven to the edge. We stood for each other as best we could, though. This team of ours is half crippled but it was good fun too.'

A few years ago, when O'Dwyer appeared on a popular phone-in programme on Radio Kerry, there was a momentary silence which crackled with tension when it was announced that the first caller was Paudie O'Mahoney.

'He was shitting himself, I'd say, thinking I'd cut loose on him. I'd only good things to say, though. There's a closeness there because of it all. I was the first person to arrive at his mother's funeral. He told me that. I think when I was drinking he always had an understanding of it. I liked him and I still like him.'

The boys don't see too much of John Egan these times. He has lived over the border in Cork for many years and, as it did even in the great days, geography has kept him apart. They say, though, that if anyone is bitter about O'Dwyer it is John Egan.

John was taken off during the 1984 All-Ireland final when he was struggling on Mick Holden. He walked off the field and wasn't seen in green and gold again.

He shrugs when 1984 and Mick O'Dwyer are mentioned in the same sentence.

'I never enjoyed 1984, for some reason. If you are playing for as long as I had been, you expect a pass in certain circumstances. When I wouldn't get it I'd get cranky.

'Mick was never close to players. He always kept the distance. He wouldn't be your friend, it wouldn't be the thing to do. He wasn't a drinker. If he golfed he went with some of the lads all right. I didn't blame him for 1984. Maybe [I did] for a while, because initially I was very disappointed. It's so hard to drop off that ladder. Suddenly you're out. It all goes on without you. It was your whole life, and then it's gone. You're on the terrace and as a spectator it's a foreign world. I was disappointed. I made no comment about Mick O'Dwyer then, though. I've nothing bad to say now.'

If there was fear of Heffernan in the Dublin camp, sometimes there was never more than exasperation with O'Dwyer among the Kerrymen. He knew what made his players tick and he used that knowledge, treated each one differently.

'I had a fierce competitive edge,' says Egan. 'He knew that. It hurt me to be dropped or taken off. I would say to myself, "Why didn't that other fella come off?" You have to be that way. That's why nobody takes your ground. You're like a farmer with a field. You have your patch. I thought about it for a long time, brooded. I blamed Dwyer, but it was always going to end some way.'

O'Dwyer's prolonged absence from the Kerry scene as he coaches other counties has perhaps cost his boys as the years go past. In Dublin, Lorcan Redmond and Donal Colfer worked hard to keep the group together and close when it all ended. Tony Hanahoe has taken up the task of preserving the unity and integrity of the group. In Kerry, the youth of the team and the revolving captaincy system meant that Kerry ended up with no natural leaders to draw them together, and O'Dwyer, who had many different selectors in his time, is perhaps the only man who could draw all his old players in again under one tent. He's sentimental and the idea appeals to him. He still has a life to live and sessions to take, though. Always moving.

Jack O'Shea remembers a spat between himself and O'Dwyer in the mid- to late eighties.

Kerry had played a league match in Tralee. Jacko thinks it might have been against Donegal – the years have misted the memory. Jacko gave a ball into Bomber Liston but it was winter and out of season for the Bomber. The big man wasn't the fittest.

'Bomber didn't make much of a move for it, and the ball didn't reach him. It was intercepted, Donegal went down the field, got a goal and beat us.'

The following weekend Jacko was dropped for a game against Armagh. The demotion came as a shock.

'In midwinter I'd still be looking after myself, doing everything he wanted. I was playing well. I thought he just did it to teach me a lesson, and I was so hurt. The team was announced and I wasn't in it. They were to travel from Kerry, and because I lived in Leixlip I'd drive up on Sunday morning. For a while I wasn't even going to go. In the end I went. I togged out on the sideline and it was a day when Armagh tore into us and after about ten or fifteen minutes they were winning six points to no score. Dwyer turned to me and said, "Get ready, you're going on." I said I wouldn't go on. I told him to stick with what he started with.

'I always felt since that that he always respected me a lot more. I was so hurt. I wasn't going to go at all. I wasn't going to get up and go in and help save it all. That was the only time I ever stood up to him and said anything. He never mentioned it again! It's funny, he put no fear in you. Just respect. A lot of affection. He gave me a fair crack of the whip, except that once. I knew I didn't deserve to be dropped. I was back in the following week, of course.'

When it all finished with Kerry, Mick O'Dwyer was ready for quiet twilight. He had a boat built in Derrynane. He'd bought his lobster pots and nets. He was going to fish and run his business and enjoy watching football.

Then Kildare came calling and, after two spells there, Laois wanted a slice of the magic, and suddenly he was seventy years old and still running county teams, still cajoling players who had grandfathers younger than him.

Several nights a week now he sleeps in the Burlington Hotel. As Laois prepare for the championship, it suits him to be nearby. He loves driving, but Laois to Waterville three nights a week stretched his affections too far. As he strides through the airy lobby of the Burlington, you can inhale the odd scent of his celebrity. Every Irishman in the place recognizes O'Dwyer instantly and takes a second glance. No tourist has a notion who he is.

The game has changed, and he hasn't got the natural talents to work with in Laois as he had in Kerry all those years ago; but, as with any team he has ever taken, he keeps them competitive and disciplined and within striking distance of glory.

He has adapted, too. He has brought in physical trainers, learned the wisdom of being cautious with injuries, taken the best that can be taken from modern team-preparation techniques. One thing distinguishes him still, though, makes him Micko. The enthusiasm.

He loves a good game of football. He loves talking about footballers, watching footballers and evaluating footballers. He loves talking about the seventies. He's still competitive about the era and can tell you each precise bounce of the ball which cost Kerry the chance of winning twelve titles in a row.

Eight All-Irelands for a team represents an unscalable Everest of achievement, but in Mick O'Dwyer's passionately competitive heart the ones that got away still hurt.

He is not close with Heffernan, never has been. Whatever their teams shared, whatever legacy got passed on, O'Dwyer and Heffernan have never been inclined to sit down and reminisce. The comradeship which has grown between the players of the era has never got a grip of their leaders.

'Heffernan was one of the best,' says O'Dwyer politely when asked about his old rival. 'He brought them from nowhere. He was top class. Hanahoe did a great job afterwards. He had the right ideas, Heffernan. He saw the rural fellas giving small Dublin teams the works and he got big fellas.'

Heffernan would argue that it was much more than that. He enjoyed the game best when it was played at a certain level, when he could detect signs of an active brain on the other bench. And that's what people forget, perhaps, when they moan about Heffernan being the catalyst for the era of the manager. Before Heffernan, football was just a tactical black hole. Kerry had their gurus, Cavan and Down and Antrim had their moments, but the game never experienced a revolution like that of the 1970s. Ask Heffernan now which of those he played against he had a lot of time for, and he smiles across the table.

'None of them.'

You clarify the question. Not liked. Just respected.

He laughs again. Not arrogance, just amusement at the gulf in understanding.

'At the time I would have had no time for any of them.'

So you drag the answers out little by little.

Eugene Magee?

'In the seventies Magee and I would have spat at each other up and down sidelines, first when he was with UCD and I was with Vincent's, and then when he was with Offaly and I was with Dublin. We would have disliked each other intensely.

'Now we can be civil to each other. Now we can have a chat, and I think we're both surprised to find that we have a lot of views in common about the GAA. Back then, though, he was the enemy.'

And Mick O'Dwyer?

Just polite evasion here. A tricky one. O'Dwyer would be the nemesis, the living, breathing incarnation of all the dread Kerry cutery.

Heffernan doesn't want to talk about O'Dwyer. 'He certainly played the game at that level.'

Too intuitively, though. For O'Dwyer it was never a chess game. For Heffernan the challenge was in the intellect.

The Dubs believed O'Dwyer to be an ungracious loser. The Kerrymen believed Heffernan to be coldly ruthless. In 1986, when O'Dwyer was passed over for the job of managing the first Irish squad to travel to Australia for the modern International Rules games, Heffernan was given the job. Some Kerry players withdrew from the tour in protest.

Others, like Pat Spillane and Jack O'Shea, travelled and got the opportunity to consort with the enemy. They found Heffernan more remote than O'Dwyer, but similar in his heart.

'The two most competitive divils ever put on this earth, I'd say,' says Spillane. 'They'd have different ways of handling people but would be able to see right through you from the time you shook hands and said hello.'

O'Shea was made squad captain by Heffernan for the tour. He remembers one conversation with Bomber Liston when the big man implored him not to go.

'I could see Bomber's point, and he was closer than any of us, I suppose, to Dwyer. Not going wasn't going to make any difference, though. It was a chance to play for Ireland and a chance to play for Heffernan. I found him extraordinary, and when I look back at it that's one of the privileges of my career. I was one of the few to have played for both men.'

The perspective of history will enhance that distinction.

20

Sure isn't that what horses are for!

Jimmy Deenihan

On excursions to Dublin it's a treat for old Kerry players to run
into certain of their Dublin counterparts. Mikey Sheehy remembers fondly long nights in the company of a range of Dubs. Eoin
Liston recalls ringing Sean Doherty one day and disturbing him at
a funeral.

'Where are you?' Doherty whispered into his mobile phone.

'The Burlington.'

'Hang on. I'll be there in half an hour.'

It works the other way, too, of course. The Dubs still like to
travel to Listowel. Robbie Kelleher has a house near Páidí Ó Sé
in Ventry, Hanahoe a place out in Caherdaniel.

Tommy Drumm was in Kenmare once with eighteen clients of
McInerney's, the engineering firm of which he is a director. He
ran into Mickey Ned O'Sullivan, and Tommy and his entire party
ended up having dinner in the home of Mickey Ned and his wife
Marion.

One day, the same Mickey Ned O'Sullivan (of whom the Doc
says fondly that he can't hold very much drink) made a phone call.
It was early on a Saturday and the Doc was shining the top of the
bar in his pub when he answered.

'He asked me, would I gather up the seventy-five team. He was
going to have a reception and put us up for two nights. I said of
course we'd travel.'

'A panel of twenty-one plus partners,' Mickey Ned said.

'Well I'm afraid it's out of the question,' said the Doc. 'We've never brought the women anywhere. Not Spain, South Africa or Myrtle Beach. Thirty players and the selectors. That was it.'

Over the crackling phone line Doc thought he could hear eyebrows being raised.

That was April of 2005.

In September the Dubs descended on Kenmare. They golfed on Friday and Saturday. They did a little drinking with their old adversaries.

On Saturday night, thirty years after Sean Doherty knocked Mickey Ned O'Sullivan unconscious in Croke Park, Doherty handed the Sam Maguire Cup to his old sparring partner.

Mickey Ned gave a speech that he'd been waiting thirty years to give.

They drank with each other and to each other, the men who had made an era.

They all saw each other again much sooner than they had antici-pated. The Horse left them. The first of the gang to go.

They have a thousand and one stories about Timmy Kennelly, their big, brave centre back.

The night before the big man died, he had a half-hour conver-sation on football with Jimmy Deenihan. The two old friends spoke about the standard of contemporary football in north Kerry. Feale Rangers were in the process of organizing a twenty-fifth anniversary celebration to commemorate a landmark county final win over Austin Stack's.

The two comrades talked and they agreed that, with the way things were going, there should be just one team from north Kerry entered into the county championships. It was a variation on a million football conversations they'd had.

Timmy Kennelly and Jimmy Deenihan had been playing with each other since boyhood. They won a North Kerry cham-pionship together, playing for Listowel, in 1968. They played together in school. When the divisional side, Feale Rangers, won two county championships at the peak of their powers, one in 1978 and one in 1980, the wins had a bonus. Kennelly captained

Kerry in 1979. Deenihan led Kerry to the four-in-a-row in 1981.

Kennelly played a good portion of the 1980 final with a damaged shoulder and his arm in a sling.

They told stories after Timmy's death and captured the man with their lyrical eloquence. Billy Keane, son of John B., told how, when Deenihan was first elected to the Dáil, he was hoisted on to the shoulders of his supporters in the Ashe Memorial Hall in Tralee. Deenihan is a big man and some of his more wispy supporters were giving way under him. Kennelly pushed in and hoisted Deenihan on to his shoulders and called up to his old teammate with a grin, 'Deenihan, I've carried you all my life.'

'Sure isn't that what horses are for!' Deenihan called down.

Deenihan always wanted Kennelly to run for the local council. He was so well loved that an election would have been a formality. Kennelly always declined.

Timmy and his wife Nuala moved into Listowel from the townland of Cloonmackon and bought a pub in 1978. Timmy never really left. He went to Australia to see his son Tadhg play for the Sydney Swans occasionally, but he was a fixture of Listowel.

He knew everyone. They knew him.

'He was the sort of man who added to the joy of a town. He'll be missed off the streets in Listowel, his presence and his fun,' Deenihan says.

That sense of fun was infectious. Deenihan recalled a time when Feale Rangers were out in Deenihan's own heartland in Finuge, training for a county championship game against Austin Stack's. It was 1981 and it was Monday evening and Feale Rangers had a great team at the time.

The lads from out around Tarbert and Moyvane were passing through town on the way home from training and decided to head into Kennelly's Bar for a few sasparillas.

They had a few pints. Puck Fair was on in Killorglin. The lads suggested to Kennelly that they all head to the fair. Kennelly said no. He advised the players to have a few drinks and go home.

'They had their few drinks and went out of the pub, and Tim came after them and closed the door and they all went to Puck

Fair! It was about two in the morning. The team's trainer, Conín Riordan, was in the travelling party. They stayed for four days.'

Worse was to come. Those of the team who didn't go were out training the following night and heard that the lads had gone to Puck Fair. They got into the cars and went off to join them.

They all arrived back for training on Thursday evening. There were men getting sick on the sidelines. On Sunday they lost by a point.

Deenihan asked innocently afterwards how the entire expedition to Killorglin was financed. Kennelly replied with a twinkle that one of the lads had a chequebook.

It was a beautiful winter's day when they buried Timmy Kennelly. The Christmas lights were up in his beloved town as the long procession moved slowly down from the mortuary. It took four hours for sympathizers to be done shaking the Kennelly family's hands. The atmosphere of loss and grief was palpable in the winter air.

At the church, just as the Horse's funeral was to begin, there was the sound of footsteps in the centre aisle. Heads turned. The Dubs.

Greying men in long Bugatti coats and sombre hats. They marched up the aisle all together.

'Here come the mafia,' somebody whispered.

Kerrymen recalled later how, a couple of years previously, they had organized a surprise event to honour Timmy in his own club. They had asked Tony Hanahoe to come and be the speaker. Hanahoe had marked Kennelly and vice versa in all the clashes between the sides in the seventies. He had agreed immediately to come.

They discovered later he had cancelled a trip to the Breeder's Cup in order to be in Kerry.

They all stood together that day, their soldiering done. Men on the brink of old age. Jack O'Shea looked around with a new wonder. He'd taken these people for granted.

'I still treat the older lads with the same respect. I still feel they're looking after me. Watching me. Johnno is still our statesman.

Hanahoe with the Dubs. I know what I'm going to get with them all. The older lads, I hold them in such esteem. They'll always be senior to me. They always went before and achieved first.'

He looked around him, and in the midst of so much grief he experienced an odd moment of fleeting serenity. Every face he saw brought back memories, retrieved moments of a youth when every good thing was amplified and when nobody knew that hope wasn't an infinite thing.

The Christmas lights spread a wan glow about the place. The cold air nibbled the earlobes as the men shuffled and stamped their feet and told stories of each other. They'd be seeing themselves down for years to come, their number dwindling at each gathering, their legend becoming more remote till their splendour would be remembered only in the games they saved.

Early in 2006 David Hickey, by now an organ-transplant surgeon of international renown, became ill himself. It was one of those sunlit afternoons when life for no apparent reason delivers a sickening kick to the groin.

Hickey's old marker, Páidí Ó Sé, drove from Kerry to Beaumont Hospital when he heard. Hickey had checked out by the time his old foe arrived. Páidí didn't regret the journey.

Kerry players called and wrote and rang. The Dubs gathered tight around their man, the light of their dressing room for so many years. And Heffernan was a constant and concerned presence. The small differences between them didn't matter. It was football and it was family and one lasts longer than the other.

Epilogue

For he who lives more lives than one, more deaths than one
must die.

Oscar Wilde

It is the summer of 2005. High summer, or that time when a season
starts making sense. He is climbing the concrete stairwell when he
stops and looks up to heaven.

His shirt has the precise colour of the sky. He listens. Nothing
but the din of Dub decibels above him on Hill 16. He smiles. It's
more than enough to draw him onwards. He reaches the top step
and stands there for a moment to take it all in. He inhales the scent
of the crowd. Beer breath and egg sandwiches and seething armpits.

He likes the happy noise of expectation. All these conversations
furnished with hope and enthusiasm and knowledge. All his life he's
been familiar with this hum. And down below, the long green nap-
kin of perfect football pitch stretches before him. He feels at home.

'Keep moving,' says the steward in the luminous bib. 'C'mon,
no blocking the stairs.'

He knows where he wants to stand. He knows which crush
barrier he wants to lean his weight against. He has chosen a spot
from where he can take in a view both of the game and of the
crowd. If Hill 16 had postal codes, they would radiate out from
this central position, halfway up the terrace just here where the
pitch makes a corner and the terrace crooks in gentle sympathy.

He has time on his hands. He's wearing this blue shirt and his
summer-day grin. So he just leans on the rail and lets the famous
precinct fill up around him. He half wonders if he might be
recognized. What banter might that bring?

From here, Croke Park looks like a cathedral with a dome made from sky. The stands make a high horseshoe of a horizon around the stadium and the sun makes play of light and shadow on the pitch below. The cathedral beckons and excludes Hill 16 all at once. This is the terrace. Real holy ground. Our wailing wall. This is the place where people go to worship. The occasion is experienced differently here from anywhere else.

The Dublin accents colour the air above him, the bodies beginning to press against each other as the same old jokes entertain the same old kafflers. In the distance, on the executive levels in the stands, he can see the great and the good grazing in their shirtsleeves. Men swill Chardonnays at polished bars. Bespoke suits hover over snow-white tablecloths. Every class and creed comes to a part of this church now. It's not the minority faith of bogball any more, high church of all countrymen.

The show begins with the same old ritual. Dublin emerge from a far tunnel like a blue express train and the terrace just boils over with excitment.

Warm-ups. Team news on the Tannoy. The parp, parp, parp of anthem while the Dubs stand in a long line across the pitch, facing their followers on the Hill.

The ball is thrown into the air and like a flicked switch it starts this lunatic cheering which doesn't stop until after the ball goes dead. This is a replayed match, an All-Ireland quarter-final.

There's a full house in today. Eighty-three thousand shoehorned souls. Their noise echoes out over Hill 16 and to the steep-roofed terraced houses behind.

Back in the days when he stood down there on the turf, he often wondered what it would be like to stand up here in a swaying sea of Dubs. The salty tongues and the riptide currents of their changing opinions.

It's better than he thought.

A wounded Tyrone player lies down on the field. A panel of experts convene over his body. They examine his leg. It takes forever. The Hill grows impatient.

'Jaysus. C'mon for fuck's sake. Just cut it off and hit him with the soggy end.'

Everything about Croke Park has changed, bar this place. The austere old angular stands have gone. The reeking urinals. The crêpe paper hats which ran streaks down your face when the rain arrived. The hawkers of unofficial match programmes. The cruddy dressing rooms. The rain, which always arrived. Three bars for a pound.

They still stand on Hill 16, though, and from here the world sounds blue and looks blue.

He loves it that way.

There is no place in the world like this. No other communion of people like this. A thin fence and some ability divides the blue shirts on the terrace from the blue shirts on the pitch. Nothing else. Not geography. Not upbringing. Not income. Not accent. Not class. Not colour. Not creed.

Hill 16 still represents the phenomenon of parish pride, but the pride and the parish have been fattened on urban steroid to become the preoccupation of a major city. The fundamentals are the same, though: native men, playing their native game.

Yep. He loves it.

For a period Dublin are thriving. They swagger like they so often did, back in the 1970s. Points go rat-a-tat-tatting over the Tyrone crossbar. In the excitement he is carried forward down the terraces and back up again. When he looks at his feet he notes with surprise that they aren't actually on the ground. He is fastened into this organic wad of blueness which moves about the steps with a life of its own. It's thrilling. He vows that if Dublin make the final, he'll come and stand here again in September.

Now there is a little diversion. When the teams swapped ends for the second half, the change brought Jason Sherlock close to the Hill. The warmth rolled down towards the Dublin forward. When Dublin are going well, Jayo is still emblematic of all that Dublin are capable of.

Jayo is taking digs from his marker today. The Hill registers its disgust and feigns its shock. You clatter Jayo, the Hill feels the anguish . . .

'Don't mind him, Jayo,' comes the tender roar from the man in front. 'He's only an effin racist.'

The Punch and Judy show continues. Jayo running around, taking evasive action. His stalker following, always with discreet retribution.

Again, 'Don't mind him, Jayo. He's only an effin racist.'

The Hill is getting anxious now. Opinion is divided and debate opens up.

Jayo should pop him back.

Jayo should lie down.

Jayo should hit a goal, show the hoor.

There it goes again. Another clatter. Same voice. A new thought this time.

'Don't mind him, Jayo. He's only a fucking black proddie northern bastard.'

Charlie Nelligan shakes his head and grins. Life here on the Hill is as tasty as he'd imagined it would be, all those times he'd stood down on the pitch minding the Kerry goal. He'd listened a thousand times to all the ways that his protruding ears reminded the Hill of the handles on the Sam Maguire Cup and grinned every time. Sometimes he'd turn to them and roar, 'Up the Kingdom!' They'd pay it back to him with interest. His friends, the enemy.

It was a rivalry and it was a love story, an era which saved Gaelic games for the city and in so doing saved it for the country as well. Dublin versus Kerry. They took the tiredness from our lives, opened us to the poetic tang of possibility.

It began in a time when we aspired to nothing more than the sacred laying of burgundy leatherette from shore to shore, with mountain ranges of the most handsome Formica in between. When Dublin ran out on to the field under the booming September sky for the 1974 All-Ireland final, they were greeted by a populace who had almost forgotten that the city had a team. It was widely commented that in their pristine white tracksuits the Dubs looked like Leeds United. We had no other reference point, no other measurement of sporting glamour.

In the years before that final, the game had reached its lowest ebb in the capital and the GAA had nearly died. When Kevin Heffernan leaned over and breathed life into the expiring body of the GAA in Dublin, he effected a resurrection as well as a revolution. Back then, to be seen carrying an O'Neill's kitbag or a hurley stick in public was to declare to the world that you were a redneck hick. Worse than that, you had no wish to better yourself.

You were a gahman, a bogballer, a culchie or a consorter with culchies. The brave new Ireland had no time for such things. Kevin Heffernan, remembering a different world, could imagine a different future for us. His team laid down a gauntlet and the answering challenge came, as Heffernan always knew it would, from Kerry.

You need to know where GAA was at that time. Dublin reached the All-Ireland semi-final against Cork in that heady breakthrough year of 1974. The two most populous counties in the country slugged it out on an August day. In the blue corner, The Capital, and in the red corner, The Feisty Second City. Cork were the All-Ireland champions. They had an intoxicatingly exciting team which was blessed with pure genius in the forward lines. Dublin were the next new thing.

The game was played on an afternoon which coincided with the last day of the Dublin Horse Show. RTE's outside broadcast units went to the gee-gees. Missing from the national archives is the proof of one of the greatest games of the era. In Dublin 4, where the decision was made, what went on in Croke Park was just slightly more than an irrelevance. Few demurred.

Paddy Cullen, who played in goal for Dublin that afternoon, remembers as a child the scrum to get into the one house on Seville Place which had a colour television. TV – which delivered England's World Cup win in 1966 right into Irish living rooms, and *Match of the Day* on Saturday nights – was proof that real life was elsewhere and it was better than anything we knew.

When Brazil came along in 1970, we swooned. Now this was entertainment. And Holland in 1974. Total Football? Oh yeah.

According to Larkin (Philip, not Alan), sex began in 1963, 'between the end of the "Chatterley" ban / And the Beatles' first LP'. Sex was imported, under licence and in small quantities, to Ireland some time later, but it proved just as diverting. In a tightly buttoned-up country the news that the big world was not only different but might also be having a better time when the lights went out was slightly shaming. Our confidence in the world of comely maidens and brothy GAA men seeped away. We were convinced that the path to freedom lay in earnest reproduction of all the things we saw on television and in glossy magazines.

The story is often told about the film maker David Lean coming to Kerry, a year before he began shooting *Ryan's Daughter*, his vision of an Ireland riddled with mad patriots, village idiots and scheming clergy. Scouting in Kerry for the perfect locations, he came across a pub that fitted the bill perfectly. Wood counters and dusty stout bottles and the smell of pipe tobacco.

Lean had a word with the landlord and left with him a deposit which secured the use of the pub for several months' shooting the following summer.

A year passed, and on his return the great film maker fell to his knees in despair when he returned to find that the landlord had used the cash to turn the pub into his vision of something a little more worthy of Hollywood. Three miles of leatherette, a pool table and a jukebox under a sky of neon.

Dublin and Kerry gave us something to believe in. They filled grounds and they recharged our imaginations. They played with an exuberance and a zest which sometimes seems lost now. When they left the arena and came among us again, they weren't perfumed with the sour scent of entitlement or greed. The game gave them what they wanted. They gave us plenty in return.

They were timely. They arrived at the hour of the GAA's greatest need. Kevin Heffernan will blow a stream of smoke and shake his head and say if it hadn't been him, somebody else would have come along. It's like saying that somebody else would have invented the wheel. Would they? Who knows?

On the morning of the 1974 All-Ireland final, the Dublin team broke with tradition. Normally each player made his own way to Croke Park, but on this day they met up at the grounds of Na Fianna on Mobhi Road in Glasnevin. They had a breakfast of scrambled eggs and then drove the short distance to Croke Park in a bus.

Robbie Kelleher, now one of the country's leading economists, was a student at the time. He sat beside the county chairman, Jimmy Gray. While the two men sat gazing out the window at the crowds making their way through the north side of the city, Gray sought to explain to the younger man what that moment meant. Kelleher recalls Gray saying that 'It was something to cheer about, in a place that hadn't had anything to cheer about in a long time.'

It was. When Dublin played Wexford in the opening round of the 1974 championship, the game was postponed for a week out of respect for the victims of the Dublin bombings. Dublin's performance was comically inept, but the humour was lost on a city still grieving the casualties of the bombs that exploded in Parnell Street, South Leinster Street and Talbot Street on 17 May, killing twenty-six people and injuring more than two hundred others.

It was a grey time. And when things weren't grey they were black.

It is often said that Dublin and Kerry provided a simple story of city versus country, bespoke suits jousting with freckled hayseeds. That indeed was a principal subplot of the era and a thematic strand worn threadbare in the sports pages of newspapers. Dublin and Kerry were more than that, however. Their domination of the Irish sporting stage did much to save Irish culture from plasticized homogeneity.

Ger O'Keeffe, the corner back on the Kerry team of the time, puts it succinctly.

'Our two teams, doing what we did back then, is the reason we have Croke Park as it is today. We were dead. All-Irelands were drab. The game was parochial. It would have struggled to go on.

Dublin got Hill 16 working. The colour started arriving. The Celtic Tiger in my view started slowly back then when we started to have confidence in our own game and culture. The likes of Tony Hanahoe and Kevin Heffernan and Mick O'Dwyer had a huge input there.

'A guy like Tony gave a great image to Gaelic football. He was cool, intelligent and articulate. The GAA was down on its knees. It was shamateurish and amateurish. Players were pawns. There was no respect for any of it . . . Having a guy like Tony Hanahoe out there, expressing opinions that made people stand back and listen, was a shock. He created the whole notion that GAA players aren't dumb. That team and the rivalry we had changed the whole face of more things than football.'

Dublin itself was caught in a transition period, with the population shifting from the city to the suburbs. Inner-city clubs and vocation-based clubs began to vanish and the new housing estates were open territory in which soccer thrived. Bardas, Geraldine's, St Joseph's of Terenure all went. Westerns vanished. Sean McDermott's expired in 1970, just three years after a county final appearance.

As great swaths of the new Dublin developed without GAA clubs at their heart, Dublin football sank further into the mire.

The seventies changed all that. Heffernan's team transfused the city with enthusiasm and energy. The GAA caught the wind. The number of Catholic church parishes created in the seventies in suburban Dublin was mirrored almost precisely by the spread of the GAA in those places. There was no template for planting clubs in these new sporting wildernesses. They grew from the enthusiasm of the times. Some clubs, like Naomh Mearnog, Naomh Barrog, St Jude's and Trinity Gaels, came from nothing. Smaller clubs in areas of huge population growth metamorphosed into large social and sporting institutions.

'As far as I'm concerned the most influential period of history in Gaelic football was the seventies,' says Gay O'Driscoll. 'It turned it all around. There was a time in the late sixties I wouldn't tell people I played for Dublin.

'In the seventies it became very sexy in the city. To play GAA. To be a Dub. I remember, we'd go into places like Sachs Hotel on the south side, and friends of mine in the advertising business, who wouldn't have heard of Croke Park ten years before, now they wanted to go to matches. Kerry were the only ones who had a look at what we were doing, they responded. The great rivalry came and the great era came with it. There's a great respect and affection between us ever since. We each know what we did.'

And they had fun doing it. They changed Irish lives and changed their own lives, too. Ask any Dublin player or Kerry player from that time what they remember best and value most from their time in the sun, and they each utter the same word. Friendships.

It's a crock to claim, as romantics do, that there was never a dirty blow thrown between Dublin and Kerry. There were plenty. And occasionally there were blows thrown between Dublin men at training in Parnell Park and between Kerrymen at work in Killarney. They were the squabbles of business, though, and never developed to the stage of bone-deep grudges. When the day was done, the dirty deeds were left behind. And when that golden period was over, the enmities were buried forever.

'Now it's a very sexy game,' says David Hickey, who made his debut in 1968 in Carrickmacross in deep winter, a venue and a time which were the antithesis of sexy.

When Hickey returned to Gaelic football in 1974 after a brief break, he returned from the bosom of UCD rugby. He argues that, back then, being a player on the UCD 1st XV carried far more prestige than being a Dublin footballer. The era changed all that.

'Back then, there was no question of the Irish rugby team being equated with the Dublin Gaelic football team in terms of prestige. Now, as far as I'm concerned and ninety per cent of the population of Dublin is concerned, being a Dublin footballer is far more prestigious and meaningful.'

Down on the field, Tyrone are pulling away from Dublin. As Charlie Nelligan stands with the Dubs on Hill 16 he can't make out the figure of John McCarthy sitting over in the Hogan Stand. Just as well, perhaps. The old Dublin corner forward and the Kerry goalie saw the whites of each other's eyes enough times to last a lifetime.

If they were to bump into each other today and repair to a quiet corner, Nelligan would buy the first drink. During the last waltz of the seventies, the All-Ireland final of '79, the pair of them got sent off together. Nelligan's dismissal was wrong, but he recalls two things about it. First, he knew there was not a thing that he could do about it. Second, John McCarthy stood and argued with the referee. He argued that, while he was happy to go, Charlie Nelligan didn't deserve to be sent off.

Up in his spot in the Hogan Stand, John McCarthy is sitting and watching his county's hopes vanish for another year. In the bar behind the stand he has just met the lead character in one of his favourite stories from the good days. Mickey Joe Forbes from Ardboe in Tyrone. Mickey Joe has invited him up to Ardboe. He half thinks he might go up for the crack.

Dublin are losing and the Hill has fallen quiet. The torment of Jason Sherlock reminds him again of the Mickey Joe story. A different time.

His team, John McCarthy's team, his great Dublin team of the seventies, were playing a league match on a cold winter's day in Tyrone. He was being marked by Mickey Joe and, well, Mickey Joe was good to go.

At the last fading note of the National Anthem it started. The digs in the back and the little mantra.

'I'm Mickey Joe Forbes. The hardest wee man in Ulster. C'mon, hit me. Hit me.'

Righty-o. Again it came. Bam!

'I'm Mickey Joe Forbes. The hardest wee man in Ulster. C'mon, hit me. Hit me.'

McCarthy looked to his bench for some guidance on this matter of pest control. The Dublin bench was just getting settled and warm, though, and nobody was aware that their corner forward was being held hostage by the hardest wee man in Ulster.

So it went until finally a ball broke in midfield and Brian Mullins came soloing up the field. McCarthy didn't need much encouragement to lure the hardest wee man in Ulster towards Mullins. When the moment came, Mickey Joe Forbes abandoned McCarthy and went lunging in with a tackle.

Mullins, a giant among men, hopped the ball and caught the bounce a little high and, in doing so, caught Mickey Joe Forbes. Caught him quite firmly, as it happened, planting him on the ground. Mullins soloed onwards, apparently oblivious. McCarthy surveyed Mickey Joe.

'You knew he wouldn't be getting up.'

The punchline came as Mickey Joe was being stretchered off. McCarthy leaned forward and said softly, 'Well, Mickey Joe, you've just met the hardest man in Leinster.'

He thinks of that distant day and smiles. He remembers the anecdote more clearly than the day itself, but he knows this: there'll never be another Mullins, there'll never be other days like those. He walked into Parnell Park one day in 1973 and, more than half a lifetime later, the memories still nourish him and the friendships still swaddle him.

They grew together, both teams. Some grew wealthy, some grew fat, some grew grey. Marriages broke up. Businesses bloomed and died. Health failed. The respect remained constant and the friendships deepened. Their time continues to fascinate.

Down on the field, Tyrone have just won. For Dublin it's all over for another year. The great blue tent folds again.

'You have your dreams,' says John McCarthy. 'You play. You win and you lose. Then you drift in and drift out for a while and in the end you fade away. You never forget the days when you played, but in the end we all fade away.'

Maybe not, Macker, maybe not.

Acknowledgements

Thanks to everyone at Penguin, especially to Michael McLoughlin for commissioning this book and for coaxing it out of someone as lazy as myself. Thanks also to Brendan Barrington at Penguin for his smart and heroically patient editing. To David Walsh, whose wonderful *Magill* piece in 1989 was one of the inspirations not just for this book but for this career, such as it is. To Denis Walsh, whose famous Kerry injuries article for the *Irish Times* in the early nineties nearly killed my freelance career stone dead, so enthusiastically was it received by the paper. Denis's excellence has been a benchmark ever since. To Sean Moran for the wisdom, the advice, the fine company, the great lunches and the free access to his contacts book. Special thanks to Malachy Logan, my friend and editor at the *Irish Times*, for his generosity in allowing me to have something like a real job and for giving me the space in which to write this book and others. Thanks also to the staff in the *Irish Times* library.

Thanks to my parents, John and Mary, for having the grace to be good Dubs when it was neither popular nor profitable. Having been reared for the first seven years of my life in England, I got brought to my first All-Ireland final in 1972 to see Kerry and Offaly. I fell in love on the spot, and things got even better in 1974 when I discovered that, yes, what my parents had told me in that short, awkward chat was true: Dublin had a Gaelic football team!

A short while later I joined St Vincent's and played there happily and ineffectually for eleven years before making the imperceptible move from virtual uselessness to formal retirement. It meant that I lived my teenage years in the shadow of many heroes and in the lee of great days. My proudest footballing moment was getting thrown in to make up the numbers at a senior training session in Raheny and being knocked over by Brian Mullins. When I went back to England in the eighties and needed a fake name for working on a building site, I chose Hanahoe.

This book was a chance to meet those gods who filled out those days. They say you should never meet your heroes but none of them, Dub or Kerryman, disappointed. So, in no particular order, many, many thanks to the following, all of whom gave their time and thoughts generously: Pat and Rosarii Spillane, Ger McKenna, Leslie Deegan, Stephen Rooney, Dave Billings, Paddy Cullen, Gay O'Driscoll, Sean Doherty, Robbie Kelleher, Pat O'Neill, Kevin Moran, Paddy Reilly, Tommy Drumm, Jim Brogan, Bernard Brogan, Bobby Doyle, Anton O'Toole, Jimmy Keaveney, Tony Hanahoe, David Hickey, Alan Larkin, Kevin Heffernan, Lorcan Redmond, Jimmy Gray, Mick Hickey, Pat Gogarty, Andy Roche, Mickey Ned and Marion O'Sullivan, Paudie O'Mahoney, Charlie Nelligan, John O'Keeffe, Ger O'Keeffe, Paud Lynch, Sean Walsh, Eoin Liston, Páidí Ó Sé, Mick O'Dwyer, Mikey Sheehy, Ogie Moran, Ger Power, Jimmy Deenihan, John Egan, Johnny Bunyan, Ray Prendiville, Danny Lynch, Jack O'Connor, Jack Gilroy and Mark Wilson.

Thanks to Eddie Glackin for the help and to Tommy Clancy (Dublin minor of 1973!) for sharing the memories.

For references I am indebted to *Magill* magazine and the archives of the *Irish Times*, *Irish Press* and *Irish Independent*. I am indebted also to William Nolan and those who contributed to the invaluable *The Gaelic Athletic Association in Dublin 1884–2000*, to the late Raymond Smith for his *The Football Immortals* (1968 edition) and to J. J. Barrett for his wonderful *In the Name of the Game*.

Most of all thanks to Mary, Molly and Caitlín for their patience with somebody who spends more time in the attic than he should.

Index

Aldridge, Seamus, 199, 201, 212, 214–17
All-Ireland club championships (1976), 125, 154
All-Ireland finals
  1923, 72
  1924, 72–3
  1930, 73
  1934, 245–6
  1942, 5, 246
  1955, 3–5, 7–8
  1958, 28
  1963, 15, 240
  1965, 15–16
  1966, 17
  1970, 74
  1973, 74
  1974, 54–6, 59–64, 67–8, 100, 254–5, 268–9, 271
  1975, 99–100, 102–14, 139, 166
  1976, 129, 130, 140–1, 145–6, 148–55, 156–7, 166, 187–8, 219
  1977, 146, 167–8, 170, 177–87, 193, 219
  1978, 148, 207–17, 218
  1979, 149, 220–1, 226, 274
  1982, 231
  1983, 12, 88–9
  1984, 12
  1985, 12
All-Ireland Under-21 finals
  1973, 77, 78, 79
  1975, 112
Allen, Norman, 7

An Caislean, 141
Antrim, 38, 74
Armagh, 187, 256
Artane Boys Band, 51
Austin Stack's, 73, 79, 206, 261, 262

Ballyduff, 115, 117
Ballyfermot, 241
Ballymun Kickhams, 125
Ballyseedy, 71
Barrett, J.J., 69, 73
Barrett, Jimmy, 75
Barrett, Joe, 73
Barron, Declan, 135
Behan, Billy, 84
Belvedere College, 218
Bernard, Norman, 107
Billings, Davey, 48, 96, 107, 250
Boyle, Johnny, 8
Brady, Liam, 196
Brennan, Dessie, 181
Brennan, Johnny, 116
Brogan, Alan, 153
Brogan, Bernard, 44, 139, 160, 166
  Heffernan discovers, 58–9
  1975 All-Ireland final, 107
  1976 All-Ireland final, 145
  marriage, 152–3
  1977 All-Ireland semi-final, 180, 184
  1979 Leinster final, 225
  football career ends, 221–2
  in later life, 250
Brogan, Bernard junior, 153

Brogan, Jim, 48, 50, 197, 223
  on Keaveney, 123
  on St Vincent's, 124
  squad rotation system, 127–8
  1976 All-Ireland final, 153
  1977 All-Ireland semi-final, 182,
    183
  All-Stars trip to US, 199
  on Heffernan, 249
  in later life, 250
Brosnan, Con, 71, 73
Brosnan, Donal, 192
Brosnan, Jim, 73, 193
Bryan, Willy, 44
Buckley, Mike, 87
Bunyan, Johnny, 115–18
Bunyan, Robert, 117
Burns, Michael Joe, 206
Byrne, Connie, 157
Byrne, Paul, 186

Cahirciveen, 157–8
Campbell, Ollie, 218
Cape Town, 228–9
Carlow, 38
Carmel, Mary, 90, 92
Casement, Roger, 72
Casey, Michael, 157
Casey, Paul, 157
Casey family, 231
Castleisland, 12, 70, 92
Cavan, 5, 24
Chicago, 173–5
Civil Service, 142, 164
Civil War, 71, 72
Clanna Gael, 52
Clare, 38
Clontarf, 163
Cockell, Don, 10–11
Cogan, Ann, 55
Cogan, Frank, 54, 55

Coleman, John, 20
Colfer, Donal, 32–3, 34–5, 58, 125,
    142, 250, 255
Collins, Paddy, 225
Commercial Cable Company, 252
Connell, Sam, 58
Connemara Gaels, 66–7
Cork
  1974 All-Ireland final, 54–6, 269
  1973 All-Ireland final, 26, 74
  1973 Munster final, 75, 78
  1974 Munster final, 79–80
  1975 Munster final, 98–9
  1976 Munster final, 134–6
  1977 Munster final, 178
Corn na Casca tournament (1974),
    34
Coughlan, Jim, 115
Cremins, Gus, 115
Cribben, J.J., 19
Crinnigan, Olly, 40
Cronin, Dan, 3
Cronin, Mick, 239
Cronin, Willie, 205–6
Crumlin, 241
Cuba, 240, 241
Cullen, Paddy, 19, 35, 44, 49, 100,
    146, 183
  early life, 12
  1966 All-Ireland final, 17
  ankle injury, 17
  becomes goalkeeper, 17–18
  nominated as UCD captain, 34
  1974 All-Ireland final, 269
  All-Star trips to US, 101–2, 175,
    176, 198
  team meetings, 120, 128, 129
  and Heffernan's resignation, 161
  1978 All-Ireland final, 209,
    211–12, 213, 216–17
  in later life, 250

Culloty, Johnny, 75, 76, 82, 84
Cummins, Ray, 75

Darby, Seamus, 48
Deegan, Leslie, 60, 41, 42–3, 50,
    51–2, 107
Deenihan, Jimmy, 77, 115–16, 133,
    153, 156, 160, 206, 260
  leg injury, 88, 243
  on Dublin's success, 99–100
  1976 Munster finals, 134, 135
  training, 152
  1977 All-Ireland semi-final, 179
  dropped from team, 194–5
  All-Stars trip to US, 198, 200–3
  1978 All-Ireland final, 213
  in later life, 234
  and Timmy Kennelly, 261–3
Delaney, Paddy, 19, 33
Devine, Lefty, 24, 202
Devlin, Patsy, 55
Doherty, Martin, 55
Doherty, Sean (the Doc), 34, 35, 54,
    187
  joins Dublin, 19
  1974 All-Ireland final, 26, 63–4
  training, 37
  and Mickey Ned O'Sullivan's
    injury, 109–10
  team meetings, 126, 129
  1976 All-Ireland final, 146
  and Heffernan's resignation, 161
  1977 All-Ireland semi-final, 182,
    183–4
  1978 All-Ireland final, 208, 213
  buys pub by accident, 238–9
  in later life, 250
  and Kerry players, 260–1
Donegal, 256
Donovan, Neilly, 159
Dowling, Eddie, 115

Down, 74, 148
Doyle, Bobby, 35, 47, 143
  1974 Leinster football
    championship, 40
  dropped from 1975 All-Ireland
    final, 104–8, 111, 131–2, 154
  friendship with Keaveney, 121–2
  team meetings, 121, 122–3, 125
  briefly quits Gaelic football, 131–2
  1976 All-Ireland final, 154–5
  1977 All-Ireland semi-final, 179,
    181, 184
  1978 All-Ireland finals, 148, 209
  weight training, 154
  on Hanahoe, 164–5
  fight with Reilly, 167
  friendship with Kevin Moran,
    188–9
  on Heffernan, 221
  in later life, 250
Doyle, Jim, 131–2
Doyle, Tommy, 171–2, 199, 234,
    244
Drimnagh Castle, 141
Driscoll, Paddy, 54
Drumgoole, Joe, 42
Drumm, Tommy, 219
  joins Dublin, 143–4
  team meetings, 121
  1976 All-Ireland final, 152
  1977 All-Ireland semi-final, 183,
    185
  1978 All-Ireland final, 209
  and Brian Mullins, 224–5
  and Kerry players, 260
Dublin
  1924 All-Ireland finals, 73
  1934 All-Ireland finals, 246
  1942 All-Ireland finals, 5, 246
  1953 National League final, 5–6
  1955 All-Ireland finals, 3–5, 7–8

Dublin – *cont.*
  1958 All-Ireland finals, 28
  1963 All-Ireland finals, 15
  1965 All-Ireland finals, 15–16
  1966 All-Ireland finals, 17
  1967 National League, 17
  1974 All-Ireland finals, 10, 54–6,
    59–64, 67–8, 268–9, 271
  1974 Leinster football
    championship, 38, 40–5, 47–54
  1974 matches against Kildare, 38,
    39–40
  1975 All-Ireland finals, 99–100,
    104–9, 114, 166
  1975 All-Ireland Under-21 final,
    112
  1976 All-Ireland finals, 129, 130,
    140–1, 145–6, 148–55, 166, 219
  1977 All-Ireland finals, 146, 167–8,
    177–87, 219
  1977 National League final, 173
  1978 All-Ireland finals, 148,
    207–17, 218, 219
  1979 All-Ireland finals, 220–1, 226
  1979 Leinster final, 225
  1983 All-Ireland finals, 12, 88–9
  1984 All-Ireland finals, 12
  1985 All-Ireland finals, 12
  annual All-stars trips to US, 100–2,
    173–6, 197–203
  Hanahoe replaces Heffernan, 163,
    165–8
  Heffernan becomes manager,
    32–3, 34–5
  Heffernan resigns, 161–3, 165
  Heffernan returns to, 197
  Heffernan's importance to, 1–2,
    246–51, 269–72
  improves half-back line, 137–8,
    140, 144, 160
  milk ration, 136–7
  showers, 25
  St Vincent's dominance in,
    123–5
  St Vincent's trains with, 27–8
  Saturday-morning training, 49
  scientific training, 36–7
  size of panel, 49–50
  squad rotation system, 127–8
  successes end, 221–4
  team meetings, 46–8, 119–23,
    125–30, 131, 166
  transport, 18–19
  uniform, 49
Dunne, Mick, 49, 230–1

Egan, Jerry, 206–7, 231
Egan, Jimmy, 206
Egan, John, 79, 88, 96, 134, 157
  background, 206
  1972 All-Ireland final, 71
  1975 All-Ireland final, 111, 113
  1977 All-Ireland semi-final, 182–3,
    184
  before matches, 205–6
  Fr Teahan Cup, 206–7
  1978 All-Ireland final, 207–10,
    212, 213
  as Kerry's most underrated player,
    207
  and his brother's death, 231–2
  drinking, 232, 233
  1984 All-Ireland final, 254–5
  and O'Dwyer, 254–5
Egan, Paddy, 206–7
Erin's Hope, 6
Evening Press, 33, 57, 195, 241

Fr Teahan Cup, Sneem, 206–7
Faughs, 31
Feale Rangers, 261, 262
Ferguson, Liam, 15–16

Ferguson, Snitchy, 28
Ferris, Martin, 71
Fitzgerald, Sister Consilio, 197
Fitzgerald, Dick, 71, 73
Fitzgerald, Maurice, 157
Fitzgerald, Ned, 157
Fitzgerald Stadium, Killarney,
   73
Fitzpatrick, Rev Dr William, 7
Foley, Des, 11
Forbes, Mickey Joe, 274–5
Freeney, Ollie, 3, 12
Frongoch, 71
Fuller, Stephen, 71
Furlong, John, 36
Furlong, Martin, 51

Gaelic Athletic Association (GAA),
   78, 99
  abolishes hand pass, 6
  and collective training, 8
  in Kerry, 70
  coaching manual, 71
  and Andy Roche, 195–6
  Activities Committee, 215
  Management Committee, 216
  The Sunday Game, 236
  Heffernan's importance to, 245–7,
   269, 270–2
  see also All-Ireland finals
Gaelic Park, New York, 176,
   198–202
Galvin, Bateen, 253
Galway, 74
  1934 All-Ireland finals, 246
  1942 All-Ireland finals, 5, 246
  1967 National League, 17
  1973 All-Ireland finals, 26
  1974 All-Ireland finals, 62–3
  1976 All-Ireland finals, 140–1
  1983 All-Ireland finals, 88–9

Garda, 5, 96, 125, 246
Garvey, Peter, 211
Gilroy, Jackie, 27, 31
Gogarty, Paddy, 105, 106–8, 129
Gogarty, Pat, 40
The Golden Years (video), 233
Good Counsel, 142
Gormanston, 141
Grady, Chris, 144
Gray, Jimmy, 32–3, 49, 50, 165, 210,
   216, 247, 271
Green, Johnny, 12

Halbert, Frank, 141
Hanahoe, Tony, 19, 35, 204, 250
  love of boxing, 10–11
  background, 163–5
  on Phil Markey, 22
  1974 Leinster football
   championship, 40, 52
  1975 All-Ireland final, 107, 111
  team meetings, 120, 121, 129–30,
   166
  and St Vincent's, 125
  1976 All-Ireland final, 145
  and Heffernan's resignation,
   161
  replaces Heffernan, 163, 165–8
  All-stars trips to US, 176, 199,
   202–3
  1977 All-Ireland semi-final, 181,
   183, 185, 187
  and Heffernan's return, 197
  1978 All-Ireland final, 214–15
  suspension, 215–16
  in later life, 250, 255, 260
  and Timmy Kennelly, 263
  importance of, 272
Haughey, Charlie, 170
Havana, 242
Heffernan, John, 29, 30

Heffernan, Kevin
  importance of, 1–2, 31–3, 245–51,
    269–72
  early life, 28–31, 39
  1955 All-Ireland final, 4, 7–8
  ankle injury, 6–7, 8
  style, 6
  further defeats by Kerry, 12–13
  1963 All-Ireland final, 15
  dislikes Phil Markey, 22
  takes St Vincent's players for
    county training, 27–8
  becomes Dublin manager, 32–3,
    34–5
  training, 36–7, 49
  1974 matches against Kildare, 38,
    39–40
  1974 Leinster football
    championship, 40–3, 53–4
  team meetings, 46–8, 119–21,
    122–3, 125–30, 131
  size of panel, 50
  discovers Brian Mullins, 57–60
  coaching course, 83, 84
  1974 All-Ireland final, 54–6,
    59–63, 68
  1975 All-Ireland final, 104–8, 111
  in San Francisco, 101–2
  smoking style, 122, 130
  squad rotation system, 127
  1976 All-Ireland final, 129, 130,
    145, 148–9, 152, 153–5
  improves half-back line, 137–8,
    140, 144, 160
  resignation, 161–3, 165
  1978 All-Ireland final, 208, 210
  returns to Dublin, 197
  1979 All-Ireland final, 220–1
  1983 All-Ireland final, 88–9
  manages Irish International Rules
    team in Australia, 90, 259

  and the end of Dublin's success,
    221–4
  in later life, 245
  honours, 250–1
  and O'Dwyer, 257–9
Heffernan, Mary, 30, 31–2
Heffo's Army, 57, 63, 100
Hegarty, Kevin, 20
Henderson, Ger, 117
Hickey, David, 35, 41, 104, 132, 146,
    154, 214, 273
  early life, 240–1
  1974 All-Ireland final, 50, 52, 61–2
  1975 All-Ireland final, 111
  team meetings, 120, 121, 126, 129
  1976 All-Ireland final, 145
  and Heffernan's resignation, 161–2
  1977 All-Ireland semi-final, 179,
    181, 183, 185, 186
  All-Stars trip to US, 203
  1978 All-Ireland final, 209
  on Sean Doherty, 239–40
  in later life, 240, 241–2
  death, 264
Hickey, Mick, 58, 218–19, 220–1,
    242
Higgins, Liam, 194
Hogan, Michael, 72
Holden, Mick, 143, 222–3, 255
Houlihan, Con, 156
Howth, 6–7
Huggert, Peter, 192
Hughes, Greg, 18
Hughes, Johnny, 88–9

IRA, 66, 71, 73
Irish Press, 40, 195

Jacob, Mick, 117
Jennings, Lily, 41
Jennings, Terry, 41

Jervis Street Hospital, Dublin, 16
John Paul II, Pope, 218

Kavanagh, Tommy, 211
Keane, Billy, 262
Keane, John B., 194
Kearins, Dessie, 113–14
Keating, Babs, 20–1
Keating, Brother, 158
Keaveney, Jimmy, 18, 59, 60, 106, 164
  early life, 11–12, 26, 230
  1963 All-Ireland final, 15
  1965 All-Ireland final, 15–16
  ankle injury, 15–16
  and Heffernan, 27, 248
  1974 Leinster football
    championship, 41–3, 44
  training, 44
  team meetings, 46, 120, 122–3, 129
  1974 All-Ireland final, 54–5
  1975 All-Ireland final, 107
  friendship with Bobby Doyle, 121–2
  1976 All-Ireland final, 145–6, 148–52
  1977 All-Ireland semi-final, 179, 185–6
  playing style, 146–8
  duels with O'Keeffe, 147–8
  1978 All-Ireland finals, 148, 207, 208, 218
  All-stars trips to US, 173–6, 198
  broken nose, 173–4, 176
  1979 Leinster final, 225
  1979 All-Ireland final, 226
Keaveney, Seamus, 230
Keely, Budger, 29
Kehilly, Kevin, 78, 134
Kelleher, Humphrey, 79

Kelleher, Robbie, 15, 17, 35, 41, 146, 168
  1974 Leinster football
    championship, 52, 53
  1974 All-Ireland final, 68, 271
  on St Vincent's, 124–5
  team meetings, 129
  1977 All-Ireland semi-final, 178, 179, 186–7
  on Eoin Liston, 191
  1978 All-Ireland final, 208–9, 211
  breaks leg, 219–20
  and the 1979 All-Ireland final, 220–1
  in later life, 234, 250, 260
  on Heffernan, 249
Kelly, Paddy, 239
Kelly, Paul, 91
Kenmare, 103, 114, 260–1
Kennelly, Dan, 253
Kennelly, Tadhg, 262
Kennelly, Timmy (The Horse), 82, 115–16, 243
  training, 88, 89
  misses train, 170–1
  in the Rat Pack, 172
  All-Stars trip to US, 198
  in later life, 232
  and Pat Spillane, 237–8
  and Jimmy Deenihan, 261–3
  in later life, 262
  death, 261–2, 263–4
Keohane, Joe, 194, 198
Kerry
  1923 All-Ireland finals, 72
  1924 All-Ireland finals, 72–3
  1930 All-Ireland finals, 73
  1955 All-Ireland finals, 3–5, 7–8
  1963 All-Ireland finals, 15
  1965 All-Ireland finals, 15–16
  1970 All-Ireland finals, 74

Kerry – *cont.*
  1973 All-Ireland Under-21s, 77,
    78, 79
  1973 Munster final, 75, 78
  1973 National League finals, 77
  1974 Munster final, 79–80
  1975 All-Ireland finals, 102–4,
    108–14, 166
  1975 All-Ireland Under-21 final,
    112
  1975 Munster final, 98–9
  1976 All-Ireland finals, 145–6,
    149–53, 156–7, 166
  1976 Munster finals, 134–6
  1977 All-Ireland finals, 170,
    177–87, 193–4
  1977 Munster final, 178–9
  1977 National League final, 173
  1978 All-Ireland finals, 207–17
  1979 All-Ireland finals, 149, 226
  All-Stars trips to US, 173–6,
    197–203
  The Heavies, 172
  The Golden Years (video), 233
  importance of football in, 69–74
  Jack O'Shea and, 157–61
  National League games, 91
  O'Dwyer's importance to, 82–94,
    95–6, 251, 253–7
  O'Sullivan's strategy, 9
  Páidí Ó Sé manages, 169–70
  Rat Pack, 172–3, 232
  successes, 224
  training, 8, 9, 133, 242–4
Kerry County Championship (1955),
  10
The Kerryman, 12
Kildare, 16, 74, 214, 257
  1974 Leinster football
    championship, 38, 39–40, 53
  Mick O'Dwyer manages, 86

Kilkenny, 38
Kilkenny hurlers, 102
Killarney, 229
King, Jim, 137
Kirby, Ned, 55
Knocknagoshel, 71

Laois, 16, 61, 197, 257
Larkin, Alan
  1974 All-Ireland final, 63
  and Mickey Ned O'Sullivan's
    injury, 109–10
  squad rotation system, 127
  team meetings, 129, 130
  playing style, 137
  leg injury, 197
Larkin, Philip, 270
Lavin, Jim, 4
Lawler, John, 28
Lawler, Paddy, 28, 29
Lean, David, 270
Lee, Brendan, 241
Lee, Paula, 49
Leeds United, 269
Leinster football championships, 5–6
  1957, 28
  1965, 15
  1967, 17
  1974, 38, 40–5, 53–4
  1975, 126
  1979, 225
Leinster Schools Senior Cup, 218
Lennon, Joe, 83, 84–5
Limerick, 38
Liston, Eoin (Bomber)
  and Ogie Moran, 112, 191
  joins Kerry, 191–3, 227, 256,
    259
  training, 89, 243
  in the Rat Pack, 172–3
  O'Dwyer and, 191–3

All-Stars trip to US, 198, 199, 201
1978 All-Ireland final, 207–8, 209, 212–13
in later life, 234, 235
on Pat Spillane, 237
and Dublin players, 260
Loftus, Tom, 19
London, 91–2
Long, Dinny, 79–80
Longford, 16, 23
Los Angeles, 198
Louth, 16, 24, 25
Lowry, Sean, 51
Lowth, Brinsley, 196
Lucey, Donnacha, 102–3
Lynch, Brendan, 134
Lynch, Jack, 210
Lynch, Mickey, 140
Lynch, Páidí, 160, 172, 213, 230–1
Lyne, Jackie, 76, 82, 84
Lyons, Tim 'Aeroplane', 71

McAuliffe, Dan, 10
MacBride, Tiernan, 46
McCann, Maxie, 18
McCarthy, John (Macker), 22, 24–5, 44, 61
breaks jaw, 105–6
1975 All-Ireland final, 106, 107–8, 111
team meetings, 121, 123, 128, 129
on St Vincent's, 125
improves milk ration, 136–7
1976 All-Ireland final, 150
1977 All-Ireland semi-final, 185
All-Stars trip to US, 200–2
drinking, 232
on Heffernan, 249
1979 All-Ireland final, 274
in later life, 274
Mickey Joe story, 274–5

McCarthy, Pat, 139, 152, 160, 180
McCarthy, Sean, 253
McCauley, Paddy, 60
McDermott, Sean, 31
McFlynn, Paddy, 215
MacGearailt, Seamus, 170
McGuinness, Jim, 7
McHugh family, 163
McIntyre, P.J., 103
McKenna, Gerald (Ger), 54, 80–1, 84, 85, 194, 215, 216
McTeague, Tony, 44
Magee, Eugene, 258
Magill magazine, 214, 215
Maher, Nicky, 2, 7
Malone, Baby Face, 29
Manchester United, 188–90, 210–11
Marciano, Rocky, 10–11
Marino, 5, 28–9, 163
Markey, Phil, 21–2, 24–5, 32
Mayo, 2
Meath, 1–2, 38, 53–4
Mee, Bertie, 78
Moloney, John, 135
Molyneaux, Andy, 93
Moran, Brendan, 142, 187
Moran, Kevin, 144, 146
background, 141–3
team meetings, 121, 128–9
1976 All-Ireland final, 145, 146, 152, 187–8
All-stars trip to US, 175
1977 All-Ireland semi-final, 182, 184
friendship with Bobby Doyle, 188–9
goes to Manchester United, 188–90, 195, 197, 210–11, 225
1978 All-Ireland final, 210–11
in later life, 234

Moran, Ogie, 88, 112, 115–17, 137, 205
  background, 141
  and Eoin Liston, 112, 191
  1976 All-Ireland final, 152
  in the Rat Pack, 172
  1977 All-Ireland semi-final, 181, 183
  All-Stars trip to US, 199
  Fr Teahan Cup, 206
  1978 All-Ireland final, 207–8
  All-Ireland medals, 117, 226
  in later life, 228, 234, 235
  and Pat Spillane, 236, 237
Morgan, Billy, 26, 54, 55–6, 98, 135, 149, 176
Morgan, Brian, 54
Morgan, Mary, 55
Muldoon, Marianne, 66
Mulligan, Eugene, 51
Mullin, Eugene, 21
Mullins, Brian, 25–6, 40, 136, 143, 146, 160, 161, 166
  Heffernan discovers, 57–60
  1974 All-Ireland final, 51, 55
  injured foot, 59, 60
  1975 All-Ireland final, 107
  team meetings, 120, 129
  1976 All-Ireland finals, 140, 145, 152
  1977 National League final, 173
  1977 All-Ireland semi-final, 179, 180, 183, 184
  Fr Teahan Cup, 206
  car accident, 224–5
  1979 All-Ireland final, 226
  1979 Leinster final, 225
  in later life, 250
  Mickey Joe story, 275
Munster finals, 9–10, 171–2
  1973, 74–5, 78

  1974, 79–80
  1975, 98–9
  1976, 134–6
  1977, 178–9
Murphy, Brian, 93, 135
Murphy, Dr Con, 150
Murphy, Eric, 3, 9
Murphy, Jack, 157
Murphy, Jimmy Barry, 55, 75, 78, 113, 134, 136, 200
Murphy, Sean, 135
Murray, Frank, 35, 40, 57, 59
  background, 22–4
  abilities, 43–4
  drug problems, 43, 44, 64–6, 67
  at 1974 Leinster football championship, 44–5
  tried as suspected terrorist, 64–6
  in America, 66–7
Murray, Gerry, 230
Murray, Sharon, 23–4
Musgrave family, 158

Na Fianna, 22–3, 125
na gCopaleen, Myles, 146
Naomh Barrog, 272
Naomh Mearnog, 272
National League, 91
  1953 finals, 5–6
  1967 finals, 17
  1973 finals, 77
  1975 finals, 100, 102
  1977 finals, 173
  1978 finals, 197
Naughton, Tommy, 140–1
Nelligan, Charlie, 112, 171–2, 195
  early life, 69–70, 92
  1976 All-Ireland final, 150–1, 152
  1979 All-Ireland final, 274
  before matches, 204–5
  in later life, 234, 265–8, 273–4

Nelson, Justin, 211
Nemo Rangers, 33, 56
New York, 101, 176, 197–203,
    230–1, 252
Noctor, Martin, 105
North Kerry, 10
Norton, Danny, 146

Ó Ceallacháin, Sean Óg, 33
Ó Cinnéide, Dara, 237
Ó Hehir, Micheál, 69
Ó Muircheartaigh, Micheál, 48, 97
Ó Sé, Beatrice, 173
Ó Sé, Darragh, 69
Ó Sé, Páidí, 89, 93, 112–13, 119, 126
    training, 133
    stories about, 169, 170–1
    character, 169–70
    as Kerry manager, 169–70
    O'Dwyer and, 169–70
    1977 All-Ireland finals, 170, 179,
        180, 185
    as Kerry captain, 171
    in the Rat Pack, 172–3
    on Kerry supporters, 194
    All-Stars trip to US, 202
    before matches, 205
    All-Ireland medals, 226
    drinking, 230–1
    in later life, 234, 235, 260
    and Hickey's death, 264
O'Brien, Paddy 'Hands', 2
O'Brien Institute, Marino, 29, 39
O'Callaghan, Bernie, 194
O'Connell, Mick, 10, 69–70, 76,
    79–80, 86, 157–9
O'Connor, Dee, 115
O'Doherty, Martin, 98–9
O'Donnell, John Kerry, 198
O'Donoghue, Paudie, 75, 79
O'Driscoll, Gay, 22, 60, 224, 272–3

training, 37
background, 47
insecurity, 48
1974 Leinster football
    championship, 53
1974 All-Ireland final, 63
1975 All-Ireland final, 107
team meetings, 126, 128, 129
1977 All-Ireland semi-final, 182,
    186
1978 All-Ireland final, 208
O'Driscoll, Ger, 116, 151, 157
O'Dwyer, Mick
    early life, 3, 76, 253
    Munster v. Waterford, 9–10
    Kerry County Championship, 10
    1973 Munster final, 78–9
    1974–75 National League, 80–1
    as Kerry manager, 82–94, 95–6
    rumours about, 86
    as a player, 92–3
    and Ray Prendiville, 97
    1975 Munster final, 99
    1975 All-Ireland finals, 102–4
    training, 116, 133, 242–4
    intolerance of injuries, 149–50
    1976 All-Ireland final, 150–1, 152,
        153, 156
    and Jack O'Shea, 157–9, 160
    and Páidí Ó Sé, 169–70
    and The Heavies, 172
    1977 All-Ireland semi-final,
        179–80, 181, 182, 186
    and Eoin Liston, 191–3
    selectors, 194
    drops players, 195
    1978 All-Ireland final, 208, 212,
        213
    attitude to drinking, 231
    in later life, 234, 253, 256–7
    and Pat Spillane, 236

O'Dwyer, Mick – *cont.*
  honours, 251
  importance of, 251, 253–7
  and Heffernan, 257–9
Offaly, 38, 47–9, 50–2, 225
O'Hehir, Micheál, 112, 141, 177, 184
O'Keeffe, Ger, 153
  training, 88, 89, 242–3
  1976 Munster finals, 134
  on O'Dwyer, 149
  in the Rat Pack, 172
  1977 Munster final, 178–9
  1977 All-Ireland semi-final, 179,
    181, 184
  Fr Teahan Cup, 206
  on Pat Spillane, 237
  on Dublin v. Kerry, 271–2
O'Keeffe, John, 58, 81, 112, 142, 160
  training, 133
  duels with Keaveney, 147–8
  concussion, 149
  1976 All-Ireland final, 151–2
  All-Stars trip to US, 173–4, 175
  1977 All-Ireland semi-final, 179,
    183, 185–6
  Fr Teahan Cup, 206
  in later life, 228, 234
  injuries, 244
Oliver Plunkett's, 124
O'Mahoney, Paudie
  1973 Munster final, 78–9
  1974 Munster final, 79–80
  training, 88, 133, 243
  1975 All-Ireland final, 113–14
  1976 Munster finals, 134, 136
  1976 All-Ireland final, 149
  Achilles tendon injury, 149–51
  1977 Munster final, 178–9
  1977 All-Ireland semi-final,
    179–80, 182, 184–5
  considers leaving team, 195
  in later life, 229–30, 233
  on O'Dwyer, 231, 254
O'Mahony, Gerry, 157
O'Neill, Bill, 20–1
O'Neill, Joe, 60–1, 139
O'Neill, Pat, 35, 57, 60, 142, 144
  Babs Keating incident, 20–1
  feud between St Vincent's and
    UCD, 21
  kidney problem and pulmonary
    embolism, 59–60, 138–40
  team meetings, 120, 129
  1975 All-Ireland finals, 139
  1976 All-Ireland finals, 140–1, 152
  and Keaveney's broken nose,
    173–4, 176
  1977 All-Ireland semi-final, 178,
    184, 186
  All-Stars trip to US, 199, 201–2
  1978 All-Ireland final, 209, 213,
    214
  in later life, 250
O'Reilly, Joe, 42
O'Shea, Jack, 112, 259
  background, 157–60
  and O'Dwyer, 94, 256
  selected for Kerry, 160–1
  1977 All-Ireland semi-final,
    179–80, 186
  before matches, 204–6
  1978 All-Ireland final, 209, 212–13
  on Pat Spillane, 236
  in later life, 263–4
O'Shea, Jerome, 157
O'Shea, Pat, 194
O'Sullivan, Dick, 31–2
O'Sullivan, Dr Eamonn, 8–9, 84
  *The Art and Science of Gaelic
    Football*, 8
O'Sullivan, Kevin Jer, 62
O'Sullivan, Mickey Ned, 137

background, 75–8, 79
as Kerry captain, 82–3, 84, 103
O'Dwyer becomes Kerry manager,
    83–4, 85
1975 All-Ireland finals, 102–3,
    108–11, 114, 227
training, 133
in later life, 227–8, 233, 235
on Pat Spillane, 236
and Dublin players, 260–1
O'Toole, Anton, 41
    team meetings, 47, 129
    1974 All-Ireland final, 51, 52, 55,
        61–2
    1975 All-Ireland final, 111
    on Keaveney, 148
    1976 All-Ireland final, 152
    1977 All-Ireland semi-final, 179,
        183
O'Toole, Luke, 195

Páirc Uí Chaoimh, 134
Parley, John, 239
Parnell Park, Dublin, 119–21
Pocock, Brendan, 107, 140
Portlaoise, 171
Power, Ger, 79
    All-Stars trip to US, 175, 176
    1977 All-Ireland semi-final, 185
    dropped from team, 195
    Fr Teahan Cup, 206
    1978 All-Ireland final, 211–12,
        213
    All-Ireland medals, 226
    in later life, 234, 235
Prendergast, Tom, 197
Prendeville, Mundy, 73
Prendiville, Ray, 96–8, 116

Quinn, Brendan, 15
Quinn, Niall, 189

Radio Kerry, 254
Raheny, 241
Redmond, Lorcan, 142, 250, 255
    works with Heffernan, 32–3, 34–5
    and Mullins' selection, 58
    1975 All-Ireland final, 108
    1976 All-Ireland final, 141
    and Heffernan's resignation, 162
    1977 All-Ireland semi-final, 178,
        183
Reilly, Paddy, 35, 127, 143
    1974 All-Ireland final, 50–1, 52
    team meetings, 129
    playing style, 137
    dropped from team, 166
    fight with Doyle, 167
    injury, 167
    All-Stars trip to US, 199
Revie, Don, 78
Reynolds, Hubie, 57
Ring, Eugene, 157
Riordan, Conín, 263
Roche, Andy, 195–7, 223
Roche, Ned, 3, 8, 9
Roobey, Stephen, 51
The Room, Parnell Park, 119–21,
    125–6, 127–30, 166, 235
Rooney, Michael, 62
Rooney, Stephen, 43, 57, 136
Roscommon, 35, 74, 117
RTE, 49, 110, 211, 216–17, 236,
    269
Ryan's Daughter (film), 270
Ryder, Fran, 57, 99, 107, 136, 202,
    250

St Aidan's CBS, Dublin, 196
St Finian's National School,
    Waterville, 253
St Joseph's, 124
St Jude's, 272

St Vincent's
  county championship successes, 5,
    6
  1953 National League final, 5–6
  style, 6
  further defeats, 12–13
  feud with University College
    Dublin, 21–2
  trains with Dublin, 27–8
  and the 1975 All-Ireland final, 107
  dominance and influence, 123–5
  1976 All-Ireland club
    championship, 125, 154
  Andy Roche plays for, 196
  minor hurling team, 245
  Heffernan's importance to, 246
Sam Maguire Cup, 63–4, 261
San Francisco, 101–2, 175, 198
Scartaglin, 96
Sexton, Dave, 78, 189, 210, 211
Shannon Rangers, 115
Shea, John, 206
Sheehy, John Joe, 71, 73
Sheehy, Mikey, 79, 92–3, 116, 117,
    131, 133, 169, 206
  1976 Munster finals, 134, 135
  1978 All-Ireland final, 209, 211,
    212, 216–17
  1979 All-Ireland final, 226
  All-Ireland medals, 226
  in later life, 234
  injuries, 244
  and Dublin players, 260
Sherlock, Jason, 267–8, 274
Shoot! magazine, 190
Skibbereen, 78
Smyth, Jimmy, 215
Sneem, 206–7, 231
South Africa, 228–9, 250
South Kerry, 9, 10

Spillane, Pat, 112–13, 137, 143,
    233–4, 245, 259
  training, 87–8, 133
  on O'Dwyer, 90, 91, 94
  1975 Munster final, 98
  1975 All-Ireland final, 111
  1976 Munster finals, 134, 135
  1977 All-Ireland semi-final, 184
  dropped from team, 194–5
  All-Stars trip to US, 202
  Fr Teahan Cup, 206
  1978 All-Ireland final, 209, 210
  All-Ireland medals, 226
  achievements, 235–6
  upsets other players, 236–8
  injuries, 244
Stack, Austin, 72
Stack, Sean, 117
Sweets, Christy, 37
Synott, Kevin, 140

Terenure College, 218
Thomond College, 206
Thompson, Christy, 119
Timmons, Joe, 28
Timmons, John, 4, 17, 28
Tipperary, 20–1, 96
Tobin, John, 63
Treacy, John, 181
Trimble, Brian, 36
Trinity Gaels, 272
Trinity Grounds, Dublin, 119

United States of America, annual All-
    Stars trips to, 100–2, 173–6,
    197–203
University College Dublin (UCD),
    21–2, 34, 39, 139, 218, 219

Valentia, 87

Waldron, Joe, 62
Wall, Eddie, 28
Walsh, Johnny, 77, 78, 79
Walsh, Seanie, 112, 159
   1975 All-Ireland final, 109
   1976 Munster finals, 135
   1976 All-Ireland final, 152, 153
   in the Rat Pack, 172
   1977 All-Ireland semi-final, 181,
     184
   1979 All-Ireland final, 226
   in later life, 234

   injuries, 244
Waterford, 9, 38
Waterville, 9, 84, 85, 87, 90, 91, 92,
   251–3
Webster, Eddie, 97
Westmeath, 16, 17, 20
Wexford, 23, 40, 246
Whelan, Mickey, 36, 124
Whitehall Colmcilles, 195–6, 197
Wicklow, 246
Wilson, Georgie, 44, 127, 136, 137
Wilson, Mark, 4–5, 7